GENDER RELATIONS IN THE AMERICAN EXPERIENCE
° ° ° Joan E. Cashin and Ronald G. Walters, *Series Editors*

Margaret Creighton and Lisa Norling, eds.
*Iron Men, Wooden Women: Gender and Seafaring
in the Atlantic World, 1700–1920*

Stephen M. Frank
*Life with Father: Parenthood and Masculinity
in the Nineteenth-Century American North*

Lorri Glover
*All Our Relations: Blood Ties and Emotional Bonds
among the Early South Carolina Gentry*

Richard Godbeer
Sexual Revolution in Early America

Anya Jabour
*Marriage in the Early Republic: Elizabeth
and William Wirt and the Companionate Ideal*

Angel Kwolek-Folland
*Engendering Business: Men and Women
in the Corporate Office, 1870–1930*

Catherine Gilbert Murdock
*Domesticating Drink: Women, Men,
and Alcohol in America, 1870–1940*

DOMESTICATING
DRINK

WOMEN, MEN, AND ALCOHOL IN AMERICA, 1870–1940

o o o

Catherine
Gilbert
Murdock

The Johns Hopkins University Press

Baltimore and London

© 1998 The Johns Hopkins University Press
All rights reserved. Published 1998
Printed in the United States of America on acid-free paper

Johns Hopkins Paperbacks edition, 2002
9 8 7 6 5 4 3 2 1

The Johns Hopkins University Press
2715 North Charles Street
Baltimore, Maryland 21218-4363
www.press.jhu.edu

Library of Congress Cataloging-in-Publication Data
will be found at the end of this book.
A catalog record for this book is available from the British Library.

ISBN 0-8018-6870-X (pbk.)

Wine and beer are alcoholic. This makes them as "cultural," as dependent upon civilized control and organization as bread, in that human beings have to work hard and long to grow, pick, crush, and ferment the must and the malt, and then patiently let them lie till they are ready, just as bread must be grown, harvested, ground, "fermented" with yeast, kneaded, left to rise, and baked. Care, planning, technology, and organization are required for both. Alcohol is to be treated with respect, not because it is "the staff of life" like bread, but because it is exactly the opposite: it gives pleasure, but is usually unnecessary and potentially dangerous. In ancient Greek myth, wine was a "latecomer" in human history, which meant among other things that people could live without it. Drinking it induced religious awe and direct acquaintance with Dionysus, the god of the vine, of ecstasy; of the group acting as one, of the loss of individual identity.

—*Margaret Visser*

1865

°°° CONTENTS

° ° ° ILLUSTRATIONS

° ° ° ACRONYMS

AA	Alcoholics Anonymous
AAPA	Association Against the Prohibition Amendment
ASL	Anti-Saloon League
GFWC	General Federation of Women's Clubs
LWV	League of Women Voters
NAWSA	National American Woman Suffrage Association
NJWRC	New Jersey Women's Republican Club
NWDLEL	National Woman's Democratic Law Enforcement League
USBA	United States Brewers' Association
VCL	Voluntary Committee of Lawyers
WCLE	Woman's Committee for Law Enforcement
WCTU	Woman's Christian Temperance Union
WJCC	Women's Joint Congressional Committee
WNCLE	Woman's National Committee for Law Enforcement
WONPR	Women's Organization for National Prohibition Reform
WSP	Women Strike for Peace

° ° ° ACKNOWLEDGMENTS

M y greatest gratitude extends to Karin Calvert, in whose class I first studied alcohol history, and to Murray Murphey, who has provided wise and steady guidance throughout this process. *Domesticating Drink* exists because of the University of Pennsylvania's American Civilization department. The book would not have been conceptualized elsewhere; the sources that have made this work so rewarding would never have been tapped. I owe almost as much to the staff of Penn's Van Pelt Library, particularly the Interlibrary Loan office, who made research painless and gratifying. I am also grateful to other librarians who assisted me in countless ways at the College of Physicians of Philadelphia, Hagley Museum and Library, Herbert Hoover Library, Indiana Historical Society, Library Company of Philadelphia, Library of Congress, Pennsylvania State Archives, Philadelphia Free Library, Rutger University's Center of Alcohol Studies, and Winterthur Library. In addition, Kathryn Abbott, Michelle McClellan, Robin Room, and Elizabeth Tice provided valuable research materials.

David Kyvig and Mark Lender have supported this project from its earliest days. I cannot thank them enough for their encouragement, especially David's ringing endorsement of "booze history." Robert J. Brugger, Joan Cashin, and Ronald Walters at the Johns Hopkins University Press offered detailed and thoughtful criticism of the manuscript. Numerous readers— Marie Bongiovanni, Nicholas Breyfogle, Martha Finney, Mark Meier, Susan Schulten, and PARSS members Julie Goldsmith, Russ Kazal, Liam Riordan, and Andrew Walker—now know more about women and alcohol than they ever really intended. The same applies to family members Elizabeth Gilbert, John and Carole Gilbert, Nick Gilbert, John and Janet Murdock, and of course James, who has suffered through this all with patience and excellent suggestions. Laura Root Tupper gave me her family copy of *Women and Repeal*. Bless you, Aunt Lolly, for introducing me to the WONPR. And of course my final debt of gratitude goes to Nicky and Madeleine, who have moved my focus from the past to rosy, rosy thoughts of the future.

°°° DOMESTICATING DRINK

INTRODUCTION

My grandfather Stanley Gilbert tells the story of a family picnic during national prohibition in the late 1920s, when his Aunt Grace offered him a beer. He was only fifteen at the time and his parents protested, but Grace insisted. Prohibition would not last forever, she explained, and Stanley needed to learn to appreciate beer, which was an acquired taste. Grace was correct on both counts. Stanley soon developed a healthy appetite for malt beverages, and Prohibition was repealed.

But Grace Root had more than passing interest in prohibition. She was a vice chair of the New York State chapter of the Women's Organization for National Prohibition Reform, one of the country's most powerful repeal organizations. In 1934 she would write *Women and Repeal,* the corporate history of the WONPR. The WONPR claimed to support temperance; its criticism centered on the harshness and needlessness of a national law against alcohol. But few prohibitionists would have been surprised by the spectacle of a WONPR member offering drink to a child. The Woman's Christian Temperance Union (WCTU), the preeminent women's "dry" organization, had worked for more than fifty years for temperance education and prohibition. How fitting they would have found it, a "Bacchantian maiden" of the WONPR not only predicting repeal of the "best law ever enacted" but also contributing to the creation of the nation's next generation of "drinkers."[1]

Stanley Gilbert's anecdote encapsulates the themes of this book: the omnipresence of gender in the debate over drink; the female role in moderate male consumption; the importance of beer, wine, and spirits to American sociability; and the heavy nimbus of politics that surrounded alcohol in the critical years between the Civil War and the Great Depression.

Today it is a truism that Prohibition was a mistake. According to popular opinion, the attempt by small-minded moralists to eliminate a drug so easily manufactured, so readily transported, and so essential to the national psyche was doomed from the beginning. Yet alcohol abuse in the nineteenth and early twentieth centuries existed on a scale Americans today have trouble conceptualizing. Public drunkards were a pathetic, everyday spectacle in villages and cities throughout America. Drink really did kill men and ruin families, and millions of citizens felt that the best way to meet the crisis would be to eliminate alcoholic beverages. Moreover, the nation's abusive drinking patterns were strictly gendered. At the very most, 20 percent of the alcoholic population was female.[2] Historically, it is not America that has had a drinking problem, it is American men. Male drinking gave rise to the American temperance movement, the longest, most popular social cause of the nineteenth century. Male drinking triggered formation of separatist women's groups that worked for prohibition laws to control men's alcohol abuse. Men, it must be stressed, also supported and led the temperance cause, in the same sense that men supported and voted for woman suffrage. But male drinking, like male voting rights, remained a potent badge of masculine identity. Drinking, voting, and virility formed a trinity in American politics. Alcohol flowed freely on election day. Saloons often served as polling places. Elected officials shied away from enforcing laws that regulated alcohol distribution and sales. Women's groups soon realized that prohibition would be impossible without women's political empowerment. Temperance had a profound effect on women's rights. The campaign in the 1910s for a national prohibition amendment in many ways defined the concurrent struggle for woman suffrage. Beginning in the 1820s, the controversy over drink inspired women's political participation for more than a century.

The subject of alcohol offers a fitting medium for examining gender roles outside politics as well. In the routine of home and street, in health care and leisure, patterns of alcohol use illuminate the lives of nineteenth-century men and women. From the workplace to the blue-collar saloon and blue-chip private club, alcohol promoted male bonhomie. The drink he chose, and where he chose to drink it, defined a man's profession, his ethnicity, his community standing. Abstainers relied just as fiercely on their abstinence as a form of self-definition. Moreover, myriad sources from the period reveal the integral role of alcohol in women's daily life and social standing. Fiction, advertisements, political cartoons, and photographs depict women drinking, contradicting the image of a dry and moral American womanhood that the temperance movement so often spread. Cookbooks, etiquette manuals, table-setting guides, and menu collections of the time reveal just as much about respectable American drinking. More significant still is the physical evidence of spirituous living—the wine glasses, cocktail glasses, decanters, and liquor cabinets that formed America's material culture. These objects have proved to be a most informative source on America's drinking past. Nor are these objects all alcohol related. The elaborate ice-water pitchers of the late nineteenth century speak of interest in abstemious drinking rituals as well.

Both public and private drinking, especially on the part of women, changed in the twentieth century. Although women did drink in the nineteenth century, their daughters did so more flagrantly and more self-consciously. However common the flapper may or may not have been, the very presence of this rebellious stereotype attests to the profound divisions between parent and child, old and new, good and bad, that marked America in the 1910s and 1920s. Growing acceptance of women's drinking challenged the model of pure and pious American womanhood on which the temperance movement was based. Most importantly, it dismantled the traditional linking of masculinity with drink. Subtle shifts in alcohol's gendered associations permitted ratification of the prohibition amendment in 1919. Fourteen years later, women's alcohol consumption played a far more public role in the repeal campaign that ended the Noble Experiment forever.

Readers who open *Domesticating Drink* to find thrilling stories of vamp-eyed flappers may find themselves uncomfortably mired in Victorianism— a sensation doubtless shared by vamp-eyed flappers themselves. But the nineteenth century set the stage for the legislation and behavior of the 1920s. The state of Maine was legally dry from the 1850s, and prohibition enthusiasm altered state laws and constitutions in the 1870s and 1880s and later in the 1910s. This enthusiasm culminated in the Constitution's Eighteenth Amendment, instituting prohibition, which was ratified in January 1919. Many states remained dry after repeal of the Eighteenth Amendment in late 1933. In this respect, prohibition sentiment emerged before the Civil War and lasted until World War II. *Prohibition* as used in this book refers to the period of national prohibition between 1919 and 1933 and also to the lengthier popular movement that made national prohibition possible.

Most dry legislation permitted individuals to denounce the evils of the saloon and the "liquor interests" without necessarily modifying their private drinking habits. Of the thirty-three dry states in 1920, only a third were "bone dry"—prohibiting the delivery, receipt, or possession of alcohol for personal use. Few prohibition laws sought to control the traditional domestic manufacture of wines and hard cider. (Such products are distinct from distilled liquors, the moonshining of which had been illegal for more than a century.)[3] The semantic distinction between *prohibition* and *abstinence* would become increasingly important after the passage of federal prohibition in 1920. Prohibition here means the legal movement to control or eliminate the commercial manufacture and sale of alcohol. What prohibitionists wanted—the eradication of alcohol—tended to differ significantly from dry legislation as it was written. To put it another way, prohibition sanctioned moderate domestic consumption of low-alcohol beverages—what Americans at the time would have defined as women's drinks in women's spaces.

In light of this, it is important to delineate the population *Domesticating Drink* examines. I have developed great affection for the term *respectable,* and I use it often. Respectable women supported temperance in the nineteenth century. Respectable women did not drink in speakeasies; respectable women's children, to their mothers' chagrin, often did. Respectable women tended to be "native," capable of claiming several generations of American-born ancestry. "Respectable" shows up constantly in the literature of the period. It was often spat back and forth between opposing camps. Members of the WCTU, when discussing female drinkers within their own social class, had a preference for the epithet "so-called respectable."

I have found *respectable* more useful than *middle class,* which tends to bring discussion to a halt while everyone haggles over what *middle class* actually means. A focus on the middle class overlooks the cross-class, interracial nature of both temperance activity and alcohol consumption. The term *respectable* as used here refers not so much to economic status or ethnicity as to attitude: respectable citizens, unlike prostitutes or criminals, sought to behave properly according to the parameters of their culture. Both wets and drys participated in this search to define proper behavior. Their struggles illuminate the breadth of nineteenth- and twentieth-century drinking and the parameters of American gender roles. Moreover, the public drinking of respectable women of various classes, ethnicities, and regions in the second and third decades of the twentieth century reflects a profound change in the very definitions of male and female. Temperance and social historians understand well how respectable women and men integrated abstinence into their social aspirations; this book explores how other respectable women and men integrated drinking and how, in doing so, they changed American law and custom forever.

Domesticating Drink begins by examining the relationship between alcohol and Victorian masculinity, a relationship that inspired temperance enthusiasm. Chapter 1 also surveys the close connections between temperance and the woman movement in the century before federal prohibition. The woman suffrage victory of 1920—the pinnacle of women's political achievement in the first half of the twentieth century—cannot be appreciated without full understanding of the prohibition victory of the previous year.

Both woman suffrage and prohibition emphasized male excess and potential female redemption. Chapter 2 examines drinking culture in more detail. Primary sources illustrate the breadth of drink-related roles available to women. In contrast with dry literature, these sources present drinking as normal, respectable behavior. They force us to reconsider the conflicts within Victorian social classes and the breadth and influence of the American temperance movement.

Beginning in the 1890s in the largest cities, and spreading from there to the nation's hinterlands, new forms of public socializing brought men and women together. Dance halls, cabarets, cafés, and restaurants encouraged women's public presence, including public drinking. Like the controversy surrounding women's demands for employment and financial independence, the debate over women's public drinking was lengthy, heated, and often amusingly moralistic. As chapter 3 demonstrates, concern over this new drinking remained inseparable from issues of female sexuality and self-determination.

Chapter 4 examines women's drinking and the debates surrounding it in the years of national prohibition, 1920 to 1933. As effectively as women's enfranchisement, Prohibition ended the behavior so closely linked to nineteenth-century masculinity. The Eighteenth Amendment thus forced a massive realignment of gender roles in public and at home. One could argue that it was not simply drink that was domesticated in this decade but men as well.

After 1920, alcohol control continued to dominate public discourse. Women's support of the national prohibition law was a political truism of unchallengeable veracity throughout the 1920s. More women supported prohibition in 1919 than any other single issue, including woman suffrage. Chapter 5 examines the dry sympathies of the most prominent women's groups of the decade. As weaknesses in the prohibition law became less and less deniable, these political organizations fractured. Repeal carried with it rejection of American women's separate and respected moral voice.

Chapter 6 focuses on the moral authority of the Women's Organization for National Prohibition Reform, the most popular repeal organization of the 1930s. Although attuned to home-protection rhetoric, the WONPR strove to match argument to audience, thus illustrating the decline of gender-specific rhetoric. In adroitly combining morality with American realpolitik, "wet" women created a model for effective female political activism in the later twentieth century.

The concluding chapter summarizes the evolving relationship between gender and alcohol. How did prohibition affect the evolution of feminism? The moral arguments of nineteenth-century women reformers had been based upon the most egregious male behavior. Prohibition, in eliminating much of this behavior, left these women without a suitable language for twentieth-century political discourse. Feminists continued to call for equality with men as they demanded preservation of a separate, higher standard of behavior from women. In this light, younger women's drinking may be seen as a logical effort to mediate between these two conflicting expectations, to take on male attributes while circumventing the moralism that often accompanied feminism.

Women's drinking, contrary to the fears of women drys at the time (and today), represents not a capitulation to male values but rather a domestication of male behavior. The replacement of the all-male saloon with the mixed-sex speakeasy and bar, and the integration of drinking rituals such as cocktail parties into the home, indicates more than the domestication of drink. On a fundamental level it speaks of the elimination of a masculine subculture based on exclusivity, inebriety, and violence within the United States.

GENDER, PROHIBITION, SUFFRAGE, AND POWER

From the nation's beginnings in the eighteenth century, male suffrage formed the basis of American government. The founding fathers envisioned a benevolent patriarchy in which each man voted and acted in the best interests of his family as well as his country. In the nineteenth century, legislation extended suffrage, and hence citizenship and manhood, to poor white and newly freed African American males. Yet alcohol abuse, like no other issue, highlighted the weaknesses of this patriarchal model of government. A drunkard threatened not only the ideal of a sober and responsible citizenry but also—and much more immediately—the welfare and safety of his wife and children. The masculine space of the saloon menaced women passing by, insulted them within, and promoted a sensibility at odds with respectable aspirations.

As an issue, alcohol, more than slavery or suffrage or any other single cause, effected American women's politicization. In campaigns for personal abstinence and restricted alcohol sales, dry activists confronted the restrictions placed upon women in politics, in public activities, and in the law. Women saw in temperance salvation from poverty, domestic violence, and abandonment. The Woman's Christian Temperance Union dominated the dry movement in the last quarter of the nineteenth century. It was the most popular, and by many accounts the most progressive, women's association of the nineteenth century. Although men's and women's distinct social roles precluded the notion of "equality" as we understand the concept today, the WCTU and other dry women maneuvered Victorian definitions of femininity into a persuasive demand for political emancipation.

Prohibition and temperance permeated the rhetoric of woman suffragists who blamed the "liquor interests" for the defeat of both suffrage and Prohibition. The battles over prohibition within the suffrage movement illustrate the breadth of prohibition support among American women. Alcohol and politics were intimately related—in election-day debauchery, in the local politicking of saloon keepers, in the lobbying and graft of wealthy dis-

tillers and brewers. Prohibition and woman suffrage challenged equally
the gendered boundaries of the American polity. In fact, viewing the
amendments, and their supporters and opponents, is rather like looking
through an old-fashioned stereoscope. By employing two viewpoints
slightly in contrast, we produce an image of the past with unique depth,
texture, and reality. The image of suffragists that we develop through examination of prohibition may not match current notions of appropriate social activism. But the image has the significant benefit of being correct.

ALCOHOL AND TEMPERANCE, MALE AND FEMALE

Alcohol has played a vital role in North American life since the discovery
of the continent by Europeans. Brought to the English colonies with the
first settlers, beer, hard cider, and rum were integral to colonial life. Alcohol constituted most of the limited pharmacopoeia of the era. It numbed
pain, eased headaches, lowered fever, cured infection, soothed troubled
minds, and revived low spirits. In a culture still reliant on medieval community and ritual, drink bound men together in times of sorrow and joy. Benjamin Franklin captured the communal attributes of alcohol in a 1744 *Poor
Richard's Almanac:* "He that drinks his *Cyder* alone, let him catch his *Horse*
alone."[1]

As in Europe, alcohol purified or replaced tainted water and milk—a
function it would serve throughout the nineteenth century wherever wells
were fouled and dairies questionable. Colonists considered alcohol essential to manual labor, indeed to day-to-day survival. They drank upon wak-
ing; with breakfast, lunch, and dinner; during "grog time" pauses in shop
and field work; and at every social event. Employers often paid laborers in
drink or drinking binges. Perfection of the process of distillation in the late
seventeenth century rendered this traditional consumption problematic.
New alcohol production techniques permanently surpassed civilization's
ability to incorporate drink into daily life. Cheap West Indies rum and
American whiskey soon replaced beer and cider. Whiskey in 1810 cost ten
cents a gallon, at a time when carbonated water cost five cents a glass.[2]
While citizens such as Dr. Benjamin Rush voiced concern about abusive
drinking habits as early as the 1780s, Americans from all walks of life in
the early nineteenth century began organizing to combat Demon Rum.

Temperance was never a "rural-evangelical virus," to quote historian
Richard Hofstadter's oft-cited, inaccurate phrase. Temperance advocates
did tend toward nativism, describing Irish and German immigrants with

language we find shocking today. But the movement did not consist of dour, misguided middle-class reformers forcing their notions on unwilling working-class drinkers. Middle-class temperance supporters worked to improve their own class by removing what they considered its greatest threat. Union organizers and artisans often supported temperance, not because dry shops saved their employers money and equipment but for "middle-class" motives of self-improvement and family security.[3]

From organizational beginnings in the second decade of the nineteenth century, interest in temperance exploded. *Temperance* first referred to abstention from distilled liquors and to moderate consumption of beer, wine, and hard cider, which were often not considered alcoholic. Within a generation, temperance became associated with complete abstinence from all alcohol, although prohibition's opponents—the "wets"—continued to flaunt the word's original definition. "Drys" endorsed personal abstention or (in the twentieth century) the legislative restraints of Prohibition. An estimated one-tenth of the U.S. population belonged to temperance societies in the late 1830s. Temperance was the most popular, and the longest-lasting, reform movement of the nineteenth century. Dry presses printed millions of pages a year on the dangers of drink. Educated citizens felt that alcohol was fundamentally addictive, much as modern Americans view heroin. Reformers considered drunkards victims who could be redeemed—and converted—once dried out. Thus, temperance activism evolved from an act of good will into a crucial element of evangelical Christianity.[4] Temperance advocates came to label any drinking, no matter how moderate, as pathological and set out to eliminate its source.

To complicate matters, by midcentury drinkers had moved from hard liquor to a new beverage whose popularity and supply showed no sign of abating. The United States at this time was cursed with a profound and inexorable overproduction of beer. It was one of the nation's easiest commodities to produce and—given nineteenth-century advances in transportation, refrigeration, and bottling—to distribute. National companies such as Pabst, Schlitz, and Stroh's competed with local breweries, and all competed with distillers. Breweries frequently owned saloons and demanded sales quotas. To remain solvent, most saloons broke Sunday closing and other blue laws; many financed their operations with gambling or other underworld activities, avoiding the law with graft and kickbacks. Saloon keepers washed sidewalks with beer to tempt customers. The high-license movement, intended to restrict the number of saloons by imposing large annual fees, only increased corruption and brewery involvement. Inevitably, the profession attracted men with weak principles and strong stomachs who had no aversion to alienating those most appalled by the public excess the saloon produced. Wet and dry cycles of outrage and retaliation grew more heated.

In such a climate, one of the most popular solutions to alcohol addiction was prohibition, the legal restriction of alcohol manufacture and sale. Prohibition cut to what reformers perceived as the heart of the matter, elimination of the substance to effect reform of the man. In 1851, Maine became the first state to ban the sale of alcohol for public consumption. Thirteen other states in the Northeast and Midwest quickly followed, their goal being the elimination of public drunkenness. These dry laws prohibited the commercial manufacture, sale, and public consumption of alcohol. But the implicit goal of many prohibitionists was an alcohol-free society. Prohibitionists, fearing the vagaries of state and municipal politics, sought to have these dry laws enshrined as permanent amendments to state constitutions.[5] And the primary quarry of prohibition legislation was, of course, the saloon.

The American Victorian saloon evolved from the public taverns of the eighteenth and early nineteenth centuries. (*Victorian* here defines the period from the Civil War to the turn of the twentieth century. As a temporal label, *Victorian* is indispensable—American history is quite in need of similar pithy terms for other periods.) Originally catering to a broad cross section of the community, taverns began to serve a more restricted clientele after the Revolutionary War. These public drinking spaces lost first their wealthiest customers, who retreated to more private, exclusive venues, and then the businessmen's trade, to coffee houses, private offices, and restaurants. The temperance movement in the second third of the nineteenth century drew away many middle-class abstainers. In their absence emerged the saloon, an urban, working-class, unabashed drinking space (figure 1.1). In a world lacking cheap restaurants, public rest rooms, libraries, meeting halls, even check-cashing facilities, the saloon served as an oasis. Saloon keepers could make available or easily locate pornography (which also tended to decorate the walls of the place), prostitutes, gambling, narcotics, and either union organizers or strike breakers. In small towns, particularly those with strong feelings against liquor, saloons attracted the community's worst elements, whose behavior was more visible to neighbors than in larger towns and cities.[6]

With its circle of regulars, the saloon matched in exclusivity the elite men's clubs of the era, and the saloon has often been described as the "poor man's club." It may be more accurate to describe private clubs as the rich man's saloon. In colonial America, the term *club* referred either to a group of men who gathered for drinking or to the punch itself that they drank. As clubs formalized, this emphasis on drink remained, with clubs taking pride in their elaborate bars and ingenious cocktails. Club members did not partake in the oft-criticized "treating" ritual, in which saloon drinkers shared rounds of drinks until every man in the circle had purchased. But members did take part in frequent dinnertime toasts, with doubtless the same effect.[7]

Hotel bars often merged the attributes of club and saloon, providing a public drinking space exclusive enough in appearance to guarantee a respectable presence. "Continental" saloons similarly catered to businessmen, who drank at tables rather than standing at the bar. Fraternal organi-

Figure 1.1   Saloon interior, Alburtis, Pennsylvania, ca. 1905

The saloon was "a symbol of masculinity emancipate," even in the tiny coal towns of northern Pennsylvania. Note the spittoon and the sign over the register. Pennsylvania State Archives MG–280, Arthur Bransky Photo Collection. Courtesy Pennsylvania State Archives.

zations, which attracted 20 percent of the adult male population in the late nineteenth century, also provided amenable spaces. Although many lodges officially banned liquor, they still supported drinking. Working-class lodges unable to afford their own buildings usually met in saloons' back rooms or second-story halls. Carry Nation's first husband hid in his local Masonic lodge during his drinking binges, and his fellow Masons sheltered him from his frustrated wife. In her later public campaigns, Carry Nation battled fraternal orders as passionately as she did saloons.[8]

The saloon and similar organizations were exclusive male spaces. In many cases legislation or policy explicitly excluded women; social dictum otherwise left little doubt. In the saloon, as Jack London described it, "life was different. Men talked with great voices, laughed great laughs, and there was an atmosphere of greatness." The saloon provided a bastion of maleness. A 1931 *American Mercury* magazine reminisced that the brass rail "was more than a footrest; it was a symbol of masculinity emancipate, of manhood free to put its feet on something." Even temperance organizations capitalized upon this homosociality, attempting to create alcohol-free saloons. (The term *homosocial* refers to social behavior with members of one's own sex and implies some element of choice and of preference. And like its obverse, *heterosocial, homosocial* also has some connection to sexuality. In the nineteenth and early twentieth centuries, critics of American drinking practices were quite concerned that heterosocial drinking would lead to heterosexual acts—far more concerned than they were that homosocial drinking would lead to homosexual acts.)[9]

Factors specific to nineteenth-century America made men's homosocial drinking particularly likely. Alcohol had traditionally played a central role in manual labor, as farm and mill workers marked break time with beer or whiskey. As late as the 1890s, skilled glassblowers in Muncie, Indiana, paused three or four times in their ten-hour day for beer, bought in buckets by an apprentice sent to a local saloon. Efficiency-minded industrialists sought to restrict alcohol consumption within their companies and to remove the saloons surrounding their property. As workers' productivity increased, their workday shrank, from twelve hours a day to ten and, by the early twentieth century, often to eight. Instead of amicably mingling labor and break time, alcohol was now segregated to the growing realm of after-hours "leisure." Drinking, which had been integral to work time, now became just as integral to this new leisure time. Sixty percent of all arrests in late-century Worcester, Massachusetts, were for public drunkenness. In other words, more than half the city's crime involved abusive public drinking. In many of the nation's working-class neighborhoods, one saloon existed for every four hundred residents, adult or child.[10]

Other factors contributed to male alcohol consumption and abuse. Alcohol provided recent immigrants—the Irish and their whiskey, the Germans and their beer—a form of ethnic identity. Nor was this search for identity restricted to immigrants. The industrial corporate economy forced radical changes in traditional patriarchy. As male breadwinning became problematic, other male roles took on greater significance. One simplistic yet easily attainable badge of masculinity remained drinking prowess. The association of masculinity with alcohol consumption, including abusive consumption, was well recognized in the era. Thorstein Veblen, that redoubtable critic of American conspicuous consumption (a term he coined), pointed out in 1899 that "infirmities induced by over-indulgence are among some peoples freely recognised as manly attributes." This association took on the status of a truism, a stereotype illustrating the dangers of other gendered vices. In 1881 the *New York Times* warned that "the awful . . . vice of shopping among women [is] every bit as bad as male drinking." More informal descriptions reinforce the ubiquity of abusive drinking. Henry Canby's memoir of 1890s Wilmington, Delaware, is peppered with male drunkenness—the arrests he witnessed, the weaving passage of drunken Irish laborers up his street, every family's "worthless great-uncle [who] had run away West and been drowned (presumably drunk) in the Mississippi."[11]

Considering the various elements connecting men to alcohol—class, ethnicity, leisure, labor, even public and private space—it appears as if all of nineteenth-century culture promoted alcohol consumption as essentially masculine. Yet masculinity also demanded financial success, emotional stability, and restraint—traits that drinking would obviously impair. Profound cultural ambivalence thus existed on the subject of drink. Alcohol use was a male attribute that destroyed masculinity. George Beard captured these two competing definitions of manhood in his 1881 medical text, *American Nervousness*. An early physician of mental health, Beard spent his life studying what would later be diagnosed as neurosis. Beard defined the paradox of alcohol use and masculinity. "It is much less than a century ago, that a man who could not carry many bottles of wine was thought of as effeminate—but a fraction of a man. [Today, however,] among Americans of the higher orders, those who live in-doors, drinking is becoming a lost art." In Beard's analysis, these "professional and business men" were more evolved, more civilized, than other Americans or Europeans. They were thus more prone to nervous exhaustion, a primary symptom of which was inebriety. (In the later nineteenth century, the term *inebriate* replaced *drunkard*. Considered more scientific and less moralistic, it conveyed the notion that the drinker, like a victim of tuberculosis, was subject to a disease, an addiction, beyond his control.) Beard took pride in Americans' new delicateness. In *American Nervousness* he set out to legitimize this delicacy as sufficiently masculine rather than effeminate. Yet Beard's diagnosis made possible the exculpation of alcohol abuse. Men who could hold their liquor remained among "the depressed classes," but an inebriate, a problem drinker, could also be a man of the "higher orders." Beard, in linking abuse to wealth and social standing, supported the definition of drinking as both elite and masculine.[12]

Given the confusion of definitions and expectations that surrounded it, drink became a scapegoat used to explain and excuse disreputable male behavior. Drinking permitted a loss of self-control; men attributed their brawling, bankruptcy, and domestic violence, however tertiary the relationship between alcohol and excess, to drink. Drys also scapegoated alcohol, blaming it for the financial losses, infertility, or madness of drinkers, even moderate drinkers. American courts in the late nineteenth century became increasingly willing to grant women divorces on the grounds of the inebriety of their spouses instead of solely on the grounds of physical cruelty. Male intemperance was a deciding factor in more than a quarter of American divorces between 1887 and 1906. One Kentucky judge wrote in 1892 that "while we hold in highest regard the sanctity of the marriage bond . . . , we feel that the good of society does not demand or require a wife, without fault in her marital relations, to be bound for life to a drinking, shiftless husband."[13] These objections highlight growing impatience with male drinking practices. The saloon represented a frontal assault on the values that respectable Americans, particularly respectable women, held dear.

From its start, temperance attracted the attention and support of women. As countless observers noted, women suffered from men's drinking. Barred by law or custom from divorcing inebriate husbands, unable to earn a living wage themselves, isolated in a society with few mechanisms to reform drinkers or aid their families, drunkards' wives faced brutality, poverty, and abandonment. In 1838, temperance speaker George Packard described to an audience of women a bride who, upon realizing her husband drank to excess, committed suicide rather than live "the unavoidable portion of a drunkard's wife." While probably apocryphal, the story nonetheless captures the fear that alcohol evoked. Alcohol further victimized women through the pornography and violence associated with saloons. The saloon's prostitutes, lured into disgrace through drink, transmitted syphilis and gonorrhea to their middle-class customers, who in turn infected their wives and unborn children. Fears of abandonment, brutality, destitution, and the failure of the institution of marriage were conjured by the very word "saloon." In cities and villages, respectable women traveled blocks out of their way to avoid passing stinking and raucous saloons. Even when their men did not imbibe, through temperance women could discuss their concerns about social dislocation, their frustrations with an irresponsible male culture, and their own vulnerability.[14]

It is therefore not surprising that women soon became a presence in temperance organizations. Male groups such as the Independent Order of Rechabites and the Sons of Temperance developed female auxiliaries in the 1830s and 1840s that constituted between a third and two-thirds of their total membership. As early as 1805 women founded their own temperance societies. In 1848 the Daughters of Temperance had thirty thousand members, many from the working classes, making it one of the nation's largest women's groups up to that point.[15]

Woman temperance advocates supported and personified the century's feminine ideal. Temperance, reformers believed, could be achieved if alcohol were not served privately, if children were raised and men convinced to avoid spirits, and if the home were pleasant enough that men would abandon public drinking spaces for the comforts of fireside and family. These organizations promoted an image of woman as pious, pure, domestic, and submissive: the "true woman" who obeyed her father or husband while quietly swaying him with her inherently moral nature. Such selfless femininity was intended to counteract the amoral public world of nineteenth-century men. This attitude of female patience and suffering may be seen in *Ten Nights in a Bar-room,* the most famous temperance novel of the nineteenth century.[16] Little Mary Morgan pleads with her drunkard father Joe to leave the tavern of evil Simon Slade and, in true victim fashion, is killed by a beer mug hurled by Slade himself. Slade's wife, opposed to the tavern from the start, by the end of the story goes mad from horror, and the mother of another of Slade's patrons dies of grief. Timothy Shay Arthur's novel captures women's victimization in the face of Demon Rum.

Yet rising support in the 1850s for prohibition and other political, legislative reforms left dry women with little role. Women could not vote, hold office, or otherwise participate in the legislative process. Prohibition laws also demonstrated that women's voluntary efforts, their pious tears and moral suasion, did not cure alcoholism. Dry legislation thus diminished the feminine contribution to the temperance cause. Elizabeth Cady Stanton, a leader of the woman movement in the nineteenth century, ridiculed the dismissive treatment women drys received in the hands of male "time-serving priests and politicians." Women in the 1850s began to express more actively their indignation while remaining within acceptable definitions of femininity. In several midwestern communities women defended their homes and protected their men by actually closing saloons through public prayer or—more rarely—by destroying saloons' stock and bar with axes. Little opposition arose from male temperance advocates or even from male drinkers, for the women's actions "suggested almost instinctual maternal behavior." Such activism reached its apogee with the Woman's Temperance Crusade of 1873 and 1874, when hundreds of thousands of women, in a paroxysm of activity and prayer, closed thirty thousand saloons and initiated a generation of female leadership in the temperance movement.[17]

Beginning in several small towns in Ohio and New York, the Woman's Crusade spread through the upper midwestern and eastern states. Women marched on saloons, singing hymns inside and, when locked out, on the sidewalks (figure 1.2). When a saloon keeper capitulated, they rolled his stock into the street for public destruction. By summer, the prayer and demolition had spread to thirty-one states. Not surprisingly, the crusade was most successful in small communities with a foundation of evangelical enthusiasm and a united front of respectable women. In cities with large immigrant populations, particularly German beer drinkers, crusaders risked failure and even physical attack.

Enthusiasm could not be sustained, and the crusade came to an end in the spring of 1874. Those saloons that had not closed now flourished. Others reopened quietly. Political backlash, even in small towns, brought into office scores of men committed to overturning and ignoring dry laws. Absolute alcohol consumption per capita did reach the century's lowest point during the decade of the 1870s. But the depression of 1873 and the growing popularity of beer (lower in alcohol than whiskey) affected the production and consumption of liquor more than the crusade did.[18] Reform through the aegis of enraged maternalism, while compelling in the short term, demanded too much of its participants. Public demonstrations required sustained passion, unlimited free time, and a not insignificant amount of bravery. It also required male support in the public sphere and at home. Here participants faced ambivalence even from men who supported dry principles but objected to women's curbside theatrics and quasi-legal methods. For both women and men, the crusade's disheartening aftermath led to a renewed emphasis on education, lobbying, and legislation.

Dry Republicans, sensing that the Republican Party would never travel far down the temperance path, splintered into a separate political party in 1869. The Prohibition Party crested in 1884 on the nation's second wave of temperance enthusiasm, when many states enacted antiliquor laws. Just as in the 1850s, however, most of these laws were soon repealed or diluted. By the 1890s the Prohibition Party was mired in populism. Several Ohio Methodists, disgusted with the Prohibition Party's ineffectualness and its

Figure 1.2   "Lady Crusaders" praying inside a saloon

In 1873 and 1874 the Woman's Temperance Crusade, through civil disobedience and occasional violence, closed saloons in thirty states. In this illustration, the women's devotion appears to have little effect on the barmaid, who will lose her job if their prayers are answered. James Shaw, History of the Great Temperance Reforms of the Nineteenth Century *(Cincinnati: Hitchcock and Walden, 1875), plate opposite p. 235. From the collections of the Library of Congress.*

multitude of causes, founded the Ohio Anti-Saloon League in 1893. Soon a national organization, the Anti-Saloon League (ASL), established the standard for modern political activism. In the first two decades of the twentieth century, the ASL would navigate, if not orchestrate, America's third great temperance movement. The National Intercollegiate Prohibition Association, another group, in 1892 began promoting debates on the benefits of prohibition. The association soon had chapters in more than two hundred colleges in thirty states.[19]

The most popular, effective, and well-known dry organization of Victorian America, however, was neither the Prohibition Party nor the ASL but rather a women's group founded in November 1874. From the time of the Woman's Crusade until the turn of the century, the Woman's Christian Temperance Union dominated the temperance movement, bringing fresh ideas, new adherents, and a compelling sense of purpose to the dry cause.

THE WOMAN'S CHRISTIAN TEMPERANCE UNION

The Woman's Crusade correlated with but did not necessarily create the Woman's Christian Temperance Union. The women who gathered at the WCTU's founding convention campaigned for temperance before the crusade as well as for other causes such as Sunday School and public health. The first president of the WCTU, Annie Wittenmyer, had been a national figure in the Civil War Sanitation Commission. A wealthy widow with ties to the Methodist Church, Wittenmyer had successfully kept men's groups from absorbing the Sanitation Commission. She thus came to the WCTU with a history of supporting separatist and religious organizations. Wittenmyer soon began battling the assertive national corresponding secretary and head of the Illinois WCTU, Frances Elizabeth Willard. Willard pushed the Temperance Union toward woman suffrage and other political goals rather than supporting Wittenmyer's vision of gentle moral suasion. Willard was a woman of extraordinary energy and charisma, well educated and ambitious, who had just left the presidency of a women's college under circumstances of some controversy. Although peripherally involved in the crusade in the spring of 1874 and indoctrinated in temperance sentiment by her midwestern parents, she was not committed to the dry cause before joining the WCTU.[20]

Frances Willard has been described by one biographer as "the right person, at the right place, at the right time." Once in the WCTU, she quickly rose to prominence and in 1879 replaced Wittenmyer as national president. By force of personality, she held the union together until her death in 1898. With her guidance, the WCTU endorsed the Prohibition Party and federal prohibition. Under the banner of "home protection," Willard lured conservative members toward the progressivism inherent in her philosophy. The WCTU in the early 1890s had almost 150,000 members, ten times the membership of the National American Woman Suffrage Association (NAWSA), the era's main woman suffrage organization. Unlike NAWSA or other women's organizations, the WCTU admitted only women. These "white ribboners" (from the lapel pins that denoted their temperance sympathies) set policy, organized committees, and managed volunteers.[21]

Under Willard's motto, "Do Everything," the WCTU supported numerous activities related to temperance: public water fountains, "night owl" temperance restaurants, and girls' precision drill teams complete with ceremonial brooms. The union even joined the late-century campaign for bland foods, in response to the fear that a spicy diet would foster desire for stimulating drink. Willard later promoted the White Life for Two. This program, cloaked in euphemism, endorsed alcohol-free, tobacco-free, lust-free marriages in opposition to "mediaeval . . . harem philosophies." Willard intended through her White Life for Two to elevate men to women's higher moral plane and thereby provide for women's equality. The WCTU also led the effort to ban alcohol on military bases, Indian reservations, and within the U.S. Capitol building.[22]

In the late nineteenth century, the WCTU succeeded best in its campaign for mandatory temperance education within the public schools. By the early twentieth century, teachers instructed twenty-two million school children a year, in almost every state of the nation, on the dangers of drink. The WCTU's success in this campaign was due in part to the irrefutability of their issue: who would argue against teaching the dangers of drinking? Moreover, lawmakers found education laws far less controversial than prohibition, saloons' high-license fees, or other dry attempts at alcohol control. The WCTU's lobbying did attract some opposition, particularly from scientists challenging its criticism of moderate drinking. Educators increasingly resented the WCTU's attempts to legislate their teaching activities, and temperance education laws became notoriously difficult to revise or amend. Nonetheless, the laws remained in place through passage of federal prohibition in 1919. Many historians have credited the prohibition amendment to the WCTU: the Americans who came of age in the 1910s, at the height of prohibition enthusiasm, had been raised on diagrams of inebriates' stomachs.[23]

Such efforts reflect the union's increasing politicization. The WCTU developed a national network of lobbyists capable of deluging legislators on a day's notice with petitions and pleas. Union members testified frequently in Congress and kept a paid lobbyist in residence in Washington. Willard, in 1881, even came out in support of the Prohibition Party. Her political acumen was such that the Prohibition Party changed its name to the Prohibition Home Protection Party.[24]

Frances Willard was one of the great heroines of her generation, and it is tantalizing to imagine what would have become of the WCTU if she had not died so young, at fifty-nine. Intimations of dissent in the years before her death, years she spent mostly abroad, indicate that she and the organization might have split ways. Nor did the WCTU ever monopolize temperance even in the last quarter of the nineteenth century. Thousands, possibly millions, of American women supported the image of domestic harmony that temperance promised without joining the WCTU or its offshoots.

Temperance enthusiasm touched the highest levels of government. Republican Rutherford B. Hayes did not serve alcohol in the White House after his 1876 election, and many commentators, associating women with temperance, assumed his wife Lucy had implemented the policy. But President Hayes was also dry. Like other Republicans, he sought to keep dry members in the party without actually adopting a temperance platform or alienating wet voters. The WCTU, endorsing the association of women and temperance, campaigned for funds to memorialize Lucy in a temperance portrait for the White House. In so doing, they threatened the dry-wet compromise in the Republican Party. Although other first ladies of the era, such as Sarah Polk and Frances Cleveland, had strong temperance principles, Lucy's dry stance received the most attention and criticism. Rutherford declined to run for a second term, the Hayeses returned to Ohio, and "Lemonade Lucy" became a staple of temperance textbooks.[25]

Gentle Lucy Hayes paints a striking contrast to another woman dry, the most notorious prohibitionist in American history. Carry Amelia Moore was born in Kentucky in 1846 to a family marked by mental illness. (Carry's mother believed herself to be Queen Victoria.) At the age of twenty-one, her family impoverished by the Civil War, Carry married an incorrigible drunkard. Soon widowed, burdened with a daughter of mental and physical weakness, Carry later married the ineffectual preacher and lawyer David Nation. After several moves, the couple settled in Medicine Lodge, Kansas, in 1889, where Carry Nation at last came into her own.

Possessed of a fierce if singular religious faith, Carry Nation set out to aid the downtrodden of the world. Kansas at this time was ostensibly a dry state, having ratified a prohibition amendment in 1880. But illegal "joints" in many communities operated with the connivance of local authorities. Carry Nation's life experiences only reinforced the era's temperance beliefs—particularly the theory that alcoholism caused degenerate offspring. In 1892, Carry helped found the county WCTU and worked to convert local prisoners; her fervent public prayers soon closed the community's saloons. Seven years later, Carry heard the voice of God asking her to go further. With his encouragement, she demolished several joints in a neighboring community. Her exploits reinvigorated temperance in the region; destruction of the luxurious Hotel Carey saloon in Wichita garnered national attention. For the next several years, Carry Nation performed "hatchetations" across the country. Weakened by physical attacks and public ridicule, Nation retired in 1910 from saloon wrecking and lecturing. She died in 1911 of what appears to have been congenital syphilis.[26]

During her years of political activity, mainstream temperance organizations were rather at a loss as to how to treat Nation. The woman's obvious mental instability undermined her admirable temperance principles. The WCTU eventually disavowed her, though she continued to support herself on the thousands of individual donations she received each year. Carry Nation galvanized temperance supporters across the country while becoming an icon to antiprohibition forces in the twentieth century.

While Carry Nation represents one extreme of prohibitionist sentiment, her sentiments were expressed more quietly in communities across the nation. Many of the exclusive suburbs that developed around cities' new rail and highway lines outlawed saloons, indicating general middle- and upper-class sympathy for prohibition. Planners often took this philosophy one step further, marketing new towns explicitly as "temperance towns." Dry communities such as Harvey, Illinois, designed to avoid exposure to liquor and its attendant problems, spread in the later decades of the nineteenth century.[27]

Although prohibition victories in Iowa and Kansas inspired the WCTU and other dry organizations, enthusiasm among legislators and the general public faded as the 1880s progressed. Nonetheless, prohibition would dominate the WCTU's political focus for the next forty years. As with scientific temperance education and military dry zones, prohibition entailed a legislated solution to American intemperance. In contrast with the earlier enthusiasm for moral suasion, these temperance activists now supported involuntary abstinence. Viewers today might label such measures as legislated morality, which is somewhat accurate. But we must understand why the WCTU became so dogmatic, and why their dogmatism grew until it almost destroyed the organization in the final years of federal prohibition.

The WCTU endorsed prohibition (and temperance education and dry army bases) for the same reasons that temperance advocates had endorsed prohibition since the 1840s. Prohibition focused on drink itself instead of the failure of the drinker. This censure of alcohol and forgiveness of alcohol abusers deserves detailed consideration, for it illuminates the attitudes of many nineteenth-century women. Because motherhood explicitly defined femininity, women focused on the home and their biological role within it as a source of empowerment and autonomy. This explains women's enthusiasm for temperance and the effectiveness of their public role—indeed, of their lawbreaking—as "mothers." Temperance education and dry youth organizations such as the Loyal Temperance Legion exemplified WCTU maternalism. Every issue of the *Union Signal,* the WCTU's national newspaper, contained stories and poems for children. Willard claimed in her 1890 annual address that "the W.C.T.U. gives to each boy a score of mothers"—clearly to make sure they stayed out of saloons and out of trouble. As late as the 1930s the union continued its interest in educating children.[28]

In this respect, the WCTU was only capitalizing on the traditional associations of temperance with maternity, one of the most effective images at its disposal. The most moving scene in *Ten Nights in a Bar-room* is not the death of little Mary Morgan but the murder of Willy Hammond and the death from grief of his mother. When his mother hears that Willy has been stabbed, she runs to the tavern.

"Oh! Willy, my boy! my boy!" she exclaimed, in tones of anguish that made the heart shudder. And she crouched down on the floor, the moment she reached the bed whereon he lay, and pressed her lips—oh, so tenderly and lovingly!—to his.

"Dear mother! Sweet mother! Best of mothers!" He even smiled as he said this; and, into the face that now bent over him, looked up with glances of unutterable fondness. . . .

"Who says he is dead?" came sharply from the lips of the mother, as she pressed the form of her child back upon the bed from which he had sprung to her arms, and looked wildly upon his face. One long scream of horror told of her convictions, and she fell, lifeless, across the body of her dead son![29]

For all her love and pleading, Mrs. Hammond could not stop her son's drinking or the circumstances that led to his death.

Ten Nights exposes the painful predicament of nineteenth-century maternity: women in temperance auxiliaries, in moral reform societies, in lobbying organizations, even in saloon-bashing vigilante groups, could not prevent alcohol consumption. The mother, daughter, or wife of a drunkard could thus be considered a failure, for she had failed to perform the most important duty assigned her by society and ultimately by God: to keep her family pure and temperate. Yet to admit this failure would upset the entire structure of nineteenth-century femininity. Temperance advocates mediated this dilemma by vilifying alcohol. If, as society argued, the bond between mother and son were the strongest in the world, then only the poison alcohol would dissolve this tie. Thus, when two drunken teenaged boys were arrested at a "house of ill repute," women traced the trouble "to the sale of intoxicating liquors, and . . . resolved to devote their earnest and prayerful efforts to the suppression of intemperance." The "pious mothers" refrained from faulting their own child-rearing for such outrageous behavior; rather, women endorsed the most extreme dedication to temperance. At the founding convention of the WCTU, one woman campaigned to eliminate liquor even as a medicine. She "thought of my own darling boy, just merging into manhood, and dearly as I loved him I felt that I would gladly follow him to the grave rather than see him come to the condition of one of these" drunkards. The mother of a young man shot by wets wrote the *Union Signal,* "I'd rather have the sweet memory of my pure temperate boy to cherish, than to have a living son who would touch intoxicants or advocate their use. My sorrow cannot be half so bitter as the sorrow of a drunkard's mother."[30]

Readers sympathized with her story and understood as she did the need for prohibition to prevent such tragedy. Prohibition would justify her martyred son's death and, by removing all threat of contact with alcohol, would restore the bond between mother and son. Prohibition would provide women a solid moral platform in American politics—the only platform they would need—and would ensure the survival of nineteenth-century femininity and the ideals of motherhood. The WCTU came out in support of prohibition in 1879 and fought for it through the 1940s. And it soon considered woman suffrage the catalyst for prohibition's victory.

In 1852, male drys banned two Daughters of Temperance members from speaking at a Sons of Temperance convention in Albany because of their sex. Outraged, the two women, Susan B. Anthony and Mary C. Vaughn, formed the Woman's New York State Temperance Society, appointing Elizabeth Cady Stanton president. Thus the temperance movement, albeit rather backhandedly, inspired three of the nineteenth century's most important women leaders to form separatist women's groups. The woman's rights movement was well established by 1852. The famous Seneca Falls Convention, with its "Declaration of Sentiments" based on the Declaration of Independence, had taken place four years earlier. Stanton and Anthony were also active in the abolition movement. Temperance formed as important a contribution to the woman movement as abolition. Slavery fueled discussion of the innate equality of humans of all races and sexes; intemperance forced consideration of inequality and abuse within the American family.[31]

Many women soon found themselves at odds with male temperance supporters. Elizabeth Cady Stanton advocated divorce of male inebriates—a shocking suggestion in an era when women were expected to support and cure, not abandon, their husbands. Moreover, the prohibition legislation of the 1850s left women with little voice in the dry cause. Women could not vote in local-option elections, ratify state amendments, or hold office to oversee enforcement. In their frustration, some women drys settled on suffrage as the key element to women's political and social emancipation. Such radicalism led to early schisms over whether to focus on women's rights or temperance. By the mid-1850s, Susan B. Anthony refused to hold office in the Woman's New York State Temperance Society because of its refusal "to adopt Woman's Rights as a principle."[32]

On the other hand, more conservative drys felt women's rights, particularly suffrage, menaced the traditional political unit of family. Woman suffrage implied the entry of women into the public, sordid world of nineteenth-century politics. To the general population of mid-century Americans, the issue of women's political participation remained far too threatening to the institutions of marriage and family to receive mainstream support. Many women and men drys, it should be noted, did support forms of abridged suffrage. Especially in the last quarter of the nineteenth century, women's groups advocated local "women's ballots" on causes recognized as important to women's sphere, including regulation of local liquor traffic. (Such ballots had more significance than might be apparent, for a century ago local officials wielded far more power than today.) Conservative dry women also converted to suffrage following the Woman's Temperance Crusade. In town after town, men "failed to hold the ground the women had taken."[33] If dry laws succeeded or fizzled at the whim of elected officials, then women needed a voice in these officials' election.

The WCTU, however, did not endorse woman suffrage at its 1874 founding. Indeed, when Frances Willard spoke in favor of suffrage at the 1876 national convention, she was almost dismissed from the organization. Once elected president, in 1879, she encapsulated the issues of women's rights and woman suffrage in her "home protection" movement. Willard, like many of her contemporaries, originally envisioned women voting only in local elections. In line with its commitment to temperance education, the WCTU campaigned for women's right to vote in school board elections. By 1890, women voted in such elections in nineteen states.[34]

But partial suffrage did not adequately advance the temperance cause. The national union endorsed full woman suffrage in 1881. By the mid-1880s much of the WCTU's *Union Signal* focused on political analysis and endorsements. An 1884 editorial, "Women in Politics," described the WCTU's new attitude toward enfranchisement: "Patriotism alone leads woman to the front today. . . . If her vote is necessary to obtain or maintain prohibition, she will take up this new duty in the fear of God. . . . It is not our right, but our duty, to see that our sons and brothers are protected from this fell destroyer's power." The WCTU perceived enfranchisement not so much as a right as an obligation forced on women by their inherently moral status. As the primary victims of drink, wives and mothers had a prerogative to challenge it politically.[35]

It should not be surprising, given the overlapping concerns with women's empowerment and the vote, that temperance and suffrage shared supporters. Susan B. Anthony began as an activist in the Daughters of Temperance. Amelia Bloomer founded the feminist newspaper *Lily* as a temperance journal. Lucy Stone and her husband, Henry Blackwell, supported temperance as well as equal rights, and their daughter Alice Stone Blackwell, in addition to editing the *Woman's Journal,* served as the WCTU's associate national superintendent of franchise in the 1890s. She defended temperance and prohibition throughout her life. Mary Livermore, in the late 1870s, served as president of both the American Woman Suffrage Association and the Massachusetts WCTU. Similarly, the Reverend Anna Shaw, appointed national superintendent of the WCTU's Franchise Department in 1886, left the WCTU in the 1890s to concentrate on suffrage work. She led the National American Woman Suffrage Association from 1904 to 1915. Carrie Chapman Catt, NAWSA president from 1916 through the 1920 suffrage victory, described herself as a "total abstainer" and sympathized with prohibitionists; the WCTU claimed her as a member in 1924. Links between the two causes were even stronger locally, as small-town activists combined suffrage and prohibition sentiment in one organization, typically the WCTU.[36]

Male temperance organizations recognized the significance of women's voting. The Prohibition Party endorsed woman suffrage in 1872, even before the formation of the WCTU. Temperance Union members helped dry men develop the Anti-Saloon League, and Annie Wittenmyer, the WCTU's first president, served as an ASL trustee. Not so ironically, one of the few causes the ASL endorsed beyond prohibition was woman suffrage. With thousands of chapters in towns and cities throughout the country and a generation of experience in lobbying and legislative minutiae, WCTU members helped the ASL pass dry laws and elect dry legislators. Through the 1910s, the WCTU's national network proved crucial to the ASL's local, state, and national prohibition victories. The Anti-Saloon League was quick to take credit for woman suffrage as well as prohibition triumphs.[37]

Of course, the prohibition and woman suffrage amendments did not enjoy universal support, which explains why they each required a half century of effort to pass. In the twentieth century, activists blamed many standard villains in the Progressive lexicon—the railroads, oil interests, big business—for hindering the campaigns. To be sure, conservatives opposed to the extension of federal power viewed the two amendments with suspicion, particularly as they came on the heels of amendments permitting personal income tax and the direct election of senators. Probusiness congressmen argued instead for states' rights, the rights of private industry, and the innate differences between men and women. At the other end of the political spectrum, radicals such as Mother Jones and Emma Goldman dismissed "suffrage, prohibition, and charity" as busywork disguising the real issues affecting women and workers.[38]

For obvious reasons, brewers and distillers opposed prohibition wherever they encountered it. Alcohol manufacturers listened to the rhetoric of WCTU members and soon came to fear that all women supported prohibition. Brewers at an 1881 convention swore to oppose "woman suffrage everywhere and always; for when woman has the ballot, she will vote solid for prohibition; and woman's vote is the last hope of the Prohibitionists." A 1914 letter to "Liquor Dealers and Bartenders" described "the present onslaught on the liquor business, conducted by temperance cranks backed by woman suffrage" and warned, "If [woman suffrage] should win in this state be prepared to suffer the consequences." Some liquor men even described "the fast growing prohibition and woman suffrage movement," uniting the two in a singular cause. Beyond this, many immigrants, including German American brewers, simply did not believe in woman suffrage. They feared its threat to the family—a charge that suffragists did not or could not counter. German American women even spoke against suffrage in Congress. In point of fact, state woman suffrage amendments tended to discriminate against immigrants. South Dakota passed a woman suffrage amendment only after disenfranchising all resident aliens and threatening antisuffrage agitators with sedition. Bigotry colored both suffrage and prohibition arguments: Catt complained about "begging the vote from the Negroes, immigrants, and the liquor trade."[39]

Suffragists and drys for years blamed losses on an amorphous, malevolent vice trust headed by the "liquor interests." Suffragists felt "liquor men's" antisuffrage activity predated even the establishment of the WCTU. No other opponent attracted the rhetoric and loathing that suffragists, as well as drys, aimed at the alcohol industry. Suffragists produced examples of antisuffrage campaigning and ballot tampering by Nebraska brewers in 1882, Denver saloon keepers in 1893, Oregon saloon keepers in 1906, Wisconsin brewers in 1912, and Michigan and Montana saloon keepers in 1913. They pointed out that the head of the United Liquor Dealers Association lobbied against the Illinois suffrage bill of 1913. Organizations such as the Massachusetts Liquor League opposed woman suffrage in state amendment campaigns.[40]

In 1915, the state of Texas brought suit against the Texas Brewers' Association for antisuffrage election manipulation. The following year, one hundred Pennsylvania brewers and the U.S. Brewers' Association (USBA) were indicted on similar charges. The brewers paid a million-dollar fine in lieu of a trial. These cases received wide publicity, and even such wet journals as the *New Republic* castigated brewers' antisuffrage propaganda. The USBA took to burning its monthly minutes, fueling fears of conspiracy. In 1918, at the height of World War I and anti-German sentiment, the U.S. Senate Judiciary Committee investigated the USBA and an affiliated group, the German-American Alliance. The following year it released *Brewing and Liquor Interests and German and Bolshevik Propaganda*. The report established that brewers had campaigned against woman suffrage in nine states, funded antisuffrage organizations, and published antisuffrage literature. Such evidence sealed the perception of a national conspiracy. Catt and Nettie Rogers Shuler recorded these wet machinations in *Woman Suffrage and Politics: The Inner Story of the Suffrage Movement,* published in 1923. A thorough history of the suffrage movement and its eventual victory, the book also details the opposition (and the unlimited wealth, secrecy, and power) that suffragists perceived in the alcohol industry. Suffragists had always foundered in prohibition's wake, uncertain whether to climb on board or head for the opposite shore. But as the liquor industry came to represent the nadir of monopolistic control, corruption, and treason, suffragists' anxiety over their relationship to prohibition eased. As Catt and Shuler wrote, "the methods it employed became the boomerang that gave the liquor power its final and mortal blow."[41]

The alcohol industry recognized the danger of its position and tried to reform its worst offenders. As the attacks on brewers grew more pronounced, USBA leadership distanced itself from the topic of suffrage, and even suffragists admitted that the USBA never officially opposed the amendment. The USBA's Vigilance Committee on Woman Suffrage even praised the levelheadedness (i.e., the wet voting) of western women. Others took the offensive, blaming suffrage failures on the Anti-Saloon League, "which made it a 'wet' and 'dry' issue." Although drys denied it, in reality hostility between brewers, distillers, and vintners precluded widespread cooperation or conspiracy. Each branch of the liquor industry tried to use the dry issue to its own advantage. Distillers remained a presence even in dry states by shipping liquor COD. Brewers emphasized beer's healthfulness—"bread in a bottle"—and encouraged dry laws in the mistaken belief that lighter-alcohol beers would be exempted. California vintners highlighted their contribution to the state's economy. All played on patriotism and the rights of private industry. In the end, the arrogance of the liquor interests contributed as much as anything to prohibition. Even men hostile to the dry cause could not help but wince at the "usual blindness and stupidity of the liquor dealer, who . . . chose the path which inevitably led to greater disaster."[42]

Because of the friction between the liquor interests and prohibitionists, many suffragists tried to remove their cause from the line of fire. Most women realized that arguments promising that "women vote dry" would not win converts among drinkers. Some tried to explain their sympathy for prohibition by blaming the liquor industry, which in its hostility had *forced*

them into the dry camp. Cornelia Pinchot, a prominent Pennsylvania suffragist, converted to the dry cause when "I found out that the wet lobby
was against everything in which I was interested, laws against child labor,
women suffrage. . . . As a Progressive I always found the wets on the other
side. I don't mean to imply that every reactionary is a wet. But I do think
the reactionary movement as a whole is 95 percent wet." Others were careful to stop short of actually endorsing prohibition while making it clear
that the two reforms existed fist in glove.[43]

The nation's best-known wet suffragist was Abigail Scott Duniway of
Oregon. Duniway herself felt that alcohol was dangerous and the liquor interests worse. She believed the world would be better off without intoxicating drink, and she hoped people would refrain voluntarily. But she criticized on philosophical grounds the legal restriction of alcohol. Prohibition
contradicted American equality and self-determination. Drunkards and society would be better served by legally empowering "the drunkard's wife
. . . to protect her home from a husband's debauchery." Duniway blamed
the WCTU for West Coast defeats from the 1880s to the 1910s and for this
reason hated prohibitionists passionately. Duniway was not alone in believing that prohibition alienated men from the suffrage cause, though she
spoke louder than most. Throughout its existence the NAWSA grappled
with how to approve of prohibition without endorsing it, for the association
did not want to antagonize drinking voters. Here the NAWSA followed the
lead of Susan B. Anthony. The former Daughters of Temperance organizer
refused to state publicly her opinion on prohibition or other issues until
she had been granted the vote. In an 1896 letter to Duniway she stated,
"My personal belief as to prohibition, pro or con, is nobody's business but
my own, but I have done all I could to keep the two questions (Woman Suffrage and Prohibition) separate. . . . The two movements cannot successfully unite to win for either cause. But I am glad to see women awakened
from their apathy through any movement that is backed by the churches,
since so many of them cannot be aroused in any other way." Anna Howard
Shaw, NAWSA president and former WCTU leader, took a similar stance.
Shaw stated repeatedly that women deserved enfranchisement regardless
of how, or even whether, they voted. Catt reiterated this theme. But while
few state suffrage organizations spoke publicly in favor of prohibition,
fewer still spoke against it.[44]

Although the two organizations shared leaders and membership, the
WCTU and NAWSA regarded each other warily. When the WCTU was organized in 1874, founders had grave doubts about suffrage's radicalism. At

the same time, Anthony and Elizabeth Cady Stanton worried that suffrage might become "no more than an annex to the W.C.T.U." As woman suffrage increased in respectability and power in the 1890s, suffragists began utilizing dry workers—for a price. The WCTU scheduled its 1896 national convention in San Francisco, one month before a state election on a woman suffrage amendment. After frantic letters from Anthony to her friend Frances Willard, the WCTU moved the convention site to St. Louis so that the WCTU would not prejudice drinking voters against woman suffrage. The decision to move left suffragists relieved and WCTU members, who felt suffrage never had "a ghost of a chance . . . to pass," furious. Although Anthony dismissed the incident later, at the time she wrote Willard that the WCTU was "sticking pins into the men" voters.[45]

By the late 1910s, suffragists found the topic of prohibition too polarizing even to discuss. Opponents of woman suffrage capitalized on prohibition, quoting suffragists' dry statements to wet audiences and their wet statements to dry audiences. Suffragists were therefore "exceedingly chary of discussing the question" of suffrage and prohibition, as any "expression of opinion one way or the other will be seized upon by the other side and used against suffrage."[46]

Convoluting the situation still further were the drys who criticized woman suffrage, thus violating the traditional sympathy between the two movements. The South, justifying opposition on the grounds of states' rights, remained woman suffrage's greatest foe. This, suffragists pointed out, was all the more ironic in light of southern support of federal prohibition. But prohibition in the South was predicated on the control of blacks and poor whites, and drys there capitalized on fears of drunken black men. Woman suffrage, on the other hand, challenged white male hegemony. In the North, some male temperance groups also opposed suffrage through the 1910s, feeling that immigrant, drinking women would offset any increase in the dry vote. Suffragists found these attacks particularly galling and hurtful.[47]

Women opposed to suffrage repeated ad nauseum these concerns about immigrants' wet voting. The National Association Opposed to Woman Suffrage, the largest antisuffrage group, claimed several hundred thousand women members by 1915. "Antis"—antisuffragists—argued that women were more moral, "purer," than men and thus should remain above the fray of politics. Historians have interpreted this to mean women should not enter public life, which is not exactly accurate. Antis worked in charity and labor organizations, often in positions of authority. Women such as Margaret C. Robinson of the Massachusetts Anti-Suffrage Association lobbied legislatures and campaigned for welfare and child labor reform. Robinson felt that women wielded more power as nonpartisan observers than they ever would as party cogs.[48]

Suffragists dismissed antis as being in the pocket of the liquor men. The *Woman's Journal* satirized a dowdy anti fronting for the secret political "boss" and the "liquor and vicious interests" (figure 1.3). In fact, however, women antis despised the alcohol industry. One anti wrote, "The women of America, without a vote among them, abolished slavery. The great temperance movement of to-day, which grows stronger and spreads wider every hour, is the work of women with no aid from the ballot. If we were all the right kind of women, thoughtful, wise, loving, helpful, striving to understand and do the best things, the world would move onward as fast as we could lead. The ballot is only a hindrance to such progress, for it tempts the weak and useless woman to think that it would give her power in an easy and irresponsible way."[49] Antis advocated the continuation of a separate political sphere for women, one that tapped their unique abilities and talents.

If anything, antis had more respect than their opponents for the insidious strength of the liquor interests. That is to say, they had less faith that women could overcome this evil. The frontispiece illustration of the 1915

Figure 1.3 "Anti-Allies and the Dog"

A political cartoon from the nation's leading suffrage magazine depicts female antisuffragists as frumpy and powerless and male antisuffragists as corrupt and insidious. Suffragists astride the white horse of progress would overcome both liquor and vice. Dennis Reardon, the dog in the cartoon, was a Boston machine hack who inadvertently publicized the Massachusetts Liquor League's opposition to woman suffrage. Woman's Journal 46 (2 Oct. 1915): 314.

Figure 1.4 "Politics and Home Rule"—the other side of the woman
suffrage argument

While the "Home-Rule" mother devotes herself to raising an enormous baby,
the woman in "Politics" smokes cigars, supports lady prizefighters, and
drinks whiskey and soda—adopting the most masculine elements of mascu-
line governance. The Case against Woman Suffrage *(New York: Man-*
Suffrage Association Opposed to Political Suffrage for Women, 1915),
frontispiece.

Case against Woman Suffrage shows the "Home-Rule" woman fulfilling her
political destiny by raising a healthy baby (figure 1.4). Her opposite, in
"Politics," smokes cigars, supports lady politicians and boxers, and drinks
whiskey. If women entered politics, the picture implies, they would
inevitably become corrupted. The forces of evil were too strong to be
resisted.

THE RELATIONSHIP BETWEEN SUFFRAGE AND PROHIBITION:
AN INVESTIGATION

Most Americans took one of two positions on the two amendments. Some,
predominantly male, opposed both amendments. Others, including many
women, supported both amendments. Many suffragists adopted publicly a
third stance, one of neutrality on the prohibition question. Other women
opposed to woman suffrage endorsed prohibition and felt women's votes

only threatened dry reform. Thus we have summarized the four possible positions one could take on the two amendments: wet anti, dry suffragist, wet suffragist, dry anti. The arguments these four groups employed seemed designed to baffle their listeners, as wets and drys, suffragists and antis, struggled to convince audiences of the justice of their respective causes.

As the number of dry and woman suffrage states increased in the second decade of the twentieth century, women's voting came under close analysis. Some suffragists, already enthusiastic about prohibition, sought to prove that women voters mattered and that women would improve the nation. Accordingly, they emphasized the spread of dry sentiment in woman suffrage states. Catt wrote proudly that in Illinois, "press headlines, the morning after [women's] first election, . . . announced that woman suffrage had closed one thousand saloons." But antisuffragists described this glass as half empty. With headlines such as "Women's Votes No Cure-All," antis pulled examples from state after state to establish women voters as no better than, and perhaps worse than, men.[50]

California furnished a plethora of contradictory information. The state granted women suffrage in 1911 as part of the reform platform of Progressive governor Hiram Johnson. Male voters in 1911 also passed a local-option law allowing towns to vote out saloons. Suffragists credited women voters with tripling the number of dry communities in the following three years. Suffragists also credited women for the California Red Light Injunction and Abatement Act of 1913, a law designed to suppress prostitution and vice. But antisuffragists pointed out that a state prohibition amendment did not pass in 1914 or 1916, despite the supposed efforts of women voters. In San Francisco, three times more women were registered voters than the city's entire vote for local option. Antis argued that "dissolute women" overwhelmed the "moral influence" of WCTU and YWCA members. Pasadena, dry since its founding in 1866, went wet in the first election attended by women. One anti concluded, "With alien women as well as men voting as they are bound to vote, 'wiping out the liquor traffic' looks like a very remote achievement."[51] Antisuffragists worried that indiscriminate enfranchisement eliminated respectable women's effectiveness.

Is it possible, then, to determine what effect women had on enactment of dry laws? In answering this question, we must first acknowledge the extent of prohibition sympathy in the early twentieth century. Prohibition has often been depicted as a law forced through distracted wartime legislatures by the Machiavellian Anti-Saloon League. But state amendments ratified by popular vote, and draconian dry legislation that even the ASL opposed, indicate that dry sentiment outstripped ASL control and expectations. More than two-thirds of the twenty-three prohibition states in 1916 went dry directly through voter referendums. Prohibition enthusiasm peaked in the late 1910s, boosted in part by World War I and patriotic arguments for grain conservation and personal asceticism. By 1918 brewers and distillers could find few public supporters willing to risk stigmatization as a tool of the liquor interests.[52] National momentum for prohibition thus extended far beyond the issue and regions of woman suffrage.

The role of women voters in the passage of state prohibition amendments is difficult to establish. The wide variety of local and state prohibition laws and the numerous forms of woman suffrage obscure the extent to which drys supported woman suffrage and women voted dry. With the exception of California, the full-suffrage states of the American West all had statewide prohibition by 1920. At the same time twenty-three other states were dry without women's votes. One female observer in Colorado stated in 1909, "though the passage of the local-option law was doubtless made less difficult by the fact that the women of the state vote, this, like other recent victories of the temperance cause, seems to have been primarily a result of the wave of temperance enthusiasm which has swept over the whole United States." She felt that women contributed mainly by dissuading saloon keepers from running for office.[53]

Voting data from the period help to establish women's dry sympathies. In Portland, Oregon, in 1914, women voters supported prohibition more enthusiastically than twenty-five other referendums, including abolition of the death penalty and establishment of an eight-hour workday. In Chicago in 1919, twice as many women as men supported a local prohibition measure. Women constituted 37.9 percent of Chicago voters in the presidential election the following year; analysis revealed that these women contributed one-third of the votes for Democratic and Republican candidates but more than half the votes for the Prohibition Party. An Oregon historian writing on the state prohibition amendment of 1916 estimated, "a fair approximation would give a ratio of two to one for prohibition among the women, and three to two among the men."[54]

Observers assumed beyond question an inextricable relationship between woman suffrage and prohibition. In 1913 the muckraking magazine *Collier's,* criticizing the antisuffrage intrigues of the liquor interests, concluded, "All women are not paragons of virtue and wisdom; far from it; 'the Lord made them to match the men,' but there are certain ancient evils,

chief among which is drunkenness, against which women have fought and
worked and prayed since time began. Suffrage is a weapon, and the first
thing that women will do with it will be to turn it against this world-old

enemy of the home." Jack London, an alcoholic, wrote in 1913 that he supported woman suffrage because women "would vote John Barleycorn out
of existence and back into the historical limbo of our vanished customs of
savagery." A 1916 writer in the *Atlantic Monthly*—a writer who opposed
woman suffrage—felt that most women opposed liquor and wanted the
vote only for this reason.[55]

37

o o o

*Gender,
Prohibition,
Suffrage,
and Power*

One intriguing incident illustrates the link between the two causes. In
1913, the Illinois Equal Suffrage Association argued for months over
whether to accept a thousand-dollar advertisement from the state Brewers'
Association. Members agreed that brewers were submitting the ad as a direct challenge to suffragists' claims to liberal broad-mindedness. But in
the end, the association refused the ad in deference to the dry sentiments
of many members, including Jane Addams and Ella Seass Stewart.[56] These
prominent women felt freedom of the press mattered less than combatting
liquor and the saloons.

Addams, Seass, London, the *Atlantic,* and *Collier's* all perceived alcohol
as inherently threatening to womankind. This belief extended beyond prohibition and suffrage organizations. In the mid-1910s, the National Conference of Charities and Correction and the even more conservative Daughters of the American Revolution endorsed federal prohibition. Temperance
and temperance education had been a frequent topic in women's clubs
since the Civil War; in 1914, the General Federation of Women's Clubs, a
national organization with more than a million affiliated members, publicly
approved both woman suffrage and prohibition. Its leaders would endorse
federal prohibition through the early 1930s.[57]

Both suffragists and antis denied formal association between women
and prohibition. From the mid-nineteenth century through the late 1910s,
suffragists described the "misapprehension" of a connection between their
cause and prohibition. Yet suffragists also refrained from painting themselves as wet, individually describing themselves as "strong believers in
temperance" or "total abstainers." When read between the lines, suffragists' continued denial of a relationship with drys indicates how strong that
relationship in fact was. At the same time, antis reprinted with glee information showing that women voters did not support prohibition or other
"women's" reforms such as child labor laws. To late-twentieth-century
readers, such reports appear designed to increase support for woman suf-

frage.[58] But such was not the case in 1915. Antisuffragists would not have gone to the trouble to allege women's lack of support for prohibition unless they felt that people believed otherwise—and that politicians and voters wanted women's dry votes.

The suffrage movement elucidates the success of the prohibition movement. Prosuffrage and antisuffrage women together demonstrate the extensiveness of public sentiment against the alcohol industry in the early twentieth century. Suffragists felt the world would be better served by elimination of an industry they considered unscrupulous and corrupting. Furthermore, as this book makes clear, prohibition enjoyed the support of suffragists' enemies, antisuffragists, as well. Antis took great offense at being associated with the liquor trusts. Their outrage and disgust illustrate how few friends saloons had among middle-class, native Americans. By the mid-1910s even drinkers such as Jack London advocated elimination of the saloon. Americans of many persuasions supported an act of trust-busting in this age of trust-busting.

Just as close examination of the woman suffrage movement explains concurrent dry enthusiasm, so too does the prohibition movement serve as a lens—one highly effective lens—into woman suffrage. The suffrage amendment did not pass because of the hard work and noble sentiments of a handful of dedicated, liberal-minded feminists. It passed because legislators in Congress and in thirty-six states, backed by several million male and female voters, voted for it. The amendment would not have been ratified without the support of politicians and voters intent on using it to further their own agendas, including prohibition. Voters with little concern for woman suffrage, objecting to the antisuffrage machinations of the Brewers' Association and the German-American Alliance, supported the enemy of their enemy. The prohibition movement illustrates the various conflicting aspirations suffragists of all stripes attached to the suffrage amendment.

The prohibition movement furthermore explains the timing of the woman suffrage amendment. Granted, it was not the sole element in suffrage's ultimate success. Like prohibitionists, suffragists realized in the early 1910s that painful, expensive state-by-state campaigns made less sense than a sweeping national one. Women by 1920 had received enough other legal and economic privileges to diffuse the radicalism of enfranchisement. Moreover, women in Great Britain, Denmark, Australia, New Zealand, Canada, and—notably—Germany now voted. All these factors contributed to the squeak-through success of woman suffrage. But the point must also be made that the Eighteenth Amendment, the prohibition amendment, was ratified, and upheld by the Supreme Court in June of 1920, before the Nineteenth Amendment, granting woman suffrage, passed that August. Suffragists at the time believed the liquor interests stopped battling woman suffrage only after they realized prohibition could not be overturned. For all the antisuffrage activities of alcohol producers and dealers, prohibition still passed. The Eighteenth Amendment thus succeeded without the votes of most American women.[59] The Nineteenth Amendment served only as an epilogue in the national battle for prohibition. Women voters simply reinforced further a law that was to all observers irrevocably permanent.

The prohibition debates of the early twentieth century capture the period's anxiety over the power women were perceived as wielding. Women who supported suffrage and prohibition felt they could only do good with votes. Other drys, fearing that too much power would be handed to women who would not use it appropriately, argued against woman suffrage. Opponents of the two amendments worried that enfranchised women might carry out a little too much "good." It is striking how effective each of these factions considered women to be. Supporters and opponents had deep faith in women's ability to effect change, even if women antisuffragists feared this would be lost, not enhanced, with enfranchisement.

Even more striking, however, is the manner in which debates about gender roles and gendered behavior became conflated in these two issues. Both woman suffrage and prohibition challenged traditional male public behavior. Supporters of the two amendments considered alcohol and politics pathologically intertwined: both male drinking and male politics required female intervention. One woman spoke in favor of suffrage and prohibition with a single example—the use of saloons as polling places. "You will not have ballot-boxes in saloons when your wives and daughters have votes," she explained, implying as well that you would not have political machines or vice or even saloons themselves once women voted. Another suffragist wrote in 1886 of the effort to keep men from "billiard rooms, club-houses, saloons, hotel parlors, and political headquarters, where so many men forget their duties to wives and children, and contract habits which rob them of manhood." Suffragists took great pride in the California Red Light Injunction and Abatement Act, passage of which they credited to new female voters.[60] In a 1914 *Chicago Tribune* political cartoon, a man in a bar promises the votes of his wife, daughters, "and mebbe the cook" to "Alderman Barleycorn" and staggers off to instruct them (figure 1.5). But the following morning the man's house is plastered with posters for respectable "James Dry." The cartoon appeared two weeks before the first election following women's enfranchisement in the state of Illinois.

In *Woman Suffrage and Politics: The Inner Story of the Suffrage Movement,* Carrie Catt captured this melding of men, liquor, and politics in her description of the final days of the campaign for woman suffrage. Tennessee, the last state needed to ratify the Nineteenth Amendment, had been dry since 1909 and had ratified the prohibition amendment eighteen months earlier.

> With nothing to do, [state representatives] again accepted the invitation to the eighth floor, where a group of anti-suffrage men dispensed old Bourbon and moonshine whisky with lavish insistence. . . . Denial

Figure 1.5
"Delivering the
Woman Vote"

The Chicago Tribune
*printed this front-page
cartoon shortly before
the first Illinois election
in which women participated. Here men,
obeying their saloon
keepers, vote for
"Barleycorn"; women,
doubtless upset over
their loss of sleep, for
the very dry-looking
"Dry." The newspaper
could not have stated
more clearly the anticipated effect of women
voters on the liquor
interests.* Chicago
Sunday Tribune, 5
Apr. 1914, 1. Courtesy
Chicago Tribune.

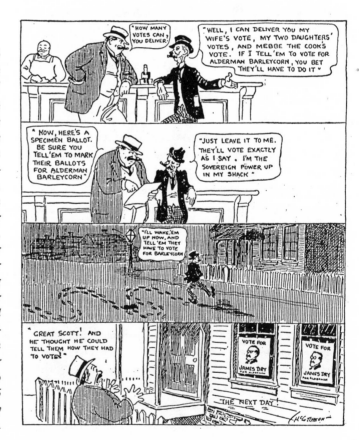

of this traditional license when a great issue was at stake would be resented as an interference with established custom by suffragists and anti-suffragists—"This is the Tennessee way." Suffragists were plunged into helpless despair. Hour by hour suffrage men and women who went to the different hotels of the city to talk with the legislators came back to the Hermitage headquarters to report. And every report told the same story—the Legislature was drunk! "How many legislators?" was the abashed query. No one knew. "Are none sober?" was the next asked. "Possibly," was the answer.

Tennessee ultimately ratified the amendment. But Catt and her fellow suffragists had no patience with the drunkenness that male suffrage permitted. Women, they felt, would eliminate the worst excesses of traditional masculine political behavior.[61]

Nor were suffragists alone in this perception. When Wyoming Territory granted women the vote in 1870, one male editor wrote, "There was plenty of drinking and noise at the saloons, . . . but the men would not remain, after voting, around the polls. It seemed more like Sunday than election day." Clearly, many men and women enjoyed seeing election day turned into a more serious and controlled event. In the 1912 comedy film *A Suffragette in Spite of Himself,* the ambivalent hero fought off both suffragists and antisuffragists "and staggered home only to find that his maid had impishly planted a 'Votes for Women' banner beneath his bourbon bottle."[62] To the film's creators, no other image captured as well the manner in which woman suffrage would permeate—and alter—man's life.

Politics, masculinity, and alcohol were a powerful triumvirate in the early years of the twentieth century. It is, therefore, not surprising that women accused drinking politicians of opposing woman suffrage. The liquor interests had every reason to oppose woman suffrage as zealously as prohibition. For the women who spoke in favor of prohibition and of suffrage were not describing simply a saloon-free America but were arguing for elimination of the entire masculine culture that made institutions such as the saloon possible. Thus the brewers, saloon keepers, and liquor men were fighting for far more than the preservation of their jobs. On a fundamental level they were engaged in a losing struggle to preserve their very self-identity.

DOMESTIC DRINKING IN VICTORIAN AMERICA

Victorian drinking practices have already been the subject of some discussion in *Domesticating Drink*. Men's drinking fueled formation of the Woman's Christian Temperance Union and other organizations within the nineteenth-century woman movement, groups that sought to control not only male alcohol consumption but also male sexuality, warfare, and politics. Indeed, the concurrent campaigns for prohibition and woman suffrage were in many ways inseparable. In highlighting the gender divisions of the nineteenth century, male drinking inspired women's demands for a public presence.

Activists within the woman movement depicted women as the moral opposites of men: pious, domestic, community-spirited, and thus essential to effective reform, temperance or otherwise. Temperance activists utilized a second set of polarities, as well. If men were hard-drinking and therefore disreputable, then women were, as a sex, abstemious. This construct was essential to dry women's political activism. It has since become a truism permeating scholarship on the temperance movement and nineteenth-century womanhood.

But the polarity of dry women and wet men so crucial to the success of the WCTU merits closer examination. For if respectable, middle-class women did in fact drink, much is at stake. We must rethink gender antagonism and the nature of Victorian gendered spaces. Victorian women's alcohol consumption, should it be discovered, would inspire dramatic reinterpretation of the generational "revolution in manners and morals" in early twentieth-century life. Most importantly, Victorian women's drinking forces further consideration of the popularity of the WCTU and other dry women's groups and of the frictions that separated dry and drinking women. It is therefore imperative to examine drinking practices in Victorian America, that period between the 1850s and the first years of the twentieth century.

This chapter focuses on the reality of drinking within the home. Advice literature such as etiquette manuals, cookbooks, table-setting guides, and home entertainment handbooks describes alcohol's pervasive presence in respectable sociability in the late nineteenth and early twentieth centuries. Fictional sources, including temperance stories in publications of the Woman's Christian Temperance Union, reiterate the relationship between alcohol and the attentive hostess. Although certainly affected by regional and class differences, alcohol use remained remarkably consistent over these fifty years. The wealth of discussion within primary sources demonstrates that alcohol had a distinct and accepted role in the home long before the domestic excess of flappers and cocktail parties in 1920s America. We have long understood the connection between social aspiration and temperance enthusiasm. Closer research drives home the connection between respectability and drinking.

THE RHETORICAL USES OF WOMEN'S DRINKING

In nineteenth-century America, the gendered dyad of male and female spheres had a powerful material component. Men and women to a great degree occupied separate spaces, distinct worlds permeated with masculine and feminine values. Industrialization moved male artisans and farmers out of the home, the traditional workplace, into sex-segregated factories and offices. The work environment was no longer defined by the routines and interactions of gender and family; instead, men and women now labored with members of their own sex. While the cult of domesticity may have trapped women in the home, it also provided them unprecedented authority within it. Men, still nominally heads of the household, often found themselves treated as boarders, outsiders to the affection and rhythm of domestic America.

Discussion of women's drinking and alcohol abuse was thus rendered most problematic by the fact that drinking was, for the most part, a public, male activity conducted in public, male spaces. Women drinkers threatened this gender division. Both fictitious and "truthful" descriptions of women inebriates dwelt with particular horror on the public nature of their drunkenness: the daughter of a judge arrested while walking the streets "in her night costume," for example, or the businessman's wife who insisted on going into "public places where she makes a show of herself." The general association of women's drinking with sexual depravity and with prostitution—a profession connected to public spaces and particularly to male saloons—reinforced this horror over public drunkenness. As early as the 1840s some women's temperance groups had difficulty empathizing with women inebriates, associating them too closely with prostitutes and immorality. The temperance movement, after all, was profoundly vested in domesticity and in the contrast between public male drinking and private female abstinence. Women, expected to be "angels," suffered especially when exposed as human.[1]

Fear of women's alcohol abuse excited a great many people who molded the situation to their own ends. Female inebriates were used to illustrate male selfishness, thoughtlessness, and brutality. Concern about women drinkers fostered the creation of separate medical institutions and heightened criticism of common medical practices. Most of all, women's abusive drinking drove home the destructive potential of alcohol. We must, therefore, turn to these descriptions to begin to understand a fuller range of drinking behavior. Such rhetoric and hyperbole illustrate the barriers to rational discussion of women's moderate drinking.

Temperance advocates used the spectacle of women inebriates to attack male insensitivity and cruelty. In the 1870 short story "A Victim of Excitement," debutante Anne Weston develops a taste for drink through her father's "lavish indulgence," worsened by her husband's "unyielding distrust." Another woman with a drunkard husband begins drinking only "to seek in that which gratifies his appetite, some solace in her misery." Writers criticized physicians who blithely prescribed drink for women patients, thereby "bring[ing] an unspeakable curse upon the hapless and innocent." The WCTU even produced a handbook of temperance medical treatments, *Alcohol: A Dangerous and Unnecessary Medicine.* The book described "a lady, Mrs. A., tenderly nurtured, refined, cultured, moving in an influential position, [who] belonged to a family in whom the tendency to intemperance existed." Although she strove to remain abstinent, her husband and doctor insisted she take wine for an illness. She became an inebriate and, after twice entering asylums, "fell into the lowest degradation and utter ruin, surely deserving our deepest pity." The story damningly concludes, "her doctor and her husband had persisted in working her fall in spite of her own strongest convictions."[2] Men not only harmed women by their own drinking but drove them to intemperance, as well.

Both physicians and drys stressed women's unique medical needs. Menstruation, pregnancy, childbirth, and menopause created pain that doctors and patients treated with drink—with the ominous results described above. One doctor advised that "a careful practitioner should remember the peculiar sensitivity of women during certain portions of their life. . . . Hence, if he prescribes alcohol for them at all, it should not be for trivial ailments, which are liable to recur frequently." Etiquette writer Mrs. John Farrar blamed the use of "stimulating liquors" on "sedentary habits, hot rooms, tight lacing, late hours, improper diet, want of bathing, &c." *Alcohol: A Dangerous and Unnecessary Medicine* listed nonalcoholic remedies to medical complaints, including baths, simple stretching exercise, hot water bottles, and the Victorian panacea of regular bowels.[3]

Others blamed the cultural oppression of women for their drinking problems. British traveler Harriet Martineau in the 1830s described "the vacuity of mind of many women" that led to "the habit of intemperance . . . among women of station and education in the most enlightened parts of the country." If American women could "ever so far cast off self-restraint, shame, domestic affection, and the deep prejudices of education, as to plunge into the living hell of intemperance, there must be something fearfully wrong in their position." *One Thousand Temperance Anecdotes* included the story of a woman who insisted, against her husband's warnings, on using alcohol in her cooking, medicine, and socializing, particularly with their five sons. Two of the sons died drunkards. "By the [remaining] three the mother was often, when they were sober, upbraided as the prime instrument of their degradation and ruin."[4] When women were not equipped to manage their responsibilities, tragedy ensued.

Much of the concern over women's drinking and social responsibility stemmed from fears of race suicide. According to scientists of the period, inebriety was an inherited trait that would worsen with succeeding generations. Thus, not only abusive but also moderate drinkers put their children and grandchildren at risk. One article that should have been banned from the public mails describes a family's three-generation descent from moderate drinking to incest, prostitution, drug addiction, sodomy, and miscegenation. Others analyzed women's drinking through social Darwinist principles. A doctor wrote in 1892 that women charged with drunkenness "are always profoundly degenerate, both mentally and physically . . . the unfit and the last remnants of the race-stock hurried on to death by a law that knows no shade or shadow of turning." The implication, of course, is that these drinkers were barely human, not fully women. Physicians thus proposed sterilization as a long-term solution to inebriety. Dr. Agnes Sparks considered "desexualization" a last resort. Her recommendation bears particular mention because she herself considered alcohol addiction more environmental than hereditary. Her comments thus illustrate the ubiquity of eugenicist thought in the alcohol debate.[5]

Commentators at the time pointed out how society marginalized women inebriates. Most writers criticized society's forgiveness of men's drinking problems rather than advocating acceptance of women's drinking. But others stressed that society's disgust with woman drunkards made their recovery especially difficult. Women with drinking problems would stoop to any deceit to avoid being labeled as drunkards, as would their families. Harriet Martineau described how a man begins drinking "with conviviality, and only arrives at solitary intemperance as the ultimate degradation. A woman indulges in the vice in solitude and secrecy, as long as secrecy is possible." T. D. Crothers, writing for the WCTU's *Union Signal,* leveled a bitter assault on women who punished, instead of aiding, woman drunkards. In the *Quarterly Journal of Inebriety,* Crothers compared public disdain to "the old persecution of witches."[6]

Crothers had a professional interest in seeing inebriety treatment modernized. Inebriates, he continued, were not sinful but "sick and diseased, and need care, treatment, and restraint." This contrasted with the more common belief among late-century temperance advocates and physicians that alcoholism represented a moral failing on the part of the individual—an attitude that was particularly hard on women. The American Association for the Cure of Inebriates, an organization of physicians within asylums and treatment centers, established the *Quarterly Journal of Inebriety* in 1876. The association and the journal argued that alcoholism was a disease rather than a moral failing. Both focused upon the benefits and treatments within inebriate asylums.[7] The *Quarterly Journal of Inebriety* was therefore unusual for discussing repeatedly and in detail women's abusive drinking.

UNCOVERING THE REALITY OF WOMEN'S ALCOHOL ABUSE

Institutions to cure, or at least dry out, problem drinkers were a common feature of the late Victorian landscape. Between the Civil War and the turn of the century, more than a hundred inebriates' hospitals opened in the United States. Many of these institutions had begun as boarding houses catering to the Washingtonians, a short-lived working-class temperance group. The most successful (financially, at least) and well-known hospital was Dr. Leslie Keeley's Dwight Institute, where sufferers received daily injections of his secret "Gold Cure." Although other physicians such as Crothers dismissed Keeley as a quack, by 1901 Keeley had thirty-nine branch institutes and a network of three hundred Keeley League chapters.

Other models existed as well. The Franklin Reformatory Home for Inebriates in Philadelphia opened in 1872 with a staff of recovered inebriates. All
admissions were voluntary, and the home did not accept "tramps"—two
factors that may have accounted for its success. The home offered medical
care to acute cases, dormitory housing when necessary, and regular
evening meetings with public confession and prayer. Besides bed rest and
close supervision, an institute's treatment might include strychnine, ar-
senic, or electrical shock.[8]

Men constituted a significant majority of the drunkard population and
were recognized more willingly by American society. Accordingly, asylums
sought out and catered to men. Institutions that did admit women operated within expected cultural boundaries. Separating women and men patients proved one challenge, particularly when treatment involved public
confession or activity that might offend feminine delicacy. The Dwight Institute, which admitted women, guaranteed them private rooms and private injections.[9]

Even before the Civil War, temperance reformers advocated separate
hospitals for women, particularly those of "respectable families." To its
great credit, the WCTU pledged to work for "Homes for Inebriate Women"
at its founding convention in 1874. The union established at least five
homes, staffed in part by women, in New York, Philadelphia, and Manchester, New Hampshire, and two in Chicago. There "women who are victims of strong drink can have the chemical cure applied to their diseased
bodies and the gospel cure to their diseased souls." Treatment in the
WCTU homes consisted mainly of a Christian and sympathetic environment free of alcohol.[10] The brief lives of these institutions indicates that
the needs of woman drinkers and their would-be saviors did not, for financial, philosophical, or other reasons, coincide. Nowhere was this clearer
than in the Woman's National Hospital. In the early 1880s, J. Edward
Turner, founder of the New York State Inebriate Asylum in Binghamton,
set out to create an institution for women, staffed by women, in Wilton,
Connecticut (figure 2.1). Reports in the national press on Turner's mis-
management combined with ecclesiastical and public opposition. The Connecticut state legislature rejected the hospital's charter in 1885, although
ground had already been broken for the project.[11] Like WCTU caregivers,
Turner, for all his good intentions, could not overcome the social opprobrium women inebriates faced.

Much of the discussion on women's asylums revolved around drug
rather than alcohol abuse. In the late nineteenth century, Americans ac-

Figure 2.1   The Woman's National Hospital

A model of Victorian institutional architecture, the Woman's National
Hospital was intended to house respectable women alcoholics. The Connecti-
cut State Legislature, finding the project far too controversial, withdrew
funding in 1885 after ground had been broken. J. Edward Turner, The
History of the First Inebriate Asylum in the World *(New York: privately*
printed, 1888), x.

knowledged women's opium addiction far more readily than their alcohol
addiction. Available in patent medicines and by prescription, opium, lau-
danum, morphine, and heroin treated countless physical and emotional ailments. Women took opiates knowingly, when prescribed, and unknow-
ingly, when drugs were added to prescription and over-the-counter
medications. By the turn of the century, respectable middle-aged women
made up the majority of opium addicts. Many female asylum patients,
therefore, were admitted for drug addiction. The Dwight Institute "generally" treated women "for opium or morphine," not alcohol; at one time,
women made up 40 percent of the institute's drug addict population. Similarly, women associated with the Alabama Insane Hospital tended toward
drug rather than alcohol problems.[12]

   To be sure, narcotics and alcohol were often conflated in the public
mind; it was not uncommon to see alcohol itself described as a "narcotic"
in the popular press. This can also be seen in reports that alcohol use by
parents, particularly fathers, would lead to "a defective nervous system" in
daughters, who would "turn to narcotics for relief, using opium, chloral, or
other drugs." Turn-of-the-century pure food and drug laws required that

medications state both alcohol and opiate content. Criticisms of physicians for overprescribing alcohol for chronic female complaints recurred with opiates. Moreover, asylums tended to combine treatment of inebriety and drug addiction, often "curing" inebriety with morphine and heroin.[13]

Women's apparent preference for opiates over alcohol may be considered gendered. Observers at the time claimed that women were more inclined to opium use because of its "feminine" qualities. The *Journal of the American Medical Association* proudly asserted that "the American woman cannot constitutionally use any form of alcohol as her foreign sisters use it. . . . American women of all classes want rest, not increased excitement, hence they seek this more naturally in narcotics." One physician wrote in 1891 that "as a rule, women take opiates and men alcohol. . . . A woman is very degraded before she will consent to display drunkenness to mankind; whereas, she can obtain equally if not more pleasurable feelings with opiates, and not disgrace herself before the world." Drug abuse was solitary and private, in contrast with the public nature of drinking. Indeed, until late in the century opiate use among women may have been far more acceptable socially than drinking simply because the effects of opiates corresponded to contemporary female roles. Massachusetts druggists interviewed in 1872 described opium as "more 'genteel' than alcohol." One asserted that opium use "[is] exceedingly common among certain classes of people who crave the effects of the stimulant, but will not risk their reputation for temperance by taking alcoholic beverages." But by the turn of the century opiates were under even harsher attack than alcohol. A woman in a 1902 advertisement for premixed cocktails commented that "a Martini. . . . is so much better than a drug of any kind" (figure 2.2). As narcotics became increasingly stigmatized, liquor sellers stepped into the breach, socializing women to the benefits of drinking.[14]

The secrecy surrounding women's inebriate homes gives an apocryphal quality to the meager reports available today. Few statistics on the number of female abusers exist. Instead, drys tended to address women's drinking in a final dramatic flourish. The superintendent of an inebriates' asylum (an asylum, by the way, that did not admit women) wrote in 1887 that "the young and the old, the rich and the poor, the learned and the ignorant, and alas! too many of the women of our land, are all furnishing their quota to . . . the drunkard's grave." But he did not expand upon his final example. The difficulty of acquiring accurate statistics was recognized at the time. Crothers pointed out that even police statistics "depend on the opinions and impulses of the judges and officers who may wish to shield or expose

Figure 2.2   Heublein's Club Cocktail advertisement

At the turn of the century, liquor companies contrasted healthful and relaxing cocktails with the dangers of opium, then the addiction of choice among respectable American women. If wealthy matrons drank martinis, why shouldn't everyone? Harper's Weekly *46 (2 Nov. 1902): 1730.*

the culprit." Others stressed that upper-class women kept their abuse hidden from family members, relabeling their problem (as "nerves," for example) when in treatment. For these reasons, much of the information about women's alcohol abuse is anecdotal at best. The *Union Signal* contains frequent, vague reports on intoxicated women: one was freed from jail after her young daughter's pleadings; another, unconscious, smothered her child.[15]

Alcohol historian Mark Lender has examined six hospital and clinic surveys written between 1884 and 1912 to assess the extent of women's alcoholism. Of some 24,200 hospital admissions, the ratio of male to female patients averaged 5.5 to 1 (i.e., 15.4 percent of admissions were women). The ratio was highest at private institutions and lowest at Bellevue charity hospital, in New York City, which admitted three men to every woman. This variation, Lender points out, may be attributed to the fact that few private institutions admitted women. Other available sources reinforce Lender's conclusions. Sixteen percent of the patients admitted to the San Francisco Home for the Care of the Inebriate in 1859 were women. The same percentage existed at Homeward Retreat in Guelph, Ontario, the largest private asylum in Canada.[16]

Although hard facts were unavailable, many throughout the period believed that women's inebriety was increasing. Stephen Smith in 1874 described women's drinking as a "growing evil." The *Union Signal* reported in 1899 that the death rate from intemperance "is constantly increasing; and . . . the deaths are increasing among women far more rapidly and in a far greater ratio than among men." A *Quarterly Journal of Inebriety* article two years later repeated that "we may take it for granted that drunkenness is on the increase among women." Similar concern over the apparent increase in women's drinking was expressed in turn-of-the-century Canada and Europe. Whether or not women's drinking was actually increasing, the discussion indicated profound concern over women's "masculinization" and the perceived unwomanly, nonmaternal qualities of women drinkers.[17] Temperance advocates and physicians were more than willing to conflate all consumption into abuse, labeling any drinking destructive and in the process seeking to control other behavior of which they did not approve.

Women alcoholics, barred from treatment or sympathy by their own denial and others' prejudices, are one of the great tragedies of the period. Yet one must point out that the association of alcohol and alcoholism with men was essential to the creation of such groups as the WCTU—to the development of women's social and political consciousness based on their inherently moral image. In this emphatic gender solidarity, however, women drinkers remained marginalized. It is just as important to note that the rhetoric surrounding women's inebriety—involving reproduction, class, and sexuality—rendered discussion of women's moderate drinking almost impossible. Victorians considered alcohol a male beverage to be consumed in male environments. Its associations with public spaces, violence, excess, and leisure time further separated it from the female world of domestic respectability. Commentators were far more willing to discuss even women's opiate use, a feminine activity, than their alcohol consumption.

The dearth of primary sources on women's moderate drinking has led to the widespread conclusion that nineteenth-century women, or at least middle-class women, did not drink. But this need not be the only possible conclusion. Could it be that women did drink alcohol but drank in a manner completely at odds with contemporaneous masculine patterns? If so, it appears that Victorians were incapable of labeling this alcohol consumption "drinking" as they understood the term. In fact, significant numbers of respectable American women consumed alcohol with anonymous frequency. In the process they developed models of consumption far more familiar and reassuring to the twentieth-century observer than the abusive homosociality of the saloon and men's club. Victorian women's moderate, at-home drinking formed the foundation of alcohol consumption patterns in the twentieth century.

WOMEN'S TEMPERATE DRINKING

Myriad sources—etiquette manuals, cookbooks, and fiction, as well as preserved physical evidence—reveal that alcohol in various forms retained a secure position in many Victorian households. Women consumed alcohol in medication, particularly women's medications; in store-bought liquors acquired for cooking and for sociability; and in eating and leisure spaces. Much of this drinking behavior was labeled respectable, passing almost unmentioned by observers at the time. At other times drinking quickly became conflated with tension over definitions of female propriety and must be understood in this light. Temperance literature reveals the challenges that dry women faced from their drinking peers. We have discussed elsewhere the multiple, sometimes conflicting definitions of "temperance" available to the American public. Nowhere is this controversy more apparent than in the domestic spaces of the nineteenth century.

Medication was one form of alcohol highly popular and easy to acquire. Early in the century, temperance activists divided on whether to include alcoholic medication in the abstinence pledge. Catharine Beecher, who came from a well-known dry family and supported temperance herself, wrote in 1856 that wine, cider, and ale were appropriate for illness. Annie Wittenmyer, future president of the national WCTU, served during the Civil War on the U.S. Sanitation Commission. In 1864 she listed mulled wine, cordials, milk punch, and egg nog in her *Collection of Recipes for the Use of Special Diet Kitchens in Military Hospitals.* Other medical writers asserted that malt beer was "wholesome, if used in moderation by lean, nervous, cold, and bloodless persons;" a half or whole bottle of wine should be allowed "the moderate diners-out, and the virtuous dancing young ladies." An advertisement featuring a smiling nurse in the 1905 *New England Cook Book* promoted "Frank Jones' Nourishing Stout" for patients requiring a "liquid diet." Etiquette writer Mary Sherwood described the mishaps of "an invalid lady" traveling in London with "one bottle of port and two little bottles of champagne" and advised readers to label all drink "medicine" to avoid corkage charges.[18] Sherwood assumed women often traveled with alcoholic beverages, or at least used them.

One beverage, if that term is appropriate, had special popularity. Available in drug stores and through the mails, almost unregulated, patent medicines were one of the century's most lucrative industries. Lydia Pinkham's Vegetable Compound and other "tonics" were aimed specifically at women. The Pinkham compound was 20 percent alcohol (forty proof). The Pinkham family, all members of temperance groups, insisted the alcohol was necessary both as medication and preservative. Other patent medicines included a sizable amount of alcohol. The Montgomery Ward catalog of 1896 offered "Montgomery Ward and Co.'s Beef, Wine, and Iron": two ounces of lean beef and four grains citrate of iron suspended in sherry. Like Lydia Pinkham's tonic and other potions, it provided respectability with a kick. Scientific investigations in 1903 and 1904 analyzed several dozen patent medicines and concluded that their average alcohol content exceeded 22 percent. In the 1880s, the *Ladies' Home Journal* initiated a twenty-five-year campaign against patent medicines. Editor Edward Bok reported in 1904 that 75 percent of the WCTU members he polled "regularly took patent medicines" up to sixty proof; many of these women publicly endorsed products such as Lydia Pinkham's.[19] Victorian concerns about over-prescription and alcohol abuse among women invalids appear well founded.

Ironically, the Pinkhams went into the patent medicine business because of their refusal to sell alcohol. The family owned a grocery store in 1870s Lynn, Massachusetts, and because of their temperance principles would not carry wines and liquors. The store could not compete with nearby wet groceries, and in desperation Lydia began marketing her homemade vegetable compound. The anecdote illustrates widespread liquor marketing in groceries, common into the 1890s. Just as common was the sale of alcohol within drug stores—not unreasonable given alcohol's prominent role as medication. Temperance activists and saloon keepers united in criticizing drugstore sales, which legislators often exempted from dry statutes. Drug and grocery stores even sold whiskey from open kegs, with customers filling their own containers. As the popularity of ice cream and dry laws increased, some drug stores were even reported to sneak liquor into the sundaes of knowing customers.[20]

Temperance activists worried particularly about drugstore sales to female alcoholics. "A tippling woman can furnish a pain or an ache on short notice, and if she has a cold or a headache, the whisky has to suffer, and the drug stores in her neighborhood do a thriving business," wrote a commentator in the 1887 *Union Signal*. Indeed, Monahan's Family Wine Store promised "Special Attention Given to Ladies" in a 1913 Cambridge, Massachusetts, newspaper advertisement. Building on the tradition of grocery-store liquor sales, glamorous urban department stores in the 1890s also offered spirits. As local-option laws began to close commercial alcohol outlets at the end of the century, liquor and beer dealers offered home delivery to clients in these dry districts. Sales frequently took place over the phone.[21]

Law or custom often prohibited saloons from selling to women. Carry Nation, entering a Wichita saloon with an axe in 1900, was informed by the barkeeper, "I'm sorry Madam, but we don't serve ladies." Nonetheless, women did purchase drink there. So-called ladies' entrances into ostensibly separate drinking spaces generally served as a front for prostitutes. On the other hand, sales to women for off-premises consumption were ubiquitous in some urban areas. One self-described temperance crusader witnessed an illegal liquor sale in a saloon she "had gone [into] to buy some brandy for mince pies." More common still was the practice of "rushing the growler," bringing in buckets to be filled with beer and drunk at home. Brewers' ad campaigns promoted beer's sterility and nutritional value, a reasonable claim in light of the poor quality of urban milk and water. This alcohol was drunk at home, often by women in a homosocial atmosphere similar to that of the male saloon. Rushing the growler provided women a method of integrating alcohol into domestic sociability. Even the beer drinking of working-class couples accented but did not dominate domestic leisure time and space.[22]

If literature from the period is any indication, one of the most respected sources of alcoholic beverages remained home production. Manufacture of drink for domestic consumption has historically been a female responsibility. Beer and cider making were important tasks for colonial American women—the surname *Brewster* derives from the feminine form of *Brewer*. While beer production by the mid-nineteenth century was heavily industrialized, cookbooks described in detail home manufacture of other alcoholic beverages. They contained recipes for berry wines in addition to cordial recipes requiring the combination of store-bought brandy and fresh fruit. The Women's Centennial Committee cookbook of the International Exhibition of 1876 included blackberry, currant, rhubarb, and elderberry wine, spruce beer, cordials, bounces (a mixed drink), egg nog, and mulled wine.

Given alcohol's integral relationship to medicine, most of these cookbooks grouped "beverages" or "drinks" near chapters on care of the sick. In addition to recipes for wines and medicinal beverages such as milk punch, cookbooks discussed sauces, desserts, and confections made with alcohol. Eliza Leslie described "'a trifle,' being the contents of a very large glass bowl, filled with macaroons, &c., dissolved in wine, &c., with profuse layers of custard, sweetmeats, &c., and covered in at the top with a dome of whipt cream heaped high and thick over the whole"—scarcely a dessert for the modern weak of heart! Even ostensibly temperate writers felt it proper to retain wine and brandy in recipes.[23]

Cookbook authors offered readers more than food; they offered advice as well. Mary F. Henderson's 1876 *Practical Cooking and Dinner Giving,* while providing recipes, was much more specific about how to present them. It is these discussions that clarify the exact position of alcohol in the American home. Henderson's book included separate chapters titled "Beverages" (with eleven punch recipes using alcohol) and "How to Serve Wine." She considered serving many different wines during dinner "ostentatious. . . . Four different kinds of wine are quite enough for the grandest occasion imaginable." The first edition of Fannie Farmer's classic cookbook in 1896 detailed the wines to be served with each course. And bear in mind that these books were aimed at the middle class. Catharine Beecher wrote for the inexperienced housekeeper "in moderate circumstances." Henderson listed courses that could be purchased in cans to save labor and time. Christine Herrick's *Consolidated Library of Modern Cooking and Household Recipes* sought out the "average American wife." Linda Hull Larned provided instruction for those "fortunate enough to be able to run the domestic machine with one maid-of-all-work." While modern readers might consider a maid-of-all-work the lap of luxury, a century ago domestic help was one minimum requirement of middle-class status.[24]

Another excellent window into the drinking behavior of respectable American women is the etiquette manual. Victorian America produced hundreds of guidebooks on etiquette. These manuals aimed for an American ideal. In doing so, however, they inadvertently revealed much about the realities of American society. Mrs. John Farrar's admonition that "a gentlewoman should never . . . run, jump, scream, scramble, and push, in order to get a good seat anywhere" indicates that too many gentlewomen in 1836 were doing exactly that. Often, etiquette writers made only oblique references to alcohol consumption, such as Sarah Josepha Hale's description of how to clean glassware "encrusted with the dregs of port wine."

Mrs. H. O. Ward, in *The Young Lady's Friend* (1880), advised readers to drink water instead of wine after eating artichokes because it improved their flavor. On other occasions, however, authors were quite explicit about what beverage to serve and how to drink it. Eliza Leslie specified that "on no consideration let any lady be persuaded to take two glasses of champagne. It is more than the head of an American female can bear." Others listed champagne without comment in menus, even recommending it as the sole wine for simple dinners.[25]

For these writers, wine and other alcoholic beverages were to be included in a wide variety of social events: afternoon teas, caudle parties to celebrate a birth, wedding breakfasts, and garden parties. Balls and evening parties demanded punch and champagne. Menus for ladies' luncheons appeared in manuals and cookbooks published throughout the later nineteenth and early twentieth centuries. These menus included soup, roast, salad, and dessert and specified sherry, claret, port, sauterne, champagne, cordials, and wine in various combinations. The names themselves indicate familiarity with the beverages. Mary Henderson differentiated these meals from men's dinners: "Nearly the same dishes are served for suppers as for lunches, although gentlemen generally prefer more game and wine." May Wright Sewall, prominent in woman suffrage and the president of the International Council of Women, at a 1904 Berlin council hosted a breakfast at which she served wine. (One of the guests reported that "some of the temperance ladies appeared very upset" by this.)[26]

Formal dinners constituted the bulk of alcohol-related discussion in both etiquette manuals and cookbooks. The Victorian formal dinner was a mind-boggling enterprise involving hors d'oeuvres, one or two soups, fish, a vegetable, a roast, game such as duck or goose, salad, cheeses, dessert, fruit, and coffee. (Research into this, one soon learns, should not be conducted when hungry.) Each of these dishes was served in a separate course with its own wine, champagne, or sherry, the whole event taking roughly two hours. Smaller, more informal dinners, writers assured panicked American hostesses, could make do with fewer courses and only claret and champagne for beverages. Writers specified every detail. For "the hostess of today," "everything pertaining or belonging to one course should be removed before the next course is served, except the wineglasses. These should remain on the table from the beginning to the end, the only exception being the glasses for cordials and liqueurs, which are served after the coffee, which is sometimes served in the drawing-room."[27]

Such thorough descriptions reflect alcohol's role in Victorian domestic life (figure 2.3).

Similar depth of detail may be seen in the physical evidence of spirituous living. Victorians excelled at creating objects for specific tasks and collecting as many task-specific objects as possible. Ice cream, for example, was not complete without the ice cream knife, nor the Saratoga (potato) chip without the Saratoga chip server. Thus it is not surprising that etiquette manual and cookbook writers expounded on the glassware and accoutrements that should accompany beverages. In her history of Victorian dining, Susan Williams lists the "plates, finger bowls, compotes, jelly glasses, bowls, dishes, decanters, molasses 'cans,' wine, champagne, and cordial glasses, and footed sweetmeat dishes with covers, intended as vessels for 'liquid confects'" that no bride could be without. The *New Cyclopaedia of Domestic Economy* of 1873 recommended that aspiring housekeepers obtain "three dozen wine glasses, two dozen champagne glasses, two

57

○ ○ ○

Domestic Drinking in Victorian America

Figure 2.3   "The Modern Dinner-Table"

Like all etiquette writers, Mary Sherwood aimed high: most nineteenth-century housewives lacked the furnishings, let alone the courage, to attempt a formal dinner for twenty-four. Nonetheless, the five glasses at each place setting—for water, sherry, champagne, claret, and probably Madeira—illustrate the unquestioned position of alcohol in American entertaining. Mary Elizabeth (Mrs. John) Sherwood, Manners and Social Usages *(New York: Harper and Brothers, 1884), frontispiece. Courtesy Library Company of Philadelphia.*

dozen claret glasses, three dozen goblets, six water carafes, six decanters, one liqueur stand, twelve liqueur glasses, two glass pitchers, one celery glass, one trifle bowl, eight dessert dishes, one full dinner service, one common set for kitchen, one common tea service for kitchen, one 'good' tea service, one breakfast service, and one 'good' dessert service."[28]

This glassware could be expensive lead crystal or new, cheaper machine-pressed glass. Montgomery Ward sold through the mails two "Wine Sets" of decanter, six stemmed glasses, and a glass tray, as well as individual decanters, wine glasses, and beer mugs. The 1896 catalog also offered a "Whisky Tumbler," "Fancy Pressed Glass Champagne or Sherry Tumbler," "Hot Whiskey Glass," and "Wine or Apple Wine Glass." Water pitchers, tumblers, and "Plain Water Goblet[s]" were sold for water drinking; "Goblets, Plain and Engraved" appear to have been all-purpose, used for both intoxicating and nonintoxicating drinks. Sears, Roebuck, which explained it sold spirituous liquors only in medication, listed glassware as nonspecific "water tumblers" and "goblets." The catalog did offer two silver flasks cited as "whiskey flasks" in its index. Even furniture formalized alcohol consumption. Elaborate sideboards held the wine, which was also displayed in cut-glass decanters. Liquor cabinets featured locks (to keep alcohol from the servants) and "handsome mahogany" finishes.[29]

The detailed names within these department-store catalogues demonstrate widespread familiarity with and acceptance of alcoholic beverages. A middle-class woman who supported temperance would not order whiskey tumblers when she could have plain water goblets. But a woman who did not care about temperance, or who actually wanted the whiskey tumbler, might very well have. This materialism illustrates yet another paradox of Victorian drinking, how to balance the excessive consumption of objects with restraint in the consumption of the beverages they held.

For further proof of alcohol's role in domestic sociability, one need only turn to dry writers, who were forced to confront the fact that some women drank socially and in moderation. These temperance activists reveal incontrovertibly the popularity and significance of alcohol consumption in late-nineteenth-century America. Participants in the Woman's Crusade and the WCTU had to address their own drinking. Mother Stewart asked, "Have you crusaded your own cellars and closets before coming to me? What about your home-made wines, your wines and brandies for your pies, cakes, and puddings?" One thousand crusading young women in Cleveland, Ohio, "promised not to use wine, [and] to discourage its use among young gentlemen." When creating the WCTU, founding members devised "a special pledge for women, involving the instruction and pledging of themselves, their children, and *so far as possible,* their households; banishing alcohol in all its forms from the side-board and the kitchen, enjoining quiet, persistent work for temperance in their own social circles." Admissions of women's drinking are visible as well in the confessional stories of new WCTU members such as the "conscientious young woman who . . . 'never yet sat down to dinner without wine, but I am now determined never to taste it or offer it again.'"[30] These anecdotes hint at established female drinking behavior. Temperance pledges by WCTU members might be interpreted as a symbolic gesture. But the detail within these descriptions indicates that these women were familiar with alcohol, that they regularly cooked with and drank it.

Even more disturbing to drys than women's drinking were the rituals that facilitated interactions between the two sexes. Several alcohol-related traditions even encouraged drinking in mixed company—a direct affront to dry beliefs that women should not only abstain but restrict male drinking as well. Nineteenth-century etiquette writers discussed as a matter of course the tradition of "challenging" women to drink, which appears to have evolved from all-male drinking rituals. After the soup course (at formal dinners, presumably), a man could "quietly" lift his glass to a woman, who was expected to at least raise her glass to her lips as an act of courtesy. Eliza Leslie specified in 1864 that "it was not customary, in America, for a lady to empty her glass" but only to take a sip or two. Women asked by strangers to take wine during hotel dinners should "refuse at once, positively and coldly, to prove that you consider it an unwarrantable freedom." But it was perfectly acceptable for a woman to drink when challenged by an acquaintance or companion.[31] Challenging appears fraught with complication and meaning, implying male sovereignty and female obligation, and hinting at both sexual union and alcoholic excess.

Challenging required women to drink at the invitation of men. Most horrifying to drys, however, was the opposite social ritual: men drinking at the insistence of women. A temperance speaker described "the evils resulting from the offering of wine by the hostess at her entertainments. . . . Many a young man has accepted the glass of wine because it was offered to him by the fair hand of one whom he admired, and because he felt that it would be uncourteous to refuse." The speaker concluded that "one who tempts such an one to drink, under the mistaken idea that hospitality requires it, is unconsciously doing the devil's work in a most effective way." In one temperance story, a mother insisted on packing a bottle of homemade wine in her grown son's picnic lunch, knowing his companion was battling intemperance. The friend returned from the outing inebriated and remained so. Another woman who "found a prominent place on her table" for wine could not understand her own grown son's intemperance. In these stories, far too many women are willing, even eager, to serve wine and other beverages socially.[32]

Women had available to them alcoholic medication, recipes for alcoholic beverages and foods, and a substantial body of literature detailing when and how alcohol might be integrated into domestic life. None of this is to imply, however, that women drank to excess. Sources imply just the opposite. Mary Sherwood warned in 1884 that "the overfilling of the glass should be avoided, and servants should be watched, to see that they give champagne only to those who wish it, and that they do not overfill glasses for ladies, who rarely drink anything."[33] This statement that "ladies rarely drink anything" may be interpreted two ways. *Manners and Social Usages* was a prescriptive work: the instruction that ladies *ought not* has no tangible relation to what ladies actually *did*. As with the 1836 gentlewomen who scrambled for good seats, the ladies Sherwood hoped to mold may in fact have drunk quite a bit. On the other hand, Sherwood would have been much harsher in her criticism had she actually suspected women of intemperance. All evidence indicates Sherwood was calmly speaking the truth.

It is also worthwhile to iterate the significance of other drinks. Cookbooks, etiquette manuals, and domestic handbooks present water, tea, lemonade, and other nonalcoholic beverages as common and unquestioned elements of sociability. Water—ice water, soda water, mineral water, fresh "tea water"—enjoyed great popularity in Victorian America, the "favorite beverage" as Sherwood herself described it. The water enthusiasm produced insulated silver-plated ice-water pitchers and even "cold-water gift books" promoting temperate sentimentality. Coffee and tea also grew in popularity throughout this period, leading to a similar plethora of drink-related objects and rituals. Middle-class hostesses self-consciously prepared lemonade from expensive sugar, ice, and imported lemons.[34]

Such conspicuous consumption may also be seen in the purchase of alcohol. In the late nineteenth century most wine was imported from France and cost four times the price of whiskey. It was thus far less popular than whiskey or increasingly ubiquitous beer. One writer in 1901 estimated that wine accounted for half the cost of a formal dinner. Wine's expense and formality explain its declared absence at everyday meals. Marion Harland in 1891 published the *Dinner Year-Book,* providing menus and recipes for

365 dinners. No mention was made of alcohol, implying that it had no prescribed role in the everyday (and very filling!) meals of the average American middle-class family. Fannie Farmer's *Boston Cooking-School Cook Book* similarly listed only café noir as a beverage for everyday dinners. Per capita consumption of wine between 1870 and 1900 averaged slightly less than eight ounces, or two glasses, a month—quite enough for formal dinners. These statistics did not take into account home production. Yet such numbers establish the moderate pattern of Victorian wine consumption.[35]

Drys' outrage was aimed mainly at these male and female moderate drinkers. Most temperance activists genuinely worried about problem drinkers—prohibition legislation, after all, came about as a compulsory cure for inebriety. Drys felt, accurately, that moderate drinkers only muddied the waters of the antialcohol debate, because moderation demonstrated that alcohol was not inherently addictive or poisonous. Moderate drinkers, therefore, received the harshest criticism, much of the dry discussion focusing on their decay over several generations.

Drinkers, not surprisingly, found this indictment of moderate alcohol consumption singularly alienating. Etiquette writers had little patience for aggressively dry guests or heated dinner-table discussions on the merits of temperance. *Every-Day Etiquette: A Manual of Good Manners* asserted that "the need of 'a perfect self-containedness' at a dinner-table, where food and sentiments may not be to our liking, often makes itself felt. If wine is provided, and the guest does not approve of it, a private table is not a suitable place for expressing individual convictions. He may receive the wine in the different glasses sparingly and make no comment. If toasts are proposed, he will lift his glass and be courteous." Another author in a discussion of proper wine service concurred: "Experienced diners will always refuse anything that is to them especially injurious, and are expected to do so, but it is bad form to parade one's objections; a quiet refusal by a glance or a motion is all that is necessary." Christine Herrick wrote that "it [is not] bad form to decline wine at a dinner if you do not wish to drink it. The rudeness lies in making a display of your temperance principles by any conspicuous refusal when the waiter appears to serve you."[36]

Other writers also hinted at the cultural ambivalence surrounding temperance. Although scathing about American women's excessive drinking, Harriet Martineau was careful to inform her readers that she herself did not abstain. Emily Edson Briggs, who attended dry meals in President Rutherford Hayes's White House, felt the lack of drink "added unnecessary tedium to the three-hour state dinners." A visitor to New York in 1883 described with distaste the amount of alcohol provided at formal dinners because hosts feared the label of a "dry party." Another writer in the 1930s "well recall[ed] the curious or pitying glances directed politely toward the one who turned down the wine glass to indicate that none was desired."[37]

Criticism of the temperance position may be found even in temperance writings, as dry authors answer their offstage censors. In a short story published in 1870, a guest refused wine at a formal dinner. "Many voices were lifted in condemnation against him, for excluding one of the gladdeners of existence, what the Scriptures themselves recommended, and the Saviour of men had consecrated by a miracle." A suitor in a *Union Signal* story reprimands his fiancée for demanding he swear to abstinence: "'Have your own views, my little love,' he added more gently, 'but allow me also the same privilege.'" Dry writers, like etiquette writers, addressed alcohol's role in sociability and entertaining. In "Mrs. Myrtle's Parlor-Meeting," Mrs. Myrtle stews to her husband: "'Why, you know, John, how everybody here has wine on their tables, and it is always offered when you pay afternoon calls. Mrs. Traill always has sherry and port on her sideboard on her reception day.'" In another story, the narrator "heard [a] mother, in discussing a wine party with one of her fashionable friends, say, 'I didn't know whether I could walk straight when I got up from the table, but I fixed my eyes on the easel in the corner, and aimed for it, and reached it safely.'" Conversely, in yet another story, a young woman doubted her pledge and wished to revoke it because of the dissent it caused. She was the only guest to ask for water at a party.[38] Although in each of these stories the temperance cause ultimately triumphs, wet criticism and its sting to the WCTU remain apparent.

CLASS, ASPIRATION, AND ALCOHOL IN VICTORIAN AMERICA

Victorians equated wine—alcohol—with hospitality. Bubbling champagne, Rhine wine, claret, sherry, port, and cordials all formalized the act of entertaining while at the same time easing its formality. Alcoholic beverages raised the status of the events at which they were served—note their display in decanters and on dinner tables in private homes. An 1865 temperance newspaper regretted that in "social circles wine is, with lamentable frequency, proffered to guests. At tables, both private and public, malt and other liquors are a constant beverage." Cookbook author Helen Saunders

Wright described the Victorian tradition of afternoon calling, "a very serious affair [at which] cake and wine were invariably served." Mary Sherwood advised hosts to "send around the champagne early to unloose the tongues; and this has generally a good effect if the party be dull."[39]

In the iconography of Victorian ornament, literal-minded Victorians decorated household objects in a manner that marked their function, their meaning. The fruit and dead game carved into sideboards manifested the meal. In light of this, consider a late-century dinner invitation featuring a watercolor sketch of a stag coming upon a bottle of wine. If carved animals and vegetables defined Victorian dining, then the sketched stag and wine defined Victorian entertaining. A 1905 magazine on mission furniture advertised a dining table set with one plate and one stemmed glass filled with wine—an image epitomizing the domestic social experience.[40]

Indeed, alcohol's integral social role may be witnessed in the constant claim that a host could be acceptably social without serving wine. "Such [dry] dinners are in quite good taste," wrote Mary Henderson in 1876. "Those whose principles forbid alcoholic beverages . . . nevertheless give excellent dinners without them," assured Sherwood eight years later. Linda Larned stated in 1899 that "both formal and informal dinners are in equally good taste without wine as with it." In 1905, Christine Herrick repeated that "in giving a wineless dinner one breaks no rule of etiquette or of good taste."[41] Throughout the period, etiquette and cookbook writers assured their readers that entertaining did not require wine. Yet the monotony of this assurance indicates that many readers felt quite the opposite.

Temperance historians have emphasized the elitism of drys who sought to control working-class behavior and leisure. But the reverse snobbery of drys is also noteworthy. Dry fiction is replete with criticism of the drinking habits among the "so-called upper class of society." The *Union Signal* in 1899 bemoaned, "We have preached well for twenty-five years, but we have barely begun. . . . 'Highly respectable' people who never go to church and care nothing for reform and reformers, use beer, wine, and whisky on every social occasion." A temperance newspaper in 1867 stated that "the names of 1,800 rich men's daughters in New York are . . . on the list of applicants [to the state inebriate asylum]. This is the result of social drinking which is carried on to an extent in fashionable circles!" The WCTU might mention that intoxicated "middle-class ladies" were "by no means an unusual occurrence." But the union was far more likely to describe how "half the ladies of wealth and fashion . . . disguised" their abusive drinking. (In these stories, "fashionable" women describe WCTU members as "quite of the common sort," revealing how drys felt they were viewed.)[42]

Most scholars of the American temperance movement consider the temperance movement to be middle class and the middle class, ergo, temperate. Yes, working-class temperance societies often flourished, and the middle-class WCTU focused mainly on drinking among the working class. But it worried most about the bad example that "so-called respectables" set to their social inferiors. Yet Victorians' terms—"rich," "fashionable," "respectable"—remain frustratingly vague. What was the dividing line between the acceptable "self-supporting class whose chief pleasures in life center in and about the home" and the derided "so-called respectables?"[43] This question becomes particularly baffling when one considers how much respectable (or would it be "so-called respectable"?) social activity involved the domestic consumption of alcohol.

We have already established that middle-class men drank and often suffered from their drinking. Club life, businessmen's saloons, and the inebriate and insane asylums all contained a significant middle-class element. Cynics at the time pointed out that ostensibly dry middle-class neighborhoods were surrounded by saloons accessible by street car. Wherever dry laws closed public drinking spaces, liquor distributors reaped profits by shipping COD. Middle-class drinking can also be witnessed in physician George Beard's separation of inebriety among "brain-workers" from "the simple vice of drinking to excess." In distinguishing inebriety from simple excess, Beard was providing a medical definition, and thus rationalization, for what had been perceived as a moral problem. The lower orders might be immoral dissipates, Beard states, but middle-class drinkers had justifiable medical complaints.[44]

The "fact" that middle-class women "did not drink" has also become a truism. But it appears that WCTU women actually reversed this equation. In their minds, women who drank were suffering from either working-class degeneracy or upper-class snobbery. It was not that the middle class was dry; drys simply defined themselves as the only respectable members of the middle class. Values defined standing, rather than the other way around.

But alternate definitions of middle-class propriety challenged dry organizations throughout the nineteenth century. Historians have long noted the class consciousness and social aspirations of the Victorian middle class. This can be witnessed in the profusion of etiquette manuals, the formality of middle-class dinners, and the inexpensive household goods such as glassware that were fashioned after elite objects and rituals. These sources reveal the close connection between status and alcohol consumption, a connection of which Victorians were eminently conscious. Fiction and articles from the *Union Signal* illustrate that the WCTU was, from its founding in the 1870s, ill-equipped to counter the association of drink and social standing.

An 1899 article on American women's drinking in the British journal *Catholic World* summarized the diversity of drink experiences within the nation. M. E. J. Kelley, in agreement with other sources we have examined here, felt that women's drinking was increasing and that American authorities were unwilling to address this. Moreover, Kelley considered women's drinking to have a powerful regional element. "Ordinary country women in America are for the most part total abstainers. . . . In the country villages social drinking is not the custom outside the saloon, and drunkenness among women is almost unheard of." Yet even within the countryside, alcohol retained some connection to sociability: "Intoxicants are used as a treat to guests at the home only on the rarest occasions." From this beginning, Kelley then explored the use of drink by girls working in the textile mills and by "society women." "Women and the Drink Problem" drew a strong connection between alcohol consumption and the social aspirations of these women, who considered drink an indicator of urbanity and sophistication. New mill workers quickly labeled their earlier dry sentiments "awfully countrified and bigoted." Moreover, inebriety was also increasing among "middle-class women, who live in comparative ease and comfort, but whose lives are monotonous."[45]

The *Catholic World* was certainly accurate in its assessment of the connection between class and alcohol. Women in the rural Midwest, seat of the Woman's Temperance Crusade and the WCTU, did not support challenging, or wines at formal dinners, or the custom of "offer[ing] intoxicants to one's guests," which, according to Kelley, was "everywhere in the larger cities."[46] Regional differences within the nation affected drinking and temperance sentiment as strongly as did social class. But Kelley raised an interesting point in this worried discussion of itinerant mill workers and urban aspiration. Due to national migration, the population that considered temperance "countrified and bigoted" was growing. Etiquette manuals aimed not at rural readers but at this growing city audience.

The challenge faced by dry organizations, then, was far more difficult than simple elimination of alcohol sales. Much temperance rhetoric attacked male, public drinking—the saloon, the drunkard, the vice, graft, and corruption. Judging from the popularity of local dry laws and ratification of the federal prohibition amendment in 1919, voters beyond temperance circles despised this public drinking behavior just as fiercely as did drys. If one considers solely this form of drinking, it is difficult not to agree with current assessments that the middle class, women in particular, excluded alcohol from their lives and aspirations. In the eyes of both supporters and opponents, the saloon truly was the last stronghold of untempered masculinity.

Yet close reading of wet and dry sources reveals a second model of alcohol consumption that did not involve male homosociality or abusive drinking. Rather, this model entailed drinking within the home, in moderation and at precisely defined social events. Most importantly, it entailed drinking in women's presence. Often this presence was openly acknowledged, in the traditions of challenging and of women serving men. Middle- and upper-class formal social events such as dinners and balls demanded mixed company, and working-class informal gatherings around buckets of beer also mingled women and men. Alcohol was an element, often a valued element, in these entertainments. Alcohol might aid the mingling, it might mark transitions within specific activities, it might facilitate introductions between individual couples, it might even define sociability. But it did not dominate sociability as it did within saloons and other male-oriented leisure spaces.

In fact, many Americans, including some drys, did not consider women's sociable, moderate consumption "drinking," as they understood the term. This vague, rather contradictory definition of drinking parallels concurrent vague and contradictory definitions of temperance. Certainly, in the earlier decades of the century, there was some controversy as to whether wines and other light drinks were in fact alcoholic, though this issue was resolved before the Civil War. But Victorians, while considering these beverages intoxicating, often excluded wines and cordials from their definition of dangerous intoxicants. Alice Roosevelt Longworth, daughter of Theodore Roosevelt, stated this bias outright. "Drinking applied to champagne at parties, and [my parents] said that as my spirits were high, I had better not take any; then no one would be able to say that my gaiety came out of a bottle." Yet the next sentence refutes her dry stance: "A glass of sherry, or madeira, of white wine or claret was a matter of course at dinner." Another woman recalling her youth in the 1880s and 1890s asserted that "we had never been a drinking family. Wine for betrothals and christenings, champagne for weddings, a mug of hot punch for the bishop or the presiding elder who stopped with us in cold and stormy weather, these were among my childhood memories."[47] The point is not to snicker that well-intentioned ladies were inadvertent drunkards. Respectable women's drinking of cordials, light wines, and ales carries special meaning because they sought to *avoid* intoxication. These women instead strove to develop other venues by which to mark social events and leisure time. Cordials and wines permitted women a "time-out," but a more controlled and certainly more respectable time-out than that provided by the abusive drinking within exclusively male spaces.

Nonetheless, the presence of alcohol—generally associated with masculinity—within the home—an acknowledged feminine space—generated tremendous anxiety. Consider, for example, the wine decanter. Photographs from the late nineteenth century show dining room tables, end tables, sideboards, and china cupboards regularly decorated with decanters, and they appeared frequently in alcohol-related discussions. Local prohibition laws brought the "crystal decanter" to the home sideboard, a minister testified in 1867, because men no longer drank publicly. In downstate Delaware, "wine came off the sideboard [in a decanter] . . . at every thirsty look." Visitors commented on "the large display of wines and liquors [seen] in some homes." Mary Sherwood was particularly fastidious about decanters: "Sparkling wines, hock, and champagne, are not decanted, but are kept in ice-pails, and opened as required. On the sideboard is placed the wine decanted for use, and poured out as needed; after the game has been handed, decanters of choice Madeira and port are placed before the host, who serves them round to his guests."[48] Nineteenth-century sources on alcohol, be they etiquette writings, fiction, biographies, or mass-market catalogs, weight decanters with significance—the decanter as paradigm of domestic alcohol consumption.

This significance had particular meaning for women. Temperance speaker George Packard stressed the dangers that the decanter posed to women because of the threat of occasional wine sipping. A supporter of all-male saloons pointed out that "our 'lady drinkers' come from that class which adheres most strictly to the decanter." In a short story, a woman who later became a drunkard "approached a side table, and turning out a glass of rich cordial, drank it." Another who would later die of a drug overdose "looked down into the hall below, . . . [and saw] the tray of tall glasses and silver-collared decanters which the butler had just placed on a low table near the fire."[49] The decanter feminized alcohol enough to render it respectable. The decanter stored wine, sherry, and cordials in a limited, and thus more acceptable, amount. It displayed alcohol, and in so displaying rendered alcohol itself a decorative item in the elaborately decorated Victorian interior. Brought out when visitors called, it integrated alcohol into socializing. Most significantly, the decanter, as the excerpts above illustrate, made alcohol easily available to women within their domestic sphere. Unobtrusive as it may seem, the decanter reconfigured the relationship between gender and alcohol in nineteenth-century America. Drys, in discussing women's dangerous relationship to alcohol, therefore had every reason for singling out the decanter.

One alcohol-related scandal, a incident that shook the WCTU badly, encapsulates the temperance movement's inability to accept or redefine the association between sociability and drink. In the late summer of 1894, a rumor spread that Frances Willard had been seen in upstate New York drinking a bottle of wine with her friend Lady Henry Somerset. In truth, Willard and Lady Henry did drink together. But the liquid "was a brand of unfermented wine which had been largely consumed here this season . . . pour[ed] out of a regulation wine bottle." Nonetheless, according to a contemporary press report, "the majority of the people were, temperance or otherwise, inclined to censure Miss Willard for her act; for as President of the great W.C.T.U., they held she should, of all people, avoid the mere appearance of evil."[50]

The two women were staying in a dry hotel in the dry community of Chautauqua, drinking a popular local temperance beverage. The "evil" that so offended Willard's constituents was the act of drinking socially. Willard's authority as president of the WCTU was at this point under the greatest strain of her tenure, compounded by the WCTU's financial difficulties from the 1893 depression. The rumor represented a double challenge to her leadership: members' outrage at her consumption of "alcohol" was heightened by the elitist, social connotations of drinking itself.

Temperance activists self-consciously created "temperance beverages," akin to the nonintoxicating wine drunk by the hapless Frances Willard, in order to capitalize upon this association and so tame it. Just as they sought out "substitutes for the saloon," they also sought out alternatives to alcohol. But the incident involving Frances Willard illustrates the difficulty of this undertaking. As time would show, the Anti-Saloon League and the WCTU were far more successful at battling the institution of the saloon than the substance of alcohol. Prohibitionists failed to distinguish between saloon drinking and social drinking. Worse, they failed to recognize the support for alcoholic social events among respectable American women.

Temperance advocates painted the saloon as the polar opposite of the home, stressing how alcohol ruined domesticity. Yet the domestic drinking that has been uncovered in this discussion suggests a method by which alcohol-related benefits such as male companionship might be integrated into women's separate sphere. A professional bartender in an 1892 drink-mixing manual hoped for the day "when reasonable drinking is not looked upon as a crime; . . . when around the table the whole family sits chatting and whiling idle hours away, while the sparkling bowl sharpens their wit and loosens their tongues; when father and grown-up sons will not leave home to seek recreation, but when they will spend their leisure time in the family circle." Others, too, suggested that melding the home with the club (merging male restraint and female hospitality, as one author described it) would benefit the domestic circle. A humorous cartoon from late in the century shows a young wife turning her drawing room into a saloon to ensure her husband's presence.[51]

Doubtless, drys were outraged at the suggestion that women in effect capitulate to men's drinking. Their own words, however, reveal the frequency with which women already joined their men. Abusive male public drinking instigated local, state, and ultimately federal antialcohol laws. Yet a model of respectable, temperate drinking within the home was in place by the later decades of the nineteenth century. Alcohol's integral relation to sociability and entertaining—spheres that American women traditionally controlled—would prove the temperance movement's undoing. With alcohol consumption so virulently associated with beer-soaked saloons and gutter drunkards, few in the late nineteenth century spoke publicly on the benefits or prevalence of nonabusive practices. But federal prohibition in 1920 would do more than close the saloon. It would also let domestic drinking out of the closet.

° ° ° 3

STARTLING CHANGES
IN THE PUBLIC REALM

In 1909 the city of Denver banned unescorted women from drinking at night in restaurants and cafés. The Woman's Public Service League protested the ban, criticizing "any measure which places restrictions upon the freedom of action of women which are not placed upon the freedom of action of men." Because Colorado had granted women the vote in 1893, antisuffragists used the league's protest to illustrate the degeneracy that woman suffrage would produce. They felt that "political women," in the name of equality, would drag women down to men's level in public drinking spaces and elsewhere. The Woman's Public Service League perceived the situation differently, however, feeling that access to public institutions should not be gendered. The incident illustrates the clash in values between Victorian notions of female propriety and the burgeoning woman's rights movement. Denver had passed the law in response to complaints of women's drunkenness, and the Public Service League withdrew its protest after the city presented this explanation.[1] Denver legislators and antisuffragists were not alone in linking women's drinking to the concurrent campaign for female equality. The Denver controversy encapsulates the battles over the proper sphere and behavior of the modern woman.

Alcohol in the nineteenth century had been an integral element in home entertaining, particularly at formal dinners and at other events requiring the company of both men and women. In the second decade of the twentieth century, temperance enthusiasm would dim this association. At the same time, however, acceptance of mixed-company public drinking was growing within urban environments, an acceptance that spanned social class. Legislation to control or eliminate the liquor industry, and with it public drinking, spread in popularity, culminating ultimately in the Eighteenth Amendment. Yet most temperance rhetoric continued to focus on masculinity—male saloon attendance, male political corruption, male inebriety and its dangers to industry. Prohibition and public heterosocial drinking were two concurrent social movements that developed in reaction to each other.

THE NEW WOMAN

"Almost every number of the leading periodicals has a paper about Woman—written probably by a woman," grumbled *Harper's Magazine* in 1890. "Woman Today, Woman Yesterday, Woman Tomorrow. . . . The inquiry is daily made in the press as to what is expected of woman, and the new requirements laid upon her by reason of her opportunities, her entrance in to various occupations, her education." Indeed, the male editor concluded, "the impartial observer is likely to be confused, if he is not swept away by the rising tide of femininity in modern life."[2]

From the 1880s through the 1920s, discussion of women—praise, criticism, advice, reminiscence—filled the pages of the popular press. Articles and books titled "The Unrest of Modern Woman," "Women's Wild Oats," "The Unadjusted Girl," "The Restless Sex" described their state and status. The "New Woman," as the term developed in the early 1880s, was an unmarried woman with a college degree and a job. Beyond economic independence, the New Woman model encompassed such vigorous popular sports as cycling, tennis, and golf and increasingly included suffrage. In a humorous caricature from 1901, a New Woman dubbed "Gibson Girl" announces, "I can do everything my brothers do; and do it rather better, I fancy. . . . My point of view is free from narrow influences, and quite outside of the home boundaries." By 1910, Margaret Deland, in "The Change in the Feminine Ideal," felt that the New Woman "is almost ceasing to be 'new,'" so many American women were independently minded. The Syracuse, New York, *Wesleyan Methodist* in 1913 captured conservative anxiety over this New Woman in a discussion of the year's fashions: "If girls had a faint idea of the disgusting sight they presented, or could hear some of the unmanly, dissolute remarks made about them as they pass along the streets clad in . . . one of those short, outlandish, tight-gripping . . . skirts, they would feel so ashamed that if they had a spark of virtue left in them they would go to their rooms or get out of sight somewhere till they had a sensible dress to put on. How can they expect people to distinguish them from the low and corrupt if they dress exactly like them?"[3] An assertive public presence, overt sexuality, the dissolution of class boundaries—such were the topics the New Woman raised in pre–World War I America. The postwar flapper did not emerge like Venus from the sea, fully developed and in need of only a light wrap. Part of the charm of the *Wesleyan Methodist* quotation lies in its date. We expect such shocking behavior in the 1920s, but not a decade before.

In the nineteenth century, women who worked for pay outside the home did so out of impoverishment. (Women's paid employment remained shameful in part because of its connections to male inebriety.) By the early years of the twentieth century women worked outside of the home far more commonly. Women made up less than 10 percent of the labor force in 1860. Due to growing public acceptance and female desperation, fifty years later almost one in four employees was female. The percentage of female jobs in domestic service declined as clerical and manufacturing positions increased. Even middle-class women were encouraged to enter public life, to stop "fluttering about inside four walls under the delusion that these mark their proper sphere of activity."[4]

Respectable women began to appear not only in traditionally male workplaces but in equally threatening locales such as the barber shop. Ballroom dancer and fashion leader Irene Castle appeared in public with cropped hair in the first years of the 1910s; by 1924 bobbed hair was "practically universal." Mark Sullivan wrote bemusedly at the time about this invasion of "man's last retreat." Male customers complained of being overwhelmed with women's magazines, and male barbers attempted to restrict their shops to "Men Only." Department stores also created separate men's sections decorated in masculine themes to provide men some environment free of feminine influence.[5]

In Victorian America, leisure time had been heavily gendered. For men, leisure meant time away from work, physical separation from the work and home environments (see figure 1.1). Leisure, in fact, permitted an opportunity to engage in behavior normally unacceptable. While this "time-out" did not require drunkenness, alcohol and leisure for many men intertwined. A Wyoming woman homesteader described how male farmhands marked time off with binge drinking lasting several days. Women's domestic responsibilities did not permit such discrete scheduling of work and play.[6] In the new century, female wage earners also experienced the spatial and temporal separation of labor and leisure. This female leisure encompassed traditional male associations with time-out. At the same time, female leisure built upon alcohol's associations with mixed-company entertaining. Just as alcohol had formalized and ritualized male-female interactions within the home, it now did so in public, making possible introductions, conviviality, and relaxation. Concern over women's public drinking behavior, over their demands for social equality, preceded and in many ways introduced discussion of their potential economic and political equality.

Women of the middle and upper classes had at times visited commercial Victorian drinking establishments. Dining rooms in fashionable hotels served mixed drinks—juleps, cobblers, and the like—to women throughout the nineteenth century. German immigrants brought with them the tradition of beer gardens, indoor or outdoor spaces that provided music, beer, and family entertainment. Afternoon visits to local beer gardens were a common weekend leisure activity for many respectable couples in the late nineteenth century. In the 1870s, Temperance Crusaders campaigned against beer gardens as well as saloons and drug stores. Yet these public drinking and dining spaces remained problematic. Temperance writers whispered of "certain quiet 'ladies' restaurants' in all the seaboard cities, so quiet and modest in appearance that gentlemen are not tempted into them, where respectable women resort for the stimulant which is probably inaccessible at home." Restaurants maintained a strong association with the demimonde, some establishments providing private rooms in which men might join consorts. Delmonico's, the most prestigious and well-known restaurant in the country, in the 1860s would not admit unescorted women to its dining room. The policy served both to prevent prostitutes from soliciting diners and to keep diners from soliciting respectable women guests.[7] Public dining spaces had an aura of disrepute for much of the nineteenth century.

Elegant public dining became more popular at the end of the century, with New York City leading the way. Restrictions on unescorted women eased, even at Delmonico's. Public dining retained a risqué quality, however, with respectable patrons likely to encounter chorus girls and their wealthy dates out for a late-night champagne-and-lobster repast. Indeed, such interaction was expected, part of the spectacle of public entertainment as essential to dining as the alcohol itself. Theodore Dreiser, in the novel *Sister Carrie,* described a meal Carrie shared with three friends at Sherry's, a rival of Delmonico's. "Several bottles of wine [were] brought, . . . [and] set down beside the table in a wicker basket." These restaurants served alcohol to women without comment. Other turn-of-the-century leisure institutions catering to young urban revelers also accepted—within limits—women's drinking. Cabarets had existed in New York before the 1910s, in saloons or red-light districts, as underground performance spaces. As couple-oriented forms of sociability, notably dancing, spread in popularity, entrepreneurs moved cabarets to street level, cleaned them up, and began catering to respectable audiences.[8]

Alcohol consumption remained an important element in these new establishments. Many cabarets did not offer couples the traditional stand-up, men-only bar. Instead, waiters served drinks to seated patrons, an innovation that made women's drinking far less conspicuous. Even more remarkable, owners developed separate women's drinking spaces. Most of the cabarets that offered table service to couples—men and women—maintained a separate "men's café" for male stand-up socializing. In 1913, New York's Café des Beaux Arts improvised on this custom, providing a "ladies' bar" catering to women. The ladies' bar served men only when they were accompanied by a female escort. According to news reports, the ruse succeeded, for "prostitutes avoided it, while society women, actresses, and social climbers paid attendance."[9] Although originating as a publicity stunt, the appearance of the ladies' bar illustrates the drama and rapid evolution of women's public drinking.

More shocking than ladies' bars, and certainly more significant, afternoon dances in cabarets and hotel ballrooms spread in popularity around 1912. Dubbed tango teas, tea dances, or (for Francophiles) *thé dansants,* these events permitted married and single women an afternoon of dancing with professional male dancers. Tea dances built upon familiarity with afternoon tea, an increasingly popular social event in which women might visit several homes in as many hours for tea, sweets, and conversation. They differed in several key respects, however, from this model of domestic sociability. Tea dances took place in commercial establishments that charged an entrance fee; they focused on dancing instead of conversation; they provided an easy and attentive male presence; and they offered alcohol. *Harper's Weekly* advised mothers to visit a tea dance "and see the young girls, many of them obviously of breeding and refinement, who, cheek by jowl with professionals whose repute is not even doubtful, are footing it gaily, and learning the insidious habit of the early cocktail." The article described girls "dizzily endeavoring to right themselves" before returning home.[10] In the opinion of this author, commercial drinking places left young women at grave risk.

Within working-class communities, women saloon habitués also challenged earlier standards of male and female behavior. Women, working-class women in particular, had always had some presence in the saloon, going back to the colonial tavern. In the nineteenth century, most saloons were family operations in which female relatives prepared the free lunch and served customers. Irish immigrants brought with them the tradition of the shebeen, a kitchen grog shop run by a widow whose clients considered their patronage to be a form of charity. These women certainly contradicted the moral code of Victorian femininity. And at times they broke prohibition laws just as male members of the liquor industry did, serving after hours or within dry communities. Illegal kitchen bars in Maine, a state that had been dry since the 1850s, brought the tradition of shebeens into the early twentieth century. Members of the Woman's Temperance Crusade of 1873 and 1874 described these women operators as much more abusive than their husbands. One saloon keeper's wife threatened to scald crusaders who entered her shop. Another foul-mouthed woman was, following their prayers, struck dumb, "though she kept on at her soul-destroying business, making signs for the price of her beverage of eternal woe." A Columbus, Ohio, crusade leader was "severely choked by Mrs. Wagner," a proprietor of the Holly Tree Coffee and Lunch Rooms.[11]

Woman's Crusaders, by kneeling in saloons and praying outside them, were recognized as violating the boundaries of Victorian womanhood. In light of this, one could argue, the female saloon keepers' verbal and physical abuse was only a form of retaliatory deviance. Certainly, with their livelihoods at stake they were just as committed to selling drink as crusaders were to its elimination, and as women they could attack crusaders as their husbands could not (see figure 2.1). The constant presence of women within the saloon—the *Union Signal* in 1893 reported five thousand women working "the liquor business" in Chicago alone—weakened dry women's assertions of universal female condemnation of the liquor traffic. After 1900 several states and many communities banned women from serving liquor or working in establishments that did. Although waitresses protested this restriction to their livelihood, reformers sought to protect them from immoral influences and to curtail prostitution.[12]

Women utilized the saloon as customers as well as proprietors and waitresses. In the late nineteenth century, most working-class women's drinking consisted of purchasing beer within saloons for off-premises consumption. This practice would continue until federal prohibition closed the saloon for good. Women capitalized as well on other saloon features, particularly the free lunch that most saloons offered as a lure to customers. Reformers worriedly discussed this matter in the 1910s, pointing out that the sustenance that came with a five-cent beer could not overcome the environment in which it was served. With the growing public understanding (shaky as it might have been) of germs and nutrition, "white-enamel" luncheon cafeterias began to appear. But not until federal prohibition ended the free-lunch saloon did restaurants truly cater to and serve women.[13]

Like men, women also visited the saloon to socialize. Shop girls, after a long day's work, stopped at saloons or dance halls for a glass of wine. In 1899 the reformer John Koren pointed out that "in some cases married couples go to these saloons . . . because the place, bare though it may be, is really more comfortable and cheery than their own so-called homes." Courtship, difficult in tiny railroad flats full of family, was easier in gilded barrooms. Larger gatherings—weddings, balls, club dances—required space that working-class and most middle-class families simply did not have. While the middle class might rent hotel ballrooms, working-class organizers turned to municipal halls and, most importantly, to saloons.[14]

Certain saloons in Victorian America had offered space for dancing. Such public events in drinking spaces were inextricably connected to prostitution. As dancing grew in popularity in the 1890s, a new institution developed: the dance hall. These brightly lit and festive spaces were often located in the back room or second floor of a saloon. At the turn of the century, 80 percent of New York's East Side dance halls adjoined a saloon. Often, dance halls relied solely on drink sales to remain solvent, interspersing five minutes of dancing with fifteen-minute refreshment breaks. Waiters "circle among the dancers, importuning them to drink," wrote a 1910 observer. More reputable halls and those rented for private functions, supported by admission and rental fees, split dancing and drink time more equitably.[15] A handful of dance halls established by municipal reform organizations explicitly banned liquor. The bulk, however, made their profits from the sale of alcohol. Like tea dances and cabarets, dance halls commercialized leisure. But it is important to stress that these entertainments commercialized heterosocial leisure. Men in the nineteenth century paid—quite dearly at times—for the privilege of the all-male drinking space. New social events sought, and in dancing situations required, the mingling of couples. A massive transformation was taking place: the integration (or, more accurately, the reintegration) of women into public drinking rituals, an integration unplanned, unanticipated, and, for many, heartily unendorsed.

Middle-class reformers found particularly disturbing the ritual of treating. For the working-class male drinkers of nineteenth- and early-twentieth-century America, treating required that every man buy a round of drinks for the group. Women present in the saloon did not participate in this masculine ritual. As saloons and related drinking spaces such as dance halls became a location for working-class courtship, a new treating ritual evolved: men's purchasing of drinks for their female companions. This form of treating extended to food, gifts, and even clothing, depending on the seriousness of the relationship.[16] Treating, like the "challenging" practiced at formal dinners, brought tension, mystery, and ambiguity to male-female relationships. Unlike challenging, which required only the raising of glasses, treating placed this gendered interaction in an overt economic realm. The economics were to a certain level only practical, in that most women wage earners simply did not earn enough to pay for admission, drinks, car fare, or fancy clothing. Without treating, women could not go out. All participants and observers recognized, however, that women were obliged to compensate their consorts in some way for this gift of cash: with the charm of their company, their agreement to marry, or their sexual favors.

Because of the connection between drinking and dancing, because of the vigorousness and physical contact many popular dance steps required, because of the ambiguity of treating itself, reformers continued to question the safety and morality of dance halls. Unlike middle-class social events that men and women attended as couples, public dance halls admitted individuals and single-sex groups. Working-class men and women then mingled within the hall, men passing between tables to ask for dances, often offering drinks for the privilege. Middle-class observers considered such behavior akin to solicitation, one step removed from the historic connection of dance halls and prostitution. Jane Addams' 1912 *A New Conscience and an Ancient Evil* described in graphic detail the dangers of dance halls and saloons. In fact, observers found particularly frustrating the difficulty of telling respectable working-class girls from prostitutes soliciting clients. Some women straddled this boundary, "charity girls" who offered themselves to men for the price of a night out. Reformers repeatedly outlined the course of this fall: a young girl begins to attend dances, there falls in with unruly companions, learns to exchange personal favors for entertainment, and ultimately ends up a prostitute. The crucial element in the downfall was, of course, alcohol.[17]

Many scholars today emphasize the separatist, woman-centered aspect of the New Woman—the single-sex schools, the "loving female friendships." But the New Woman's contemporaries seemed most concerned with her rampant heterosexuality. Sex by this time pervaded the country. The 1913 article "Sex O'Clock in America" began, "A wave of sex hysteria and sex discussion seems to have invaded this country. Our former reti-

cence on matters of sex is giving way to a frankness that would even star-
tle Paris. Prostitution . . . is the chief topic of polite conversation. . . . The
White Slave appears in the headlines of our newspapers." After 1910, wrote
another observer, "Freud and his three slaves, Inhibition, Complex, and Li-
bido, . . . got to working on sex and marriage and love life generally. . . .
The very kindergarten children knew ALL." Although first denounced, Sig-
mund Freud's theories, as interpreted by American popularizers, soon
swept the country, attributing "every human motive" to sex. The birth control movement, begun in the 1910s by Emma Goldman and Margaret
Sanger, rapidly lost its radical and immoral associations, though contra-
ception remained illegal. Studies in the late 1920s established that middle-
class women coming of age in the first two decades of the twentieth century were far more likely to engage in premarital sex than were earlier
generations.[18]

Not surprisingly, concerns about women's sexuality also appeared in
temperance literature. A 1913 Anti-Saloon League poster announced that
"alcohol inflames the passions, thus making the temptation to sex unusually
strong. *Alcohol decreases the power of control,* thus making the resisting of
temptation especially difficult. . . . *Avoid all alcoholic drink absolutely.* The
control of the sex impulses will then be easy, and disease, dishonor, disgrace, and degradation will be avoided."[19] Temperance advocates in the
nineteenth century had criticized women's drinking within the home, associating it with lower- and upper-class degeneracy. But the public drinking that women engaged in from the 1890s onward presented a far more
insidious threat. After the turn of the century, discussion of alcohol usage
remained inseparable from discussion of women's sexuality, oppression,
and physical danger.

The most extreme and certainly most sensational example of alcohol-
related degeneracy was white slavery. In the early twentieth century,
Americans panicked about men who reputedly lured girls into movie
houses or saloons, administered a drugged drink or injection, and then entrapped their victims in a life of prostitution. The *Independent* reported in
1900 on "four young men of respectable families" in Paterson, New Jersey,
who took a young girl to a saloon, drugged her, and "then carried her off
unconscious for purposes as vile as provoke lynchings in some States."
The girl died, and the boys were tried for murder. Commentators often
considered alcohol and prostitution inseparable. "Prostitution and Alcohol," in the Progressive journal *Social Hygiene,* described the numerous
ways the two vices interacted. Alcohol entrapped women into prostitution.

The promise of a drink lured men into drinking spaces that also housed prostitutes. It then lowered the men's resistance to prostitutes' entreaties. Drinking enabled prostitutes to work, stimulating them while suppressing any residual morality. And the sale of alcohol provided brothels a crucial income source. Hysteria over white slavery and venereal disease peaked around 1909, encapsulating social concern about urban evils, female independence, and drinking. The *Independent* article on the New Jersey girl who died while drugged pointed out that "the degenerate passions that give rise to such crimes are cultivated and find their opportunity in the dens of vice which are protected by law." Only by closing saloons could such crime be stopped. The famous play on venereal disease, *Damaged Goods,* concluded with a demand not only for premarital syphilis testing but also for prohibition of the manufacture and restriction of the sale of alcohol. The 1913 Webb-Kenyon Act, a federal law controlling interstate shipment of alcohol, had its legal precedent in the 1910 antiprostitution Mann Act.[20]

GROWING TEMPERANCE SUPPORT

Up to this point we have reviewed prohibition legislation in the abstract: prohibition as restriction of alcohol. But alcohol restriction took many forms. Americans today are most familiar with the prohibition amendment, a national effort to prohibit the manufacture, transportation, and sale of alcohol. Yet the prohibition amendment was preceded by eighty years of alcohol legislation at the local, state, and federal level. The passage and enforcement of these laws obviously manifest popular support of the temperance cause: unpopular legislation would not have passed. Temperance advocates, including many suffragists, considered drinking itself sinful. But if the laws passed by state and federal governments in the second decade of the twentieth century are any indication, most voters did not agree. In most instances, antiliquor legislation attempted to control the liquor industry, not personal consumption. The distinction is essential to an accurate understanding of prohibition support. It also explains the seeming contradictions between the early-twentieth-century enthusiasm for both dry laws and drinking.

At the turn of the twentieth century, thirty-seven states had local-option legislation providing towns or counties authority to vote out saloons and other liquor distributors. These laws often left drugstore sales untouched and always permitted sacramental and medicinal use of alcohol—loopholes

easily abused. Nor did local-option legislation affect the right of individuals to import alcohol into their communities for personal use. State-wide
prohibition often retained these privileges. Prohibitionists had every hope
that restricting sales would reduce drinking. But drys had too much respect for personal liberties, or too keen an appreciation of voting reality, to
attempt to legislate consumption. In its prohibition campaign, the Anti-Saloon League separated suppression of the liquor traffic, which it epony-
mously battled, from elimination of drinking, which it avoided.[21]

In 1900, Maine, Kansas, and North Dakota were dry, die-hard remnants
of the prohibition enthusiasm of the 1850s and 1880s. Prohibition enthusiasm elsewhere built slowly. Between 1914 and 1919 an average of four
states a year went dry, either by passing prohibition laws or adding amendments to their state constitutions. Of the thirty-six dry states in 1919, two-
thirds allowed some form of importation or home manufacture, or both.
Dry legislation in most cases left untouched traditional alcohol-related rituals within homes, focusing instead on the alcohol industry and on control
of public drinking spaces. Alabama's dry law allowed individual importation of "two quarts of distilled spirits or two gallons of wine or five gallons
of beer every fifteen days." North and South Carolina, Oregon, Virginia,
and West Virginia had similar provisions. A Kansas resident reported that
"the thirsty Kansan resorted to the expedient of ordering a case of his favorite beverage from Kansas City, Missouri, just across the line. In due
time a large box, conspicuously labeled 'books,' 'furniture polish,' or 'lamp
shades,' would be deposited at his door by the expressman. . . . The most
respected Kansas families . . . adopted this method." Following passage of
prohibition in Washington state, in one month alone thirty-four thousand
Spokane residents applied for permits to import alcohol—this in a city that
had only forty-four thousand registered voters! Suppression of the liquor
industry, it appears, had little relation to voters' private habits. Through
the 1910s, the most extreme bone-dry legislation was supported not by the
Anti-Saloon League but by the WCTU, radical dry campaigners, and, ironically, by wets. For years wets, in a standard legislative subterfuge, rewrote
dry bills, adding to them measures so extreme that the bills could not pass.
By 1917 wet vengefulness inadvertently merged with antisaloon sentiment
and patriotic fervor to create a potent prohibition force.[22]

This growing dry enthusiasm may also be tracked in other sources from
the period. Drinkers in the 1920s attributed temperance excess to Victorian prudery, and this stereotype has endured within both scholarship and

the popular imagination. But domestic advice literature written between the Civil War and World War I describes a different evolution in dry sentiment. According to these manuals, temperance did not begin to affect respectables' domestic drinking until the second decade of the twentieth century. It appears that temperance enthusiasm was not a multigenerational, deeply rooted movement but rather a shallow vine (as it were) that would wilt in the dry years of the 1920s. Etiquette and cookbook authors in the first two decades of the twentieth century discussed and supported temperance principles far more than their predecessors had. Writers continued to specify the glasses and wines required with each course. Yet disclaimers crept into their texts. The *New England Cook Book* of 1905 stated that "goblets and wine-glasses, if the latter be used, should be on the table at the start." These writers felt that both formal dinners and ladies' luncheons were drying out.[23]

Florence Howe Hall provides one of the more intriguing illustrations of the growth in temperance sentiment. The daughter of the social reformer and suffragist Julia Ward Howe, Hall published the etiquette manual *Social Customs* in 1887. There, she reiterated much of the common drinking wisdom of Victorian America: the proper arrangement and use of stemware, the wines to be served with dessert and after dinner, the timing and placement of wine decanters. This first edition of *Social Customs* unabashedly endorsed drinking. In 1911, Hall issued a new edition of *Social Customs* filled with temperance endorsements: "Wine is not usually put on the dinner-table at the present time. . . . The temperance movement has made great headway in recent years." Whereas "several kinds of wine were formerly served" at supper parties, "the temperance movement has made a decided change in this respect." Hall attributed this growth in temperance principles not to moralism but to medicine. Reports on alcohol's effect on gout and rheumatism had turned many men into reluctant abstainers.[24]

Ellin Cravin Learned, in *The Etiquette of New York To-day* (1906), agreed. "There are so many fads about food in these days, on account of gout and other ills that flesh is heir to, that it is the fashion to have short dinners, to remain at the table a comparatively brief time, to drink few wines, and to eat less than in former times." Learned also implies that it was more acceptable in the first years of the century to refuse drink than it had been earlier. Both Learned and Hall stress the scientific—that is, rational—foundation of the twentieth-century temperance movement. Other writers from the decade did not support or dismiss temperance principles so much as circumvent discussion of alcohol, a practice that would become increasingly common in the 1920s.[25]

As this domestic advice literature illustrates, medical evidence against alcohol was converting Americans to the dry cause. Throughout the nineteenth century, temperance advocates publicized scientific evidence on the dangers of drink—witness the WCTU's efforts to promote scientific temperance education. Much of this evidence seemed too hyperbolic to be trustworthy. But by the early twentieth century scientists of unchallengeable reputation were proving alcohol's deleterious effect on moderate and abusive drinkers, the healthy and the sick. In 1917 the American Medical Association thrilled prohibitionists when it passed a resolution opposing "the use of alcohol as a beverage" and "discouraging" its use "as a therapeutic agent."[26] Drys now capitalized on scientific as well as moral and economic arguments for temperance.

By the mid-1910s temperance sympathy could be witnessed in any cross section of the general population. One man reported in 1914 that sixteen of the forty-seven banquets he attended the previous winter were dry, and eighteen "semi-arid," in that they allowed a single cocktail to each guest. He could "well remember a time when a banquet without booze was considered a barren ideality, worse than Hamlet with the melancholy Dane omitted." Dry ideology had permeated even the masculine world of clubs, toasts, and convivial excess. Temperance sentiment fueled to a certain extent new, non-alcohol-related leisure activities, though other factors were equally significant in this development. Movies, for example, became increasingly popular in the first decade of the twentieth century. Originally associated with vaudeville, silent films retained much of vaudeville's appeal to working-class values. Theaters charging a nickel admission attracted an audience that crossed age, ethnic, and, increasingly, class boundaries. Movies have been hailed as a tool for the Americanization of immigrants and for the liberation of women, encouraging as they did the daytime attendance of otherwise sheltered wives and daughters. They were also widely recognized at the time as promoting temperance. One film industry analyst in 1915 stated that movie theaters bankrupted local saloons; the *Cyclopedia of Temperance* asserted that "motion picture houses" reduced saloon attendance by 50 percent. Movies were cheaper than saloons—admission equaled the price of one beer—and could be enjoyed by the entire family.[27]

Amusement parks such as Coney Island also sought out couples and families. In the nineteenth century, Coney Island catered to a male audience. Individual resorts offered drink, gambling, brothels, and taxi-dance houses. By the 1890s, however, concert and vaudeville halls throughout the country encouraged female attendance. Family picnic grounds and pleasure parks often did not sell alcohol or banned its use. Such regulations were not simply an effort to control historic forms of working-class leisure, although there is some truth in this assessment. They were more an attempt to control the traditional male culture of excess, excess facilitated by alcohol. Like movie houses, dry picnic grounds and amusement parks illustrate how commercial entertainment was rapidly losing its male, working-class associations.[28]

Not insignificantly, improvements in urban housing stock also threatened traditional masculine spaces. A Massachusetts union official in 1883 complained about the small size of local tenements, the lack of private space within them. "If a man had a little room where he could go and read his paper and be comfortable, I think he would be more likely to stay at home instead of going abroad to seek other kinds of enjoyment." Young working-class couples unwilling to use or unable to afford public meeting spaces gathered for rooftop or alley "can rackets" centered on a bucket of beer. But by the turn of the century tenements were cleaner, more comfortable, and better built. Working-class housing now provided a "livable home." A similar transformation took place in middle-class housing, as "dens" and other male spaces facilitated the reintegration of husbands into women's separate domestic sphere.[29]

By the second decade of the century, the traditional saloon was "decaying from within." Men who had patronized the saloon in their youth continued to do so as they aged, but younger generations did not join them. The average saloon patron in 1910s Worcester was in his sixties. Entertainment places such as dance halls, movie theaters, and picnic grounds tapped potential saloon customers. Professional organizations—unions, fraternal groups—now shied away from meeting in saloons' back rooms and paying their rent in beer purchases. Child labor laws, boys' clubs, and public schools now impaired the brass-rail indoctrination of potential young customers. New patterns of immigration involved families (instead of bachelors) and ethnic groups (Jews, Italians) that lacked the public drinking traditions of the Irish, the Germans, and Eastern Europeans. The saloon remained a segregated male space in an increasingly integrated nation. Declining acceptance of homosociality left it obsolescent. Women's public drinking and public interaction with men reflected the cross-class revolution in morals and manners taking place before the first World War.[30] Just as prohibitionists and other temperance-minded reformers focused on male drinking, so too did young women, but with opposing goals in mind. For these women, rejection of the saloon did not equal rejection of drinking or drinking spaces.

THE COALESCING SPHERES OF WOMAN AND MAN

In the nineteenth century, women—that is, respectable women of every class—did not experience leisure as a public phenomenon. Except for beer gardens and a handful of respectable restaurants, most socializing took place at home, at afternoon calls, luncheons, teas, and dinners. Domestic rituals involving women and men continued after the turn of the century. Etiquette writers and others in the first two decades of the twentieth century emphasized the temperance now present at these formal domestic affairs. Their prose illustrates the growth in middle-class support for temperance legislation. It also presents the intriguing notion that the dry puritanism ascribed to Victorians by young rebels in the 1920s, and by historians since, may have been a twentieth-century development. Dry enthusiasm in the 1910s was one wave in the temperance cycle, not a multi-generation plateau. Yet in the face of this new drive for temperance even within the home, the majority of state and local prohibition laws either overlooked or specifically permitted home consumption and home production. In 1920, 86 percent of Americans had had no experience with bone-dry prohibition. As state prohibition laws show, legislators were keenly aware that voters intent on abolishing the saloon had very different sentiments about their own sideboards and liquor cabinets.[31] While prohibition laws might eliminate the public liquor trade (trade, not incidentally, dominated by men), they did not begin to control this domestic drinking and the implication of female hegemony that accompanied it.

Two different, rather contradictory movements thus marked early-twentieth-century America. On the one hand, women, particularly young urban women, exhibited an ever greater presence in public drinking arenas, in the process desiccating the all-male saloon. On the other hand, prohibition enthusiasm spread from drys to much of the general population, contributing to dry laws within the majority of states and ultimately to the federal prohibition amendment. Concern over female drinking fueled prohibition sentiment. This concern also played a minor role in the dry enthusiasm of the 1910s. What, then, one must ask, did these two movements have to do with one another?

To answer this question, we need first to review others' analysis of gender in the early twentieth century. In the past decades, women's historians have examined the new male presence in fiction, domesticity, religion, and other cultural spaces after the turn of the century, spaces that had been the domain of women in Victorian America. Some of these historians have considered this new male presence an indication of the breakdown of woman's separate sphere, a loss of female prerogative. Others proffer a related view of woman suffrage, that women were enfranchised when suffrage carried less power: Women got the vote when it no longer mattered that *women* got the vote. The authority women were now allowed to assert within a traditionally male realm was, in this final analysis, no authority at all.[32] In other words, at the same time that women in the early twentieth century were losing authority within their own arena, they were begrudgingly admitted to male venues that no longer entailed privilege.

Few historians have considered the connections between this gender turmoil and the prohibition movement. Yet the connection between two concurrent social trends—women's public drinking and prohibition—appears more than coincidental. I would argue that just as male religious movements, increasing interest in fatherhood, and changing emphases in fiction indicate the decline of a separate female hegemony, so, too, does women's public drinking represent the dissolution of the male sphere. Alcohol use, like the right to vote, was no longer a uniquely masculine attribute.

If this is in fact the case, then the popularity of prohibition sentiment in the second decade of the twentieth century makes a great deal more sense. If alcohol were no longer male, then men could support prohibition. Men, granted, had led the temperance movement for part of its existence. Women maintained an active presence and dominated temperance discussion from the 1870s to the 1890s. But their presence, combined with the traditional association of alcohol with masculinity, rendered the status of dry men problematic. Wet critics described temperance supporters as a "shrieking sisterhood." In hard-drinking Idaho a man might have trouble finding work if he was "a lemonade son of a bitch." A dry congressman beset by wet lobbyists defended himself as "no namby-pamby teetotaler!" The connection between temperance sympathy and accusations of effeminacy remains only a proposition here, but a proposition worthy of future examination. For it appears that by the 1910s this association had weakened. Since "real men" did not need alcohol—or, rather, no longer required alcohol in "real-men" environments—real men could vote dry. In 1921 a newspaper editor admitted grudgingly, "I voted for prohibition . . . not that I don't take a drink now and then, because I do, but because I thought it was the best thing for the coming generation." In the early twentieth century, even male drinkers supported such historically feminine issues as children's welfare and prohibition. Just as the responsibilities and future of American women—of the New Woman—came under close scrutiny at the turn of the century, so, too, did those of American men.[33]

Three examples strengthen this hypothesis. From the 1850s through the 1920s, advice writers described the tradition of women leaving the dining room at the completion of formal dinners so that male guests could smoke and drink. As early as 1851 one temperance writer criticized the hypocrisy of the ritual, feeling that men's drinking neutralized their regard for woman's "superior taste." By the beginning of the twentieth century such criticism was widespread. Advice writers were now eliminating the sole domestic tradition that permitted respectable male excess. Yet the replacements writers offered for this ritual did not require abstinence from drink. In *Table Service* (1915), Lucy Allen described how men and women now drank cordials together after dinner as they did wine during dinner— in other words, formal heterosocial drinking! Domestic drinking rituals were now almost completely ungendered.[34]

Our earlier discussion of Victorian drinking concluded with the words of a professional bartender who hoped that a time would come when the whole family sat at home with "the sparkling bowl," the bowl that would keep "father and grown-up sons . . . in the family circle." In 1914, *Bonfort's Wine and Spirit Circular* repeated this hope in a scenario even more shocking to drys, who subsequently reprinted it in *The Cyclopedia of Temperance, Prohibition, and Public Morals.* Describing prohibition's attack on the saloon, the *Circular* editors concluded that "the American saloon with its bar and its screens and its perpendicular drinking and its treating habit must be changed into a café, which a man may enter without hesitation accompanied by his wife and daughter." Brewers and liquor dealers often campaigned against prohibition in order to preserve masculine gender roles. More astute members of the liquor industry, putting the horse before the cart, recognized that public drinking spaces must be made acceptable to women and couples if prohibition were to be avoided.[35] In other words, they advocated elimination of the all-male saloon.

Finally, consider a criticism of women's drinking also published in 1915. Although writing about England, Arthur Shadwell's words merit international comparison. He ascribed a perceived increase in female drunkenness to women's new independence, particularly the economic freedom granted by wage earning and "the imitation of masculine ways. This [woman] movement was [intended] to regenerate man by feminine example and competition. I am afraid the opposite result is more conspicuous up to the present."[36] Shadwell, like American reformers distressed by dance halls and cabarets, could not accept the spectacle of women's "masculine" behavior. Yet his distress illustrates the boundary crossings taking place in the 1910s, the startling changes within the public realms of alcohol consumption and employment. Women, expected to raise men's morals, were, instead, discovered to be imitating them. Shadwell, unlike Lucy Allen in *Table Service* or the editors of *Bonfort's Wine and Spirits Circular,* did not recognize how women's presence might mitigate men's behavior. Female public drinking and male public temperance permitted ratification of the prohibition amendment. These same gendered sentiments a decade later would lead to its downfall.

PROHIBITION, COCKTAILS, LAW OBSERVANCE, AND THE AMERICAN HOME

Alcohol in many ways defined the domestic social life of nine-teenth-century American women. It marked the arrival and departure of guests, the presence of men, the rituals of hospitality and entertainment. In the early twentieth century, alcohol's association with domestic sociability continued, though discussion and criticism shifted to the far more radical behavior of young women and men within new public drinking spaces. By 1920, domestic drinking returned to public scrutiny as a stringent new federal prohibition law closed all public drinking establishments while permitting private consumption. It should not be surprising, therefore, that new drinking rituals focused on the home and on the drink-related interactions of American women and men.

Prohibition transformed both drinking and the broader national culture in which this behavior took place. Alcohol, cocktails in particular, facilitated the evolution from Victorian to modern America. Mixed drinks, with their elaborate instructions and fancy names, provided Demon Rum with sophisticated fashionability. Cocktails brought the saloon into the home at the same time that they brought women into the saloon's illicit prodigy, the speakeasy. When drys referred to Al Smith and later to Franklin Roosevelt as "cocktail presidents," they were not simply describing the men's drinking habits.[1] They were also criticizing a way of life, a worldview far distant from dry values and from separate spheres.

This chapter begins with a close look at the prohibition legislation of the 1920s. Federal prohibition effectively dismantled the public drinking culture of the saloon and in this respect should be considered a success. But other effects were less positive. Contrary to popular belief today, dry lawmakers permitted numerous outlets to legal alcohol, outlets that elaborated upon traditional drinking practices. After 1920 wets used familiar dry arguments on alcohol's dangers to society to criticize Prohibition.

Drys, on the other hand, insisted that Americans stop drinking, even though drinking was legal, in order to support the law. Discussions of alcohol within the media and domestic advice literature reveal a growing acceptance of new alcohol-dominated rituals within the home. In fact, home drinking and home manufacturing reinforced—often with a tinge of nostalgia—women's historic domestic responsibilities.

FEDERAL PROHIBITION

The stringency of national prohibition was not at first apparent. The Eighteenth Amendment approved by Congress and forty-six state legislatures (ten more than necessary for ratification) prohibited "the manufacture, sale, or transportation of intoxicating liquors within, the importation thereof into, or the exportation thereof from the United States and all territory subject to the jurisdiction thereof for beverage purposes." A subsequent section granted "the Congress and the several States . . . concurrent power to enforce this article by appropriate legislation." A third section added by disgruntled wets, and, as it turned out, unnecessary, required ratification within seven years. The amendment also provided a one-year grace period between ratification and enforcement to give liquor manufacturers time to convert their facilities to other uses. Unlike earlier state dry laws that permitted importation for personal use, federal prohibition specifically banned importation. Moreover, the national scope of the law rendered illegal acquisition problematic: thirsty residents could no longer simply cross into adjoining wet states in search of a drink or a bottle. Most significantly, the Eighteenth Amendment did not prohibit purchase of liquor. This loophole, which had been created to obtain purchasers' testimony against sellers, created an ethical morass. Drys argued that no difference existed between selling liquor and buying and drinking it. But the fact remained that drinkers did not get arrested and did not go to jail. In the 1920s a citizen could complain about the failure of government efforts and the breakdown of law and order while tapping comfortably into a new supply of bootleg hooch.[2]

The prohibition amendment ratified in January 1919 also left unspecified the definition of "intoxicating liquors." Congress's related War Time Prohibition Act ended production and sale of most alcoholic beverages even before federal prohibition began. It defined intoxicating liquors as those containing more than 2.75 percent alcohol. Some legislators voted for the prohibition amendment with the expectation that it, too, would permit light beers and wines. Yet Congress, overriding President Woodrow Wilson's veto, in October 1919 passed an enforcement law of remarkable severity. It was sponsored in the House of Representatives by Andrew Volstead of Minnesota and forever bore his name, though in point of fact it was written by the Anti-Saloon League. The Volstead Act defined "intoxicating liquors" as any beverage containing more than 0.5 percent alcohol.

While ostensibly banning all alcohol and all drinking, the Volstead Act contained several important caveats that left alcohol consumption legal. The twenty-fifth section of the second title of the Volstead Act specifically permitted possession and consumption of alcohol within the home by the homeowner, his family, and his guests. Some conservative legislators were of the opinion that the home was sacrosanct and the federal government had no justifiable presence there. Others felt that drinking within the home was not immoral or questionable in the same way that saloon drinking was. Serious doubt exists as to whether an amendment explicitly prohibiting domestic drinking could have been ratified. Moreover, the law nicely circumvented the delicate issue of what to do with the several million gallons of alcohol already in private possession. They would be drunk, lawmakers hoped, and the matter solved forever.[3]

Drys permitted personal possession in part because they believed the issue would shortly become moot. Throughout the history of the United States, drys considered alcohol a drug that was pushed, as it were, onto innocent users by the liquor industry. The connection in the second decade of the twentieth century between the liquor industry and such evils as political corruption and antisuffrage campaigning further reinforced this attitude. That women and men might seek out, enjoy, and even become addicted to alcohol voluntarily did not enter this worldview. With the traffic eliminated, drys felt, drinkers could return to their true abstemious natures. It is all the more ironic, therefore, that one of the more notable loopholes of the Volstead Act permitted the domestic production of wine and hard cider—in effect moving the liquor industry into the home. Households in the 1920s could legally produce up to two hundred gallons a year of wine or hard cider for family consumption. Numerous cookbooks from the decade described wine making with the same detail and tone as works a half-century earlier.[4] These cookbooks built upon the traditional associations between wine making and other woman-controlled elements of domestic food production.

The Volstead Act did not permit home-brewed beer. But home brewing capitalized on the sentiments and marketing of domestic viniculture. Department stores legally displayed and sold cans of malt syrup, capping machines, and gauges that had few uses other than alcohol production but which the courts did not consider inherently illegal. Drys frowned upon the tax that Michigan imposed on malt syrup and wort in the early 1930s, feeling that taxing the ingredients of prohibited beverages suggested certain ethical irregularities. Legislators agreed in principle but pointed out that Detroit residents had produced almost fifteen million gallons of beer in the first half of 1932. The impoverished state government desired a slice of the pie.[5]

91

o o o

*Prohibition,
Law
Observance,
and the
American
Home*

Far more questionable than home brewing was home distilling. The federal government first taxed distilled liquor in 1791 and to this day considers moonshining a form of tax evasion to be prosecuted with particular thoroughness. Nonetheless, homeowners did set up small stills. Alice Roosevelt Longworth, daughter of Theodore Roosevelt and in the 1920s wife of the Speaker of the House, made wine, "really good beer," and also "a very passable gin from oranges" in a still in her Washington, D.C., basement. Barrel manufacturers sold family-sized containers for aging liquor. Distilling was riskier than beer or wine production, requiring as it did constant heat, elaborate equipment, ventilation to remove the stink of fermenting mash, and not a little technical knowledge. Ignorant moonshiners bottled poisonous by-products along with potable ethyl alcohol, and all moonshiners had to somehow dispose of the spent mash. While homeowners such as the Longworths experimented with distilling their own stock, most moonshiners sought payment for their product. In cities such as New York and Chicago, crime syndicates organized family production as a cottage industry, managing the police and collecting liquor and waste.[6]

Bootleggers also smuggled liquor, wine, and beer from abroad. Beverage alcohol could even be imported legally as a preservative in liquid flavorings. Although secret distilling and smuggling retain a certain romance in the popular imagination, in terms of volume they did not come close to the black market sale of industrial alcohol. The Volstead Act permitted production of grain alcohol for medicinal, sacramental, and industrial purposes. Millions of gallons were illegally diverted to beverage use. Enthusiastic bootleggers also purchased liquor flavorings, with "aroma and taste like the real thing" (figure 4.1). They mixed these flavorings with diverted alcohol, one ounce to two gallons, in the largest, cleanest household receptacles they could find—hence the birth of "bathtub gin."[7]

Prohibition, because it eliminated the legal sale of alcohol, moved public drinking from licensed saloons to any site featuring a bottle owned by

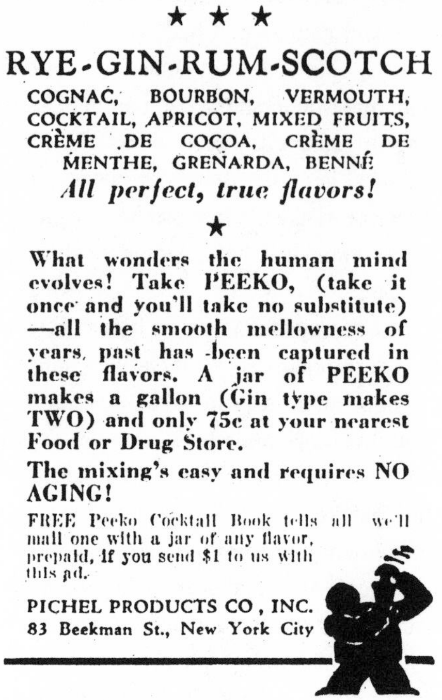

Figure 4.1
"A Wonderful Age We Live In!"

This was only one of many like-minded advertisements that appeared in urbane journals such as the New Yorker *in the last years of Prohibition. Peeko and similar products promised to flavor industrial grain alcohol "diverted" to private use. One has to ask why revelers partaking in such ghastly concoctions of bathtub gin (or bathtub rye, scotch, or crème de cocoa) would ever want to drink again.* New Yorker 8 (15 Oct. 1932): 61.

someone with a penchant for cash. Speakeasies, an ancient Irish term for illegal drinking spots, sprang up in many working-class neighborhoods for laborers who could only afford drinks by the glass. Fancier speakeasies, akin to prewar nightclubs and cabarets, emerged as well. Although New York cabaret life bottomed out in the early 1920s, after 1924 the city for all intents and purposes abandoned prohibition enforcement. Small, intimate nightclubs flourished. Harlem nightclubs catering to late-night white audiences also spread in popularity after 1925.[8]

This discussion does not begin to list all the clever ways in which drinkers and their suppliers broke the law. But it establishes the ease with which alcohol could be acquired and conveys a sense of the public nature of this law breaking. Everyone knew what the advertisements and the men in low-riding trucks were selling. Department stores prominently displayed flasks, cocktail shakers, and other equipment used only for drinking and drink making. Drys had every right to resent drinkers who in their arrogance polluted prohibition sentiment, eliminating the possibility of a truly dry America.[9]

On the other hand, enforcement officials found themselves fettered by the sizable body of wet public opinion. The Eighteenth Amendment provided federal and state governments "concurrent power" to enforce Prohibition. This stipulation acknowledged state dry laws that predated the amendment. Federal lawmakers also hoped that concurrent enforcement would spread the cost and obligation of enforcement from the national government to the forty-eight states. As it emerged, however, the clause excused states from enforcing the federal law. States could also revoke their own dry laws with constitutional impunity. State legislators and local sheriffs had little interest in alienating the wet vote through their assiduousness. To appease both wets and drys, lawmakers settled on a tactic used by states since the turn of the century: tough enforcement laws to satisfy the drys, underfunded to the point of ineffectuality in order to mollify the wets. The Woman's National Committee for Law Enforcement reported in disgust in 1931 that states were spending one-eighth as much on prohibition as on "enforcement of their game and fish laws."[10]

Drys, with some justification, blamed interest in drinking and lawbreaking on the entertainment and news industries. The news media had begun the decade commendably dry. In the mid-1910s, when Congress and the state legislatures were debating the amendment, articles in popular magazines endorsing prohibition outnumbered critical articles by twenty to one. After the prohibition amendment passed, humor and literary magazines—particularly fashionable mid-decade periodicals such as the *New Yorker* and *American Mercury*—mocked the amendment. But most major newspapers supported Prohibition until at least 1926. All periodicals, wet or dry, reported prohibition violations and controversies. Gangland killings in New York, Chicago, and other major cities captivated Americans. Magazines reported on "lady bootleggers," respectable women left bankrupt by poor investments or evil relatives who turned in desperation to driving liquor for the underworld. (The women were always anonymous; the stories may or may not have been true.) Periodicals also discussed incessantly drink's threat to youth and morality. By the end of the decade the *New York Times* reserved a full page each day for stories on hijackings, speakeasy raids, bootleggers, and wet and dry speeches. Drys complained that such sensationalism affected citizens' faith in the amendment, which is probably true. But as one writer at the time pointed out, Prohibition was "essentially the stuff of which news is made." Film and print media disseminated these images throughout the country. Hollywood in the second decade of the twentieth century had produced many temperance melodramas such as "Ten Nights in a Bar-room," films in which only evil characters drank, in the end suffering for it. In contrast, 1920s heroes and heroines drank far more often than bad guys. Glamorous parties in nightclubs or country clubs featured highballs, cocktails, fancy glassware—a world apart from the lives of the audience. Images of tippling heroines merged with those of young collegians, wealthy urbanites, and daring radicals to promote drinking as a positive quality.[11]

But how much did people actually drink? From the start of federal prohibition, wets and drys argued over whether Prohibition reduced drunkenness. A legal distinction existed between alcohol production, which was illegal, and drinking, which was not. This distinction was often overlooked, however, by adversaries presenting *consumption* (usually anecdotally) as evidence of the law's efficacy. Even at the time, opponents acknowledged that accurate data on alcohol production and consumption was notoriously poor, if not nonexistent. Consumption statistics before Prohibition are based mainly on federal tax records. Since Prohibition ostensibly eliminated beverage alcohol and thus its tax, these records had no value. In one of the decade's most thorough investigations, Clark Warburton combined raw-materials production with deathrates and arrest statistics. More recent scholars, building on his work, conclude that Americans in the first years of federal prohibition drank one-third to one-half as much as they had a decade earlier, when state prohibition laws began to go into effect. Even later in the decade consumption rose to only two-thirds of that in the early 1910s. Based on these statistics, it could be argued that Prohibition was a success because state and federal dry laws did in fact reduce consumption. Prohibition's greatest legacy has been permanent elimination of the worst excesses of the alcoholic republic. Ernest Mandeville, who traveled the country in 1925 to examine conditions under Prohibition, reported that "ten years ago it was certainly not a novel thing to see a drunken man staggering up the street or reclining on a bank. To-day in the Middle West the sight of a drunkard is so rare that when there is one he usually attracts a crowd of onlookers."[12]

The amendment's reduction in alcohol consumption affected different levels of American society in profoundly different ways. Social workers in the late 1920s described with pleasure the decline in drinking in the working-class and immigrant neighborhoods surrounding settlement houses. Saloon beer before Prohibition had cost five cents a glass; the bootleg product now cost a dollar a bottle. Poorer Americans could no longer afford to drink. Homemade concoctions such as pumpkin wine, not to mention the rubbing alcohol and Sterno sought by the most desperate, seemed designed to inspire temperance among unmoneyed drinkers. The rising cost of alcohol—which Warburton asserted tripled during Prohibition—did not affect wealthier Americans as much. In fact, under Prohibition alcohol became a rare commodity for the first time since the country's founding and therefore prized in certain circles. While beer drinking declined by two-thirds, consumption of both wine and spirits rose, spirits by 10 percent, wine by more than 60 percent. Warburton felt that "people of wealth, business men and professional men, and their families, and, perhaps, the higher paid working men and their families, are drinking in large numbers in quite frank disregard of the declared policy of the National Prohibition Act."[13]

Because Prohibition removed the most notorious public drinkers and drinking spaces from the collective consciousness, drinking could now be glamorized. Appended to praise of the decrease in public drunkenness, therefore, was criticism of the increase in domestic drinking. Prohibition, wets claimed, had simply moved the saloon into the home. The cocktail consumption of "respectable" Americans came to unavoidable prominence as dry laws eliminated the worst examples of saloon-related abuse.[14] The Eighteenth Amendment, by bringing public focus to drink's domestic presence, served to legitimize further alcohol consumption. Domestic drinking was one of the most disheartening and damning realities that prohibitionists faced.

HOME CONSUMPTION

New domestic drinking rituals did not develop immediately. In 1920 and 1921, some well-intentioned hosts and hostesses, in an effort to support the new dry law, refrained from serving any alcohol. Others explained that the alcohol they were serving had been purchased before prohibition laws had gone into effect and was thus legal. Such empathy toward dry sentiments may be found in etiquette guides and cookbooks. Although the Volstead Act did not prohibit dissemination of alcohol-related information, writers and publishers in the early years of the decade shied away from overt references to drinking. Their prose contrasts with prewar domestic literature. For example, Lucy Allen's 1915 *Table Service* specified that a maid, when pouring wine, should first serve the host. In this manner bits of cork would not end up in a guest's glass. A similar book by Mary Chambers released in 1920 described this exact ritual but for corked bottled water rather than wine. The 1922 *Book of Etiquette* and 1928 *Table Service and Decoration* mention the staff at a formal dinner serving only water; *How to Entertain at Home* (1928) avoids discussion of all beverages.[15]

A second school of writers sought to legitimize dry beverages within the rituals of sociability and drink. Sarah Adams, in *How to Set the Table for Every Occasion* (figure 4.2), describes a restaurant dinner that included the Astoria Cup, "which is made of equal parts cider, grape juice, loganberry

96

o o o

Domesticating
Drink

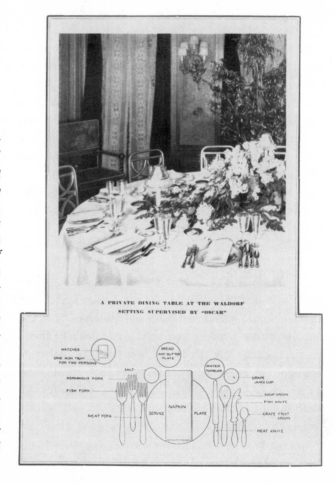

Figure 4.2   "A Private Dining Table at the Waldorf"

In the early years of federal prohibition, everyone gamely boarded the water wagon. Oscar, the Waldorf's maître d'hôtel, has provided guests a "grape juice cup" in lieu of the traditional wine glass, a temperate detail in what otherwise promised to be an intemperate evening: five courses plus bread, cigarettes, and certainly dessert. Sarah Swain Adams, How to Set the Table for Every Occasion *(New York: Derryvale Linen Co., 1921), 14. Courtesy The Winterthur Library, Printed Book and Periodical Collection.*

juice, and sparkling water." Two years later, *Everybody's Complete Etiquette* detailed the grape juice, orange juice, and other "combinations . . . made to take the place of the once familiar 'claret cup.'" A caterers' handbook mentioned the "ginger-ale cups" to be filled after the soup course of formal dinners.[16]

97

∘ ∘ ∘

*Prohibition,
Law
Observance,
and the
American
Home*

A new cookbook genre sprang up with ratification of the Eighteenth Amendment: the alcohol-free drink-mixing manual. Titles such as *On Uncle Sam's Water Wagon: Five Hundred Recipes for Delicious Drinks Which Can Be Made at Home* and the 1921 *Drinks: Formulas for Making Ozonated Non-Alcoholic Drinks to Resemble Alcoholic Cocktails and Mixed Drinks* appeared in the early years of Prohibition. In its preface, *What to Drink: Recipes and Directions for Making and Serving Non-alcoholic Drinks* acknowledged the new demands that Prohibition would put on home entertaining: "The hostess of to-day will be called upon to serve drinks in her home more than formerly, I imagine, and it were well to . . . be prepared to serve a refreshing drink in an attractive manner at a moment's notice." In other words, hostesses should be prepared to entertain couples or men who now had no place else to go. General cookbooks also supported temperance drinks. The beverage section of 1920s cookbooks often mentioned "grape-juice high-balls," "frosted orange sparkles," and nonalcoholic mint juleps. Beyond these dry cocktails, cookbooks tended to avoid references to alcohol. The 1926 everyday menu guide, *Feed the Brute,* had no beverage section at all. A French chef publishing his life's work early in the decade disconsolately substituted broth for the wine required in many recipes. Fannie Farmer, in the 1927 edition of the *Boston Cooking-School Cook Book,* was exceptional for her inclusion of wine, brandy, peach brandy, and other alcoholic sauces.[17]

Domestic advisers became increasingly bold as the decade progressed, willing to discuss without dissembling Prohibition and its effects on home alcohol consumption. In *Everybody's Complete Etiquette* (1923), Ellin Learned described how a hostess should negotiate the Volstead Act:

At the beginning of dinner the iced water or Apollinaris is poured by the butler in each glass. In these days of prohibition various mixtures are substituted for wines. White grape juice and ginger ale, with ice and mint is a popular beverage, and this is poured in wine glasses during dinner. People who still have wines in their cellars serve them as in other times, sherry, sauterne, and champagne, and, after dinner, green mint, or other liquors. When serving a wine a butler or footman mentions what it is. At present, however, he has become accustomed to say, "Grape juice, sir?"

The Book of Good Manners of the same year described the service of both alcoholic and dry beverages by the host or staff. This author was equally fastidious about legal etiquette: "Those who still have cellars and those who arrange to have some wine made in their own homes, serve wine just as they used to." He is also adamant that "a guest must never permit wine to be served and then not drink it." Etiquette writers in the nineteenth century instructed drys to accept alcohol graciously even if they did not intend to drink. But writers in the 1920s apparently considered it too precious to waste. By the end of the decade domestic advisers were acknowledging Prohibition tangentially, if at all. Lucy Allen, in her 1928 edition of *Table Service,* mentioned that ladies' luncheons sometimes began with a "light cocktail accompanied by sandwiches or small wafers."[18]

Manufacturers capitalized on the new enthusiasm for home drinking. John T. Flynn, in a 1928 *Collier's* article, listed the thirty-five different cocktail glasses he found at one New York department store, in addition to shakers, hip flasks, and a variety of wine glasses. As early as 1923, department store ads mentioned wine and cocktail glasses by name. The respectable hostess required a knowledge of glassware akin to that of her Victorian grandmother: a glassware set in Mary Chambers' 1929 *Table Etiquette* included goblet, cocktail glass, sherbet glass, "Oyster Cocktail, Luncheon Goblet, Dinner Goblet, Tumbler (water), [and] Soda Tumbler." Magazines described portable American bars available for rental or purchase by mail.[19]

Much of the public discussion of this domestic drinking centered on the fact that women, as consumers, were supporting alcohol-related products and publications and that women, as hostesses, were offering alcohol to their guests. In 1931, the journalist George Ade insightfully summarized the rise and fall of the American saloon. Home drinking differed from earlier public abuse, he explained. "The woman who never went near a boisterous bar-room or sat in a restaurant which sent drinks to the table, and the man who didn't like to find himself in any kind of boozing den, do not know how to refuse a cocktail when it is proffered by a prominent executive in a dinner jacket or a charming hostess in an evening frock." In 1928, Inez Haynes Irwin wrote a criticism of Prohibition for the *Woman's Journal,* a monthly magazine concerned with women's political issues. She described with some shock the disregard for Prohibition encountered at domestic social events. Irwin was often invited out to dinner, and these meals almost always included alcohol, sometimes "the whole pre-Volstead ritual" of cocktails, wine, and cordials. "Only once since the passage of the Amendment" had Irwin's hosts refused to serve alcohol out of respect for the law. While Irwin admitted that this disregard may be regional, she was nonetheless taken aback by hostesses' disregard of their abetting violation of the Eighteenth Amendment to the American Constitution. In the 1930 *Liberty* article "Ladies at the Bar," the muckraker Ida Tarbell, who was herself ambivalent about this turn of events, described the tittering integration of women into a sanitized, romanticized saloon culture. Two social scientists, in their 1930 discussion of social changes over the previous ten years, labeled this the "feminization of drinking." "Not for masculine shoppers," they pointed out, "are displayed the dainty array of glassware and the delicately embroidered cocktail napkins."[20] Americans were acutely aware of alcohol's regendering during federal prohibition.

99

○ ○ ○

*Prohibition,
Law
Observance,
and the
American
Home*

Dry leaders attempted to diffuse the close association between alcohol and domestic sociability with a campaign that only emphasized the intractability of this dilemma. In 1924, federal Prohibition Commissioner Roy Haynes expressed the opinion that the American woman could "save" Prohibition, "for woman largely controls social customs. . . . It is outrageous that in any American home the household should feel more ashamed of not having liquor to serve their guests, than ashamed to violate and trample under their feet the Constitution of the United States." He asked that those serving "pre-Prohibition cocktails" recognize the need for observance of Prohibition's intent. Yet even drys recognized alcohol's integral role in sociability. The director of Prohibition enforcement in northern California testified in 1926 "that he did drink occasionally because San Francisco is a wet community, and that he also served liquor to his guests because he was a gentleman and 'not a prude.'"[21]

Drys recalled warmly the prohibition enthusiasm of the previous decade, when a large majority of Americans objected to the lawlessness and corruption of alcohol manufacturers and distributors. In the 1920s, drys continued to finger this standard retinue of wet enemies. As attacks on the Eighteenth Amendment increased, so did references to the liquor interests, whom drys perceived to be behind repeal efforts. A 1930 *Woman's Journal* article, "Prohibition and Propaganda," described the "endless funds" going into repeal, providing as evidence an incident of antifeminist pamphleting by the Associated Distillery Industries of Kentucky. Other woman drys asserted that a single wet senator spent $50,000 to keep a dry from reelection as county committeewoman and that newspapers and magazines opposed Prohibition only because publishers wanted alcohol-related advertising. To be honest, in the desperate years of the early 1930s many editors would probably have advanced heroin legalization if it promised ad revenues. However, there is little evidence of secret efforts to sway public opinion on Prohibition compared with the anti-suffrage activities of brewers and saloon keepers in the 1910s.[22]

To a certain extent, drys blamed the liquor interests because the presence of other visible enemies was simply too disheartening. Drys refused to believe that "normal" women could support repeal. In 1929, a member of the League of Women Voters stated with confidence that "not, in this country, being drinkers themselves, there has been no sacrifice for women" in regards to Prohibition. "Men are sometimes a little weak and inconsistent especially under alcoholic pressure," wrote Lucy Peabody, founder of the Woman's National Committee for Law Enforcement (WNCLE), "but women who demand the traffic back are more dangerous and inconsistent. The final cure for drinking men may be drinking women. They are not fit to guide automobiles, children, or society." Drys loudly criticized the *Literary Digest's* Prohibition polls because they overlooked women. In 1932, the *Digest* addressed this criticism, mailing separate ballots to men and women participants in one city. Among those from Portland, Maine, who returned ballots, two-thirds of the women, as compared with three-fourths of the men, voted for repeal. The *Digest* concluded that women were "not so emphatically wet . . . but their wetness is decisive." Illinois, which kept its men's and women's ballots separate, reported similar findings.[23] Drys remained unconvinced.

Dry women continued to encourage their sisters toward support of Prohibition. Assistant Attorney General Mabel Walker Willebrandt, in a 1924 *Good Housekeeping* article, asked, "Will You Help Keep the Law?" Speaking before the WNCLE, she requested that every delegate "become a positive force to *inspire obedience to law*. . . . [This] means that [you] shall definitely set social standards against serving liquors at parties and clubs." President Calvin Coolidge, lukewarm at best over enforcement, repeated Willebrandt's call for law observance, and the term came to imply abstaining from alcohol out of respect for Prohibition. Law observers, it was felt, by not drinking would set a good example to their neighbors and children. The WNCLE used the slogan "Allegiance to the Constitution, Observance of Law" in its writings and, in 1931, changed its name to include "Law Observance." In 1929, wealthy Lucy Strawbridge of Philadelphia began a campaign to eliminate drinking among "socially prominent" women. Widely reported by the WNCLE and the media, Strawbridge's campaign illustrates the challenges the dry-woman stereotype now faced. Strawbridge, it should be noted, was not even asking for pledges of abstinence, only that hostesses discontinue *serving* drinks at private gatherings. Willebrandt similarly called on Republican women to ban liquor socially. A leading member of the General Federation of Women's Clubs in 1931 asked women to "start a movement in the community to make 'dry parties' popular."[24]

Wets and drys alike complained about Prohibition's unwanted presence in the home. Ida Tarbell grumbled in 1924 that she "found dinner parties giving the full time before dinner and after to 'how and where to get it,' to stories of police corruption, to the evasion of people high in office, to the corruption of boys and girls, to bitter resentment. It was an endless discussion, an obsession." H. L. Mencken cataloged the dry and wet terms that peppered everyday speech in the 1920s "and made the whole nation booze-conscious." An article on home entertaining mentioned casually, "I remember once, after dinner, when several of us were sitting about airing our views on the weather, prohibition, and all the usual topics, that we suddenly ran short of ideas." In other words, Prohibition was discussed as frequently as the weather, and with similar stimulation. A member of the New York Woman's Committee for Law Enforcement in 1931 pleaded for "less good-natured connivance at a neighbor's law-breaking, for tact and pleasantness in the patriotic duty of voicing our enjoyment in spending an evening with people who do not want to think or talk of alcohol." Carrie Chapman Catt, in the *Woman's Journal,* repeated this theme. "We do not serve liquor in our homes and we turn down our glasses on other tables. . . . We do not discuss prohibition nor the detestable character of the modern social class which finds in the violation of the law the chief charm of life."[25]

Such a request for silence was unrealistic. Prohibition remained a primary issue in the 1920s because it colored and politicized all beverages. Unlike other legal and moral issues such as graft or murder (or abortion, for that matter), Prohibition affected everyday behavior and for that reason remained in Americans' consciousness. What one drank and what one served at any social event became an explicit and highly charged political statement. Thus, participants in the most apolitical events—weddings, luncheons, club dinners, poker games—were yet again made aware of the law and the ongoing controversy over its necessity and enforcement. Drys complained that people continued to talk about and focus on alcohol. But intoxicating liquors were far too integral to the rituals of American civilization to be so quickly eliminated.

THE COCKTAIL: A BEVERAGE REDEFINES AMERICA

Alcohol had played a significant role in uniting men and women during nineteenth-century social events: witness the tradition of challenging, when a man toasted a woman with a mutual drink. A typical formal dinner in 1890s Delaware began stilted and awkward. "But with the sherry after the oysters familiarity began," wrote a young witness, "a teasing badinage of charge and counter charge, friendly, mirthful, neither noisy nor distinguished, but pleasant to hear." Yet the domestic drinking of the 1920s differed from earlier practices. In the first place, the very constraints of Prohibition rendered this drinking far more self-conscious than that of earlier generations. Beyond the legality, hostesses and hosts intent on entertaining with the lubricant alcohol faced numerous other social changes that would dramatically affect domestic heterosociality. New expectations surrounded marriage, emphasizing the time couples spent together in the home. Middle-class families sought to entertain as cheaply as possible, a concern that would become paramount in the 1930s.[26]

Related to this, the declining availability of domestic help forced the improvisation of less formal (that is, less labor-intensive) entertainments. In 1880, one-quarter of all urban or suburban households employed servants. By World War I, the number of families with help dropped dramatically, and the help that remained generally came for the day rather than living in. Young women now found better-paying and more flexible positions in factories or offices and left onerous domestic service without regret. Immigration restrictions in the 1920s further curtailed the available population of help. New electric appliances to a certain extent facilitated the housework that middle-class women were now expected to complete solo. This "proletarianization" (as the labor historian Ruth Cowan has dubbed it) of housework took its toll on home entertaining.[27]

Domestic advisers after 1900, sensitive to the labor needs of would-be hostesses, proudly emphasized the new lack of pretension at formal social events. *The Complete Hostess* (1906) considered a formal dinner "one of the most formidable of undertakings," implying an informal dinner was just as acceptable and much easier. "It is estimated that something over 90 percent of our American homes are servantless," wrote Mary Chambers in her 1920 *Breakfasts, Luncheons, and Dinners*, "and in a home which belongs to this honorable majority [a formal] dinner had better not be attempted." By the end of the decade writers had a decidedly sour-grapes attitude. *How to Entertain at Home* defined formal entertaining as that requiring a maid. "Informality is the note of the day, and happily so. Formal occasions are generally stiff and cumbersome if not stupid." In 1929, Chambers described dinners as either formal or "friendly."[28]

103

o o o

Prohibition,
Law
Observance,
and the
American
Home

Home entertainment required a substitute for the now-reviled formal dinner. "Friendly" dinners, no matter how "colorful, intimate, and almost family affair[s]" they might be, still demanded a great deal of work. The explosive interest in chafing-dish suppers illustrates this search for a method of preparing food and hosting guests simultaneously. A second, easier solution was afternoon tea. "The 'afternoon tea' is the least expensive, the least troublesome, and one of the most popular forms of social entertainment," stated the *A-B-C of Good Form* in 1915.[29] Requiring only light refreshments and a suitable gathering space, afternoon tea provided women a simple method of gathering female friends. Guests stayed for as little as five minutes, no more than an hour, and often attended several in one day.

The afternoon tea had an ambiguous relation with alcohol. The 1901 *Etiquette for All Occasions* specified wine cup for teas. Others left vague whether the punch they recommended should be wet or dry. "What if the dissipation they offer is of the mildest type?" asked dry etiquette writer Florence Hall in 1911. Yet it is unclear whether she is referring to the dangers of alcohol or of caffeine: writers advised hostesses to make the tea as weak as possible, immersing the leaves in hot water for only "a moment or two." Although teas could be wet or dry, afternoon "receptions," which were larger and more formal, generally required drink. This corresponded with receptions' heavier menu and mixed company. With the growing popularity in the 1910s of afternoon dancing, women began hosting tea dances similar to those found in hotel ballrooms and cabarets. Private tea dances, like their commercial equivalent, offered alcohol. *Dainties for Home Parties: A Cook-Book for Dance-Suppers, Bridge Parties, Receptions, Luncheons, and Other Entertainments* (1915) included ten alcoholic punches.[30]

Before federal prohibition, dry laws within many communities had inspired domestic drinking rituals. In the 1920s, these spread across the nation. Because theaters and restaurants could not serve alcohol, a night out might now begin with drinks at home. The cost and scarcity (real or imagined) of alcohol gave it new importance, an aura of modernity and hospitality. Over the course of the decade, afternoon teas gave way to cocktail parties. Even in the Midwest, an actress stated with shock, "I was invited to an afternoon tea, and when I got there, there was no tea to be had! Only quarts and quarts of cocktails." Originally a mixed drink of spirits and bitters, the cocktail in the late nineteenth century came to define as well small, distinctive portions of food served at the beginning of a meal as an appetizer. In fact, although we today think of "appetizers" as food, the term first appeared in the United States in the mid-nineteenth century in association with predinner liquors, or *apéritifs*. As the alcoholic "appetizer" came to describe foods, cocktails developed a similar association. Lucy Allen's 1915 *Table Service* describes luncheon courses of fruit or lobster cocktail—a food—in addition to cocktail drinks.[31]

This detail is significant only because advice writers in the 1920s capitalized on the dual meaning of *cocktail* as both an alcoholic beverage and a fancy but dry drink or food. In 1929, Mary Chambers mentioned serving fruit and oyster cocktails in large cocktail glasses, apparently considering a cocktail glass to be a vessel for food. Yet, building upon the etymology of *appetizer*, she also included illustrations of *apéritif* glasses. The caption reads, "Glasses for the Aperitif, or mixture made in the cocktail shaker and served just before dinner—usually in the drawing-room. Note the diminutive size of these glasses, the largest holding only three ounces. They are often refilled." Perhaps she felt dry readers would not know the meaning of *apéritif* (though surely they would deduce it from the use of a cocktail shaker). Elsewhere in the book, she described cocktail napkins "of fine linen, embroidered or lace-edged, used for Cocktail Parties." Chambers refrained from defining cocktail parties themselves, but her point is clear. Cocktail parties allowed women to entertain with some formality—note the napkins—but without much work.[32]

By the end of Prohibition, advice writers described the cocktail party as "one of the most successful forms of entertaining. It fits so snugly into the late afternoon, when a brief period of conversation and refreshment is most welcome." The pop historian Frederick Lewis Allen considered the cocktail party "a new American institution," part of the "spirit of deliberate revolt which in many communities made drinking 'the thing to do.'" Cocktail parties soon spread from urban areas to the hinterlands. The artist Leon Kroll attended cocktail parties held in his honor in Des Moines,

Iowa, in 1924. A New York Supreme Court justice defended cocktail parties from the bench in 1925, asserting that his daughter and other "nice people" often "entertained in that fashion."[33] By 1930 cocktails and cocktail parties seemed ubiquitous.

As in the nineteenth century, the medium of alcohol facilitated interaction between men and women. Etiquette maven Alma Whitaker described the mythical beginnings of the cocktail, created in desperation by the host of a dull party "in which the guests labored to make conversation. The women seemed to cackle and the men were discomfortingly dull. When it was discovered, after the host had served his nefarious mixture, that the women promptly seemed sparklingly vivacious and the men brilliantly epigrammatical, the transformation could not fail to establish the new concoction as socially acceptable." These descriptions illustrate alcohol's role in evening entertainment. A writer in the *Woman's Journal* described herself as "the most amateur of drinkers," one who disliked beer, cordials, whiskey, and brandy. She did admit to appreciating wine and champagne. "And," she wrote, "I consider that American creation, the cocktail, the greatest aid to hospitality that has ever been invented since the combination of the open fire with the luxurious couches of Chippendale, Hepplewhite, and Sheraton made sitting down more comfortable than standing up."[34] She equated cocktails with hospitality, with graciousness, with the essential elements of sociability. Incidents such as this praise of the cocktail—in the *Woman's Journal,* no less—brought to the fore the increasingly problematic connection between women as moral social leaders and women as conscientious and fashionable hostesses. The cocktail challenged this connection. Associated with conviviality, artistry, and a wealth of drink-related objects, cocktails legitimized as no other beverage could alcohol consumption within the home.

The etymologist and bon vivant H. L. Mencken declared the origins of the word *cocktail* lost to history. This did not prevent him from speculating at length on the subject nor from explaining that all the seven-hundred-odd cocktails he sampled in the course of his research were good, "though some, of course, were better than others." The earliest known reference to *cocktail* appeared in an 1806 New York newspaper, as a drink of spirits, water, sugar, and bitters. This use of bitters differentiated the cocktail from other mixed drinks of the period. Mencken described the cocktail as originally "a concoction of very precise composition—as much so as the Martini or Manhattan of today—but in a very few years it was popping up more than a thousand miles away, with an algebraic formula, $x + C_{12}H_{22}O_{11}$ $+ H_2O + y$. . . . Given any hard liquor, any diluent, and any addition of aromatic flavoring, and you have one instantly."[35]

Throughout the nineteenth century, cocktails competed with other mixed drinks and alcoholic beverages. Working-class men drank either beer or whiskey, regarding mixed drinks as effeminate. The hapless saloon patron who requested one might be asked to leave the premises, or worse. Just as significant a challenge, and one less recognized today, came from the American tradition of communal mixed drinks such as punches, cups, cobblers, flips, slings, and eggnogs. Bartenders (professional or domestic) made these drinks by the quart for two or more drinkers. Visiting America in 1842, Charles Dickens described a massive julep wreathed in flowers that he shared one evening with Washington Irving: "It was quite an enchanted julep, and carried us among innumerable people and places we both knew. The julep held out far into the night, and my memory never saw him afterwards otherwise than as bending over it, with his straw, with an attempted air of gravity (after some anecdote involving some wonderfully droll and delicate observation of character), and then as his eye caught mine, melting into that captivating laugh of his, which was the brightest and best that I have ever heard." Mrs. Alexander Orr Bradley, in the 1893 *Beverages and Sandwiches for Your Husband's Friends* (*By One Who Knows*), included thirty-five recipes for communal drinks with and without alcohol and only four recipes for individual drinks. Communal drinks, as Dickens so vividly described, created social drinking, created sociability. They brought together men (and, particularly in colonial times, women) to share in the punch bowl, the "club."[36] The treating rituals of rounds of drinks in working-class saloons may have been an attempt to recapture this experience of shared alcohol.

Communal drinks also differed from beer or whiskey in that their preparation was labor intensive. Bowls required juicing, mixing, chilling, dissolving sugar, and "resting" the mixture for hours or days before serving. Cocktails built on this tradition. The cocktails recorded in nineteenth-century drink-mixing manuals seem not only syrupy and dangerously full of egg whites but also like an awful lot of work. Bartenders in the most prestigious saloons and hotel bars had every right to treat their drink mixing as a skilled craft. They wrote detailed manuals for their peers, not the masses. Judging from the dates of these manuals, cocktails spread in popularity after the Civil War, part of the drinking culture of Victorian manhood. Jerry Thomas, one of the most famous bartenders of nineteenth-century America, defined the cocktail as "a modern invention" in his 1862 drink-mixing manual. Cocktails became particularly popular in men's clubs, perhaps because of their associations to earlier club drinks. They required skilled labor, a well-stocked bar, and an attitude of connoisseurship. As late as the 1910s, Jack London had cocktails shipped to his ranch from an Oakland, California, bar.[37]

107

o o o

Prohibition,
Law
Observance,
and the
American
Home

Toward the end of the nineteenth century, predinner cocktails came into fashion. This ritual appears based in part on the tradition of serving sherry with oysters, an omnipresent first course at Victorian formal dinners. Edna Pontellier, in Kate Chopin's 1899 novel *The Awakening,* offers a cocktail, "a tiny glass that looked and sparkled like a garnet gem," to the guests at her birthday party, but then Creole New Orleans had a long tradition of drinking. Linda Hull Larned the same year felt the practice to be as radical as smoking at dinner: "It is considered quite 'smart' in some social circles to serve cocktails just before dinner is announced or immediately after the guests are seated at table . . . ; but our hostess of to-day will lose no friends by excluding this pair of bohemians [cocktails and cigarettes] from her dinners and luncheons." Other domestic advice writers in the early twentieth century similarly described cocktails as the practice in "some fashionable houses." Florence Hall considered the custom of handing cocktails to guests before they entered the dining room "more honored in the breach than in the observance." In 1909, Francis Crowninshield listed the "sudden and violent changes that have somewhat ruffled the placid water of polite society" in the preceding decade. Included with telephones, women's rights, steam heat, and coeducation were cocktails.[38]

From colonial America forward, women retained some association with both producing and consuming mixed drinks. Mary Sherwood told readers of *Manners and Social Usages* (1884) that "every lady should know how to mix [claret] cup, as it is convenient both for supper and lawn-tennis parties, and is preferable in its effects to the heavier article so common at parties—punch." Such mixed drinks as claret cup, sherry cobbler, Roman punch (a frozen drink), and milk punch made with sherry had particular associations with women.[39] These drinks illustrate the historic gendering of alcoholic beverages. In the nineteenth century, "feminine" beverages included wines, sherry, and cordials in addition to such mixed drinks as milk punch. The ladies' entrance on many saloons led to a back "wine room," a term at times linked to brothels. The home decanter sparked debate within Victorian society because it threatened the gender boundaries associated with drink, making wine, sherry, or men's whiskey ever more accessible to women.

In the twentieth century, the cocktail would pose a similar threat. Like the decanter, the cocktail offered alcohol in a small, fashionable, dangerous package. Heublein's in 1892 began a campaign to convert women to cocktail drinking by emphasizing its healthful qualities (figure 2.2). At a dinner party in 1910, Milwaukee, "the grown-ups were served a very small Martini. They drank it in a matter of minutes, without hors d'oeuvres, and were immediately shown into the dining room. The [hosts] . . . were considered avant-garde." Dorothy Wilson, who attended this event as a child and recounted the story sixty years later, recalled that "it was especially shocking to see women drinking cocktails. . . . Women might with propriety drink wine but nothing else alcoholic." The cocktail, in other words, provided wine-drinking women hard liquor. Such stunned references must be understood in light of this distinction. In the early 1910s, cocktails appeared in reformers' descriptions of dance halls and cabarets. There, girls were induced "to drink Mamie Taylors, cocktails, and other insidious mixtures." A visitor to a hotel tea dance in 1914 described the "rickeys and pale pink, innocent looking gin beverages [that] become the 'thirst quenchers.'" When a dry Boston club woman of 1910 complained of women's cocktail drinking as "the smart thing to do," when a writer in the London *Truth* warned of "Vermouth cocktails . . . and fast men," they were not objecting to the drinking so much as to the ingredients.[40] Cocktails were mysterious, potent, and masculine. Women's consumption of alcohol in and of itself did not generate the same level of criticism.

Yet not everyone questioned the cocktail's legitimacy or danger. Cocktail recipes appeared in cookbooks of the first two decades of the twentieth century written for a domestic female audience. *A Book of Beverages,* prepared by the Daughters of the American Revolution in 1904, describes a grape-fruit cocktail of grapefruit juice, sherry, and rum. *Beverages,* the fifth volume of Christine Terhune Herrick's *Consolidated Library of Modern Cooking and Household Recipes,* included forty-eight pages of mixed-drink recipes. Herrick even enters the debate on the proper construction of a mint julep. By the early 1910s the term *cocktail* had multiple meanings and suffixes: bar, stool, shaker, lounge. Illustrators were using cocktail glasses—clear stemmed containers with angled sides—as a shortcut description of drinking and decadence. An Anti-Saloon League handbill from the 1910s asked, "Can you imagine a cocktail party in Heaven?"[41] No definition of cocktail party was needed.

Throughout the 1920s cocktails grew in popularity. Federal dry laws affected the quality as well as the volume of licit and illicit distilled liquor. Mixing helped disguise the fact that the scotch one was drinking had been aged for hours instead of years. Unlike cocktail manuals written before World War I for professional bartenders, Prohibition-era manuals aimed at the enthusiastic novice within the home. The first manuals in the late 1920s presented themselves not as guides but as museum pieces. *The Bon-Vivant's Companion; or, How to Mix Drinks* had first been published in 1862. Knopf reprinted it in 1928 with a forward by the journalist Herbert Asbury. The 1928 volume *Giggle Water* contained the subtitled explanation "eleven famous cocktails of the most exclusive club in New York, as served before the war when mixing drinks was an art." *The Home Bartender's Guide and Song Book* of 1930 included old saloon songs and illustrations of women and men in Edwardian dress, lest readers suspect the authors were not historically minded. A collection of Maryland recipes contained mixed drinks because a regional cookbook without "juleps, eggnogs, punches, bounces, and toddies . . . would not only be hopelessly incomplete but historically inaccurate." But by the end of the decade, wets were mostly making fun. Virginia Elliott and Phil D. Stong's *Shake 'Em Up! A Practical Handbook of Polite Drinking* (1930) warned readers to use only "non-alcoholic (ignore the prefix at your peril) Gin, Scotch, Rye, Corn, and Applejack." A similar disclaimer appeared in a 1932 *New Yorker* ad for maple syrup. The ad included a cocktail recipe of one part syrup, two parts fruit juice, and "four parts (more or less, depending on your strength) of non-alcoholic gin or rye."[42]

In the early 1930s, presses without blinking released guides to home cocktail production: *The Saloon in the Home, The Art of Drinking, Wet Drinks for Dry People.* With repeal imminent in 1933, this trickle of drinking advice swelled to a flood. Authors provided advice on how to select wines, mix drinks, and serve alcohol. *Redbook* published, in its women's magazine and then as a separate volume, *Civilized Drinking,* by wine expert Julian Leonard Street. Mrs. Alma Fullford Whitaker provided a lengthy criticism of Prohibition's excesses, with advice to future drinkers, in *Bacchus Behave! The Lost Art of Polite Drinking.* Dozens of drink-mixing manuals would appear in 1934 and 1935. These manuals celebrated alcohol's danger. Before Prohibition, punch recipes often had flippant or suggestive names—Whirligig, High Jinks, L'Amour, Watch Your Step!—that hinted at the potential of sexual excess. Cocktails built upon this attitude. Manuals such as *Shake 'Em Up!* described the drink to make for "The Blonde."[43] Gender did not totally disappear from this discussion, for drinks were split into feminine—gin fizzes and bee's knees—and masculine—martinis and highballs. But the drinks had the same strength; only the sugar content and garnish differed.

The cocktail epitomizes the social changes of the period, associated with other modern pursuits such as smoking and with elite activities in general. Young women considered the highballs and gin fizzes they drank at illicit country roadhouses "swanky." A laudatory article in *Vogue* described the "secure leaders of fashion" in the women's repeal movement. "They are athletic. They were the first to smoke because they liked it, and probably the first to drink cocktails." The president of the Georgia WCTU referred to her repeal enemies as "cocktail-drinking women." While the Women's Organization for National Prohibition Reform "Victory Dinner" in December 1933 did not include alcohol, cocktail parties in private homes preceded the event. Cocktail shakers and glasses and trays and manuals facilitated the American mania for objects, a mania only reinforced by the decade's financial boom (WONPR paraphernalia included matches, cigarettes, and cocktail napkins).[44] Cocktail parties embodied the elite informality and heterosocial enthusiasm of the 1920s.

In 1923 a journalist with the monthly review *The Nineteenth Century and After* described how Prohibition affected gender roles by encouraging women to drink cocktails. Because the amendment closed saloons and hotel bars and curtailed drinking in private clubs, the businessman "takes his cocktail into his house, where it is likely to be shared (it is usually mixed) by the ladies of his family. . . . There are not many ladies in well-to-do houses now—certainly in the Eastern States—who are not experts at making cocktails."[45] Women's drinking was just a fact of life. The consumption of mixed drinks had a place in the home—particularly in the fashionable home—before Prohibition. But by closing public drinking spaces, Prohibition brought this domestic consumption to new and more elaborate levels. Most importantly, Prohibition publicized domestic drinking, bringing to it the attention, criticism, and debate that women's prewar drinking had not encountered. Women in the 1910s had drunk quietly. By the late 1920s, they were doing so flagrantly. My claim that the cocktail redefined America is a bit heady—rather like cocktails themselves. But within the scope of twentieth-century America, it is absolutely accurate.

By the end of the 1920s, temperance principles had renewed support among so-called respectable violators. Much of this enthusiasm corresponded with the election of Herbert Hoover, the "dryest" president of the Prohibition era. The *New York Times,* in August 1929, reported the spread of dry parties within Washington, D.C., though "the capital is far from arid still." Margaret Banning wrote in the 1930 *Vogue,* "There are no two ways about it. Drinking is not as fashionable as it was." An article the next year in *American Mercury* stated that women in saloon days did not drink. "There were exceptions, of course: women of the smart set, the minority that is just a bit ahead of the times—the same smart minority that just now is a good deal dryer than it was five years ago—but even they did not drink in public places."[46]

This outrage increased with every news report of youth drinking— young women demanding "dividends" from their dates' flasks, the rumble that coming-out parties without cocktails were "flops." Lurid reports of roadhouses, joy rides, rural "beer farms" with rooms for rent upstairs— these only increased public suspicion that America was producing a generation of salacious alcoholics. Numerous polls revealed college drinking on the rise in the late 1920s. Wets emphasized the dangers of drinking and driving, particularly among the young.[47]

Drys, who before Prohibition had expressed great concern about youth drinking, now had the delicate task of defending the behavior and morals of the young. They asserted that, egregious examples excepted, drinking was decreasing among young adults. Prohibition's supporters criticized instead the examples that adults set in their own drinking: chaperons who drank with their charges during school dances, alumni who returned to campus with liquor. "Think of the lad who proudly displays his dad's stock of liquors to a visiting chum," asked a dry woman. She felt that wets used youth drinking as a "hypocritical cloak" to disguise their own repeal activities.[48]

Drys had sizable grounds for complaint. Prohibition era drinking, if contemporary descriptions are at all accurate, was often juvenile and destructive. A short story in *Smart Set* described three cocktails before dinner and party games dubbed "name that liquor." (On the other hand, the heroine dumps the self-righteous dry suitor for an abstemious bootlegger.) Frederick Lewis Allen, discussing the destruction wrought by heavy drinkers, felt the 1920s would one day "aptly be known as the decade of bad manners." Alice Roosevelt Longworth for a time became a Constitutional dry, "that is, one who said, 'It's in the Constitution and we ought to try to live up to it, at least give it a chance for a generation.' . . . But I was quite as apt to take the reverse position when I discussed the question with a dry. The fanatics on both sides were just about equally distasteful to me." This renewed interest in temperance corresponded with a surge of interest in repeal. Americans such as Longworth were tired of the excesses that Prohibition fostered and willing to see the law eliminated. Moreover, the nature of prohibition legislation—its awkward and unresolved treatment of home consumption, its imposition of federal law into domestic life—left both wets and drys frustrated. The Volstead Act's ambiguity only reiterated alcohol's place within American culture. To many citizens, Prohibition was the first federal presence in their daily lives. For middle-class Americans, Prohibition certainly preceded the intrusion of personal income taxes. The separate states enforced laws against murder, theft, and adultery—why should the federal government focus on, of all crimes, people's drinking?[49]

As the decade progressed, drys became increasingly defensive, if not peevish, in their efforts to convince the nation's drinkers to observe the law through the beverages they served, the news they followed, and the conversations they engaged in. Yet Americans' original dry sympathies of 1919, 1920, and 1921 faded, and some blame for this should be laid at the feet of the prohibitionists, who, in their short-sighted eagerness, wrote laws that could not be enforced. Granted, restriction of alcohol even within the home was politically if not legally impossible. Concessions that permitted domestic fermentation were also realistic. But the extreme definition of intoxicating liquor, and drys' unwillingness even to discuss modification of this definition, permitted drinking Americans to disregard the good intentions and considerable benefits of the prohibition amendment.

Alcohol buyers with legal impunity fueled a massive industry in illegal alcohol. Drinkers created new rituals within the home, most notably the cocktail party, centered on drink. In their efforts to assert their disgust with or disregard for the law, teen and adult drinkers degenerated at times into an alcoholic excess that appalled wets and drys alike. Women's participation in this process shocked dry women, who preferred to think of females as the purer sex. Young women's drinking, associated at it was with the dangers of sex and pregnancy, attracted particular concern. Arguments between wets and drys over who to blame for this situation mirror the broader prohibition debates of the 1920s.

By the late 1920s, more rational observers in both camps were losing patience with drinking Americans. Yet drinkers' excess, disturbing as it may be, in and of itself indicates the popularization of drinking ritual. Women's drinking, in removing the most masculine associations of drink, had facilitated passage of the Eighteenth Amendment. As women's drinking and attention to women's drinking increased in the following decade, the gendered associations of the proalcohol and antialcohol camps eased even further, weakening the political ideal of dry American womanhood. Dry women, however, would employ every possible rhetorical and organizational stratagem to keep this ideal alive.

113

∘ ∘ ∘

Prohibition,
Law
Observance,
and the
American
Home

PROHIBITION AND
WOMAN'S PUBLIC SPHERE
IN THE 1920S

In 1924, Marie C. Brehm ran for vice president of the United States as a candidate of the National Prohibition Party. The Prohibition Party, which had been a potent force in the 1880s, by the 1920s was struggling to remain alive. Appearing on the ballot in only fifteen states, the party garnered 57,222 votes. But Brehm campaigned hard and by all accounts was well qualified for the position. She had devoted herself to temperance, prohibition, and woman suffrage since the 1890s, representing the United States at several international temperance conferences. Brehm had already declined the vice presidential nomination in 1920. Drys had every right to be proud of their woman candidate, "the first . . . in the history of any regular political party."[1]

Prohibition had affected the woman's rights movement in the decades before enfranchisement, mobilizing both opponents and supporters of woman suffrage and defining debates on the needs and values of women voters. As the candidacy of Marie Brehm illustrates, it would have an equally profound impact on American women in their first decade of full citizenship. From ratification of the Eighteenth Amendment in 1919 through the repeal campaign in the early 1930s, women formed organizations and lobbies to promote Prohibition. The Woman's Christian Temperance Union, the Woman's National Committee for Law Enforcement, and the National Woman's Democratic Law Enforcement League were among the best-known groups of their day. In other organizations, the nation's most prominent women continued to view Prohibition as essential to women's liberty and the democratic process. Most women voters supported Prohibition, or held their tongues when they did not, until the very end of the decade. More than world peace, child labor reform, infant-maternal health, or the equal rights amendment, Prohibition provided women a distinct and respected public voice. But as public support for the law dwindled, women's groups such as the League of Women Voters, the Women's Joint Congressional Committee, and the General Federation of Women's Clubs grew silent in order to preserve some internal harmony. Repeal enthusiasm threatened not only the prohibition amendment but also the historic gender divisions that had permitted women access to the political arena.

THE WOMAN ISSUE OF PROHIBITION

Prohibition remains widely disregarded by historians of gender politics. Elimination of the liquor interests from American life has not merited the same consideration as other reforms such as equal rights, restrictions on child labor, and world peace that align more readily with late-twentieth-century sympathies. This attitude contrasts sharply with writers from the period, who considered Prohibition the single most important issue affecting women and women's political participation. In 1923, Emily Newall Blair and Harriet Taylor Upton, leaders within the Democratic and Republican parties, and Maud Wood Park, president of the National League of Women Voters, were interviewed on their opinions of Prohibition. The three agreed that women were "a solid bulwark against attacks on prohibition." As Park phrased it, "the mothers of the nation are no more likely to wipe out the Eighteenth Amendment than they are to demand the cultivation of typhoid germs in the water supply science has purified." Eunice Fuller Barnard, writing in 1928 on women in politics, began her article in the *New York Times* with a long discussion of the impact of Prohibition on women's political participation. Two years later, in "Anti-Prohibitionette," Margaret Culkin Banning asserted that Prohibition was the "first political issue that has absolutely captured the imagination of the women of the country. . . . I do not mean to juggle importances or make light of great hopes and conceptions. But it is a fact that the average woman will grow vague and disinterested in any prolonged discussion about most political subjects, and concentrated and eager in talking about prohibition." She noted Prohibition's historic "shaking" of the relationship between husband and wife and alcohol's association with prostitution and rape. She concluded that "the human relation is involved in prohibition as it is in no other modern condition." Assistant Attorney General Mabel Walker Willebrandt took this thought one step further in considering Prohibition's importance to both women and men. "Prohibition enforcement remains the chief and in fact the only real political issue of the whole nation. The tariff, immigration, banking, and other public problems are mere side issues in the estimation of most people—regardless of the fact that they involve the economic welfare of the nation. . . . Who is there not interested in prohibition?"[2] Her question neatly illuminates the greatest controversy of the decade.

Of all the women's organizations interested in prohibition, none was more closely linked than the Woman's Christian Temperance Union. The WCTU remained a multifaceted political force after 1920. It joined other women's organizations in supporting the cause of peace. Frances Willard had established a peace department in 1887, and members helped initiate the National Conference for the Cause and Cure of War in 1925. (The WCTU float in a 1929 American Legion parade included a banner that read, "Let Us Build Friendships. Between the Nations No More War, Within the Nation No More Booze.") The WCTU was also a charter member of the Women's Joint Congressional Committee (WJCC), created in late 1920 to defend women's issues in Congress. Outside Washington, the union initiated essay contests for school children on the benefits of Prohibition. Local chapters also campaigned against rising hemlines, tobacco use, and obscene films. Ella Boole, who joined the WCTU in the 1880s, became president in 1925. Boole's husband had been a Methodist preacher, and she herself was a national administrator for the Women's Home Missionary Societies of the Presbyterian Church. From her home in Brooklyn, New York, Boole organized White Ribboners in defense of the Eighteenth Amendment and the home. Like the organization she led, Boole had interests beyond prohibition. At the First Conference on Women in Industry she mediated the heated debate on whether the topic of equal rights should be included in discussion. She also ran for several public offices as a candidate of the Prohibition Party.[3]

Eradication of alcohol, however, remained foremost. To mark the fiftieth anniversary of the Woman's Crusade and the founding of the WCTU, members in 1923 poured $5,000 worth of "fine whiskies and cordials" into a Cleveland, Ohio, street. After the Pennsylvania state legislature refused to fund an enforcement law, the state WCTU donated $250,000 to Governor Gifford Pinchot "to use as he saw fit for enforcement purposes." New York WCTU members dominated lobbying for state prohibition and enforcement laws. Temperance education in the public schools, a subject that propelled the WCTU to national authority and a certain notoriety in the nineteenth century, continued to concern members. Local unions also worked to increase membership in youth Loyal Temperance Legions.

Newspapers publicized, at times bemusedly, the WCTU's alcohol-free "Prohibition Punches," and indeed the union prided itself on spreading appreciation for fruit juices. The WCTU epitomized traditional support for temperance principles and law enforcement (figure 5.1).[4]

Under Boole's leadership the WCTU played a prominent role in several of the most contested political campaigns of the decade. The union had always been involved in politics. Willard merged the union for a time with the Prohibition Party, and union members perfected lobbying and campaigning techniques in the later years of the nineteenth century. Willard's affiliations notwithstanding, WCTU members tended to identify themselves with the Republican Party and continued to do so in the 1920s. Lenna Yost, national legislative chairman of the WCTU, served in the

117

o o o

*Prohibition
and Woman's
Public Sphere
in the 1920s*

Figure 5.1   Members of the Los Angeles Woman's Christian Temperance Association assisting in the destruction of confiscated whiskey, ca. 1928.

*The Prohibition Bureau released publicity shots like this throughout the
decade, emphasizing the trickle of liquor it intercepted rather than the flood it
did not. Author Rheta Childe Dorr contrasted this image of American "coercion" with the staid state "control" of the Swedish distribution system. Rheta
Childe Dorr,* Drink: Coercion or Control *(New York: Frederick A. Stokes,
1929), frontispiece.*

P. and A. Photos

PROHIBITION IN THE UNITED STATES
The Los Angeles Women's Christian Temperance Union is invited by the Chief of Police
to smash four barrels of contraband whisky, perhaps one tenth of a bootlegger's stock.
Profits of all his remaining sales, sales of all rum runners, illicit dealers, gangsters and
hijackers go into the pockets of law breakers.

1920s on the Republican National Committee. All this helps explain the WCTU's massive effort in the presidential campaign of 1928. Herbert Hoover, savior of Belgium, food conservator, and dry supporter, ran against big-city, Irish Catholic Al Smith, who as governor of New York had officiated repeal of the state's own prohibition laws. Smith openly advocated modification of the Eighteenth Amendment. The battle lines could not have been more clearly drawn. In the process of the campaign, the WCTU distributed two million portraits of Hoover and ten million pamphlets criticizing Smith and his wet record. The union had most impact in the South, where it encouraged women "to abandon a party to which they and their forebears for generations had given allegiance." The *Union Signal* in the months before the November election exhorted readers to vote dry and listed prominent Hoover supporters. The WCTU considered Prohibition the definitive issue of the campaign and felt that dry women voters made a significant contribution to Hoover's victory.[5]

The WCTU was not alone in this suspicion. Commentators before and after the election emphasized the force of women's dry votes. The journalist Eunice Barnard felt the rank and file of women in the South and West concentrated on the race's main issues: Smith's Catholicism and Prohibition. *Good Housekeeping,* the *Ladies' Home Journal,* and the *Woman's Journal* all endorsed Hoover in part for his support of Prohibition and law enforcement. Women in previous elections had voted drier, at times much drier, than men. In municipal elections in Washington state and Chicago in 1914 and 1920, women voters supported Prohibition more than any other reform. A 1925 poll of 270,000 Americans revealed that women were more satisfied with conditions under Prohibition than were men and were more likely to consider Prohibition enforceable. A July 1928 *New York Times* headline trumpeted, "Woman Vote Plays Big Part This Year." Republican leaders believed that "in several States [women] hold the balance of power." Voter turnout for the 1928 oresidential election was 25 percent higher than in the 1924 campaign, and observers attributed the difference to women. Recent studies of the election reinforce this: women, it is estimated, constituted 49 percent of the 1928 voters, compared with 35 percent four years earlier. Prohibition was not the only issue in the debate. Nevertheless, it overlapped closely with the religious, ethnic, and regional prejudices coloring the campaign. With hindsight, some historians today feel that voter contentment in 1928 guaranteed a Republican victory. But in late 1928, the public believed that Hoover won because of Prohibition and that Prohibition won because of women.[6]

The WCTU was not the only women's organization in the 1920s concerned with enforcement of Prohibition. The Woman's National Committee for Law Enforcement, formed in 1923, defended the Eighteenth Amendment with even more single-minded vigor. Created with the guidance of Anti-Saloon League boss Wayne Wheeler, the WNCLE operated through the twenties and early thirties under Lucy W. Peabody, a wealthy Baptist widow with extensive fund-raising experience in national missionary societies.

119

∘ ∘ ∘

*Prohibition
and Woman's
Public Sphere
in the 1920s*

The WNCLE was founded to protect (unsuccessfully, as it turned out) New York State's prohibition law by uniting a number of women's groups into a single dry lobby. Founding organizations included the General Federation of Women's Clubs, the National Council of Mothers, the Daughters of the American Revolution, and the Young Women's Christian Association. Even the Parent Teacher Association participated. In April 1924, the WNCLE sponsored a law enforcement conference in Washington, D.C., chaired by Lou Henry Hoover, Herbert's wife. President Calvin Coolidge, the attorney general and secretary of the navy, and numerous governors and congressional representatives or their wives attended. The WNCLE claimed twelve million members, a figure Peabody determined by reducing by a third (for membership overlap and differences of opinion) the total membership of affiliated organizations. The WNCLE thus had the purported allegiance of one of every three adult American women. Politicians took these numbers seriously: fourteen governors attended its 1926 convention. By the early 1930s, the Parent Teacher Association and the Daughters of the American Revolution had left the WNCLE, apparently to seek less contentious pastures. But the WCTU and the Order of Kings' Daughters now belonged. The WNCLE instructed "the women of the country [to] pledge themselves to support at the polls only such candidates as will stand squarely for no repeal of the 18th Amendment nor modification through weakening of concurrent legislation." The WNCLE produced numerous books and pamphlets defending Prohibition, stressing particularly women's support.[7]

Its most famous meeting took place in 1931. When Hoover took office in 1929, he established an eleven-man committee to examine the prohibition law. Known as the Wickersham Commission for its chairman, George Wickersham, the commission released its findings in early 1931 to great controversy. The WNCLE met in Washington that April to add a "women's postscript" to the Wickersham report. The *Report of the Women's National Commission for Law Enforcement and Law Observance* included contributions from feminist Carrie Chapman Catt, Chicago lawyer Catherine Waugh McCullough, Evangeline Booth of the Salvation Army, and black leader Mary McLeod Bethune, who described the value of Prohibition in "The Second Emancipation of the Negro."[8]

State committees existed as well. In New Jersey, Miriam Lee Lippincott, a prominent suffragist and Republican who also sat on the board of the state Anti-Saloon League, chaired the state's Woman's Committee for Law Enforcement. Other women known within state political circles served on its executive committee. In Philadelphia in 1925, Mrs. Joseph M. Gazzam offered (some said demanded) the Pennsylvania WCLE's services to the National Crime Commission to combat a crime wave. The commission replied that it was primarily concerned with "crimes of violence," not Prohibition violations, and refused. Throughout the nation, state WCLE chapters campaigned to remove from office officials who criticized or did not adequately enforce the Eighteenth Amendment.[9]

The WNCLE's belief in wholehearted feminine support for the Eighteenth Amendment can be illustrated even with its name. Like the Woman's Christian Temperance Union, the Woman's National Committee for Law Enforcement utilized the singular, universal "woman." In the nineteenth century, the National American Woman Suffrage Association, the Woman's Temperance Crusade, and the WCTU helped construct the *woman movement*. The historian Nancy Cott, in *The Grounding of Modern Feminism*, traces the evolution of the term *woman movement* into *feminism*, "a more demanding and ideologically laden concept." Feminism became common in the mid-1910s, Cott argues, because the woman movement could no longer embrace women's increasingly diverse expectations. Organization names underwent a semantic evolution just as important to women's history as that of the term *feminism*. The National American Woman Suffrage Association passed to the League of Women Voters in 1919; activists united into the Women's Joint Congressional Committee and the Women's International League for Peace and Freedom. Women drys, however, remained committed to "woman"—to the nineteenth-century ideal of "the unity of the female sex." The WCTU and the WNCLE continued to believe that Prohibition mattered not just to some women but to womankind. Catherine Shaver advocated the formation of an organization of dry women voters, not a third party but simply "a woman's union." Republicans in the 1928 presidential campaign organized Woman's Work For Hoover.[10] Pointedly, the women's repeal organizations that would emerge late in the decade used the more contemporary and more divisive plural.

Southern women incensed by Al Smith's presidential nomination formed the National Woman's Democratic Law Enforcement League (NWDLEL), stepsister to the WCTU and the WNCLE. As early as May 1927, dry Democrats convening at the annual WNCLE conference warned that the party would lose support in the West and South should the Democratic leadership choose a wet candidate. That month, the newly formed NWDLEL broadcast the same message, repeated in regular, publicized meetings over the following months. Although led by Molly (Mrs. Jesse W.) Nicholson, who also sat on the WNCLE board, the NWDLEL's most famous member was Catherine Shaver. Her husband Clem chaired the Democratic National Committee and thus ran the candidacy of Al Smith. But Shaver had no intention of standing by her man. "Regardless of what Democratic leaders from top to bottom may do," Mrs. Shaver announced in July 1928, "we dry Democratic women will not support the dripping wet ticket and the joke platform named by the Tammany delegates." After 1928 the NWDLEL campaigned for the removal of Clem Shaver's successor, John J. Raskob, a wealthy businessman who had publicly criticized the Eighteenth Amendment since its inception. During the 1932 election Lucy Peabody urged the Hoover White House to subsidize NWDLEL work.[11]

Other voluntary organizations campaigned in support of Prohibition: the Conference of National Organizations Supporting the Prohibition Amendment (chaired by Ella Boole), the Women's National Committee for Education against Alcohol, the Massachusetts Committee against Repeal of the Eighteenth Amendment. Throughout the 1920s and the early 1930s, these dry women testified at congressional hearings, pressured and encouraged enforcement officials, and lobbied for stricter laws and stricter enforcement. Mabel Walker Willebrandt, assistant attorney general in charge of Prohibition, spoke frequently at WNCLE gatherings, as did a succession of attorneys general.[12] By the 1930s, beleaguered dry groups appeared to be not so much supporting federal policy as single-handedly enforcing it. But in the early years of Prohibition, federal and state agencies worked in harmony with these dedicated drys and with the vast and committed body of organized American womanhood.

DRY SUPPORT AND WOMEN'S POLITICS

The League of Women Voters (LWV), envisioned by Carrie Chapman Catt in 1919 to succeed the National American Woman Suffrage Association, trained women for citizenship and campaigned for women's causes. Although later loathe to admit it, national and state chapters campaigned vigorously in the 1920s in support of Prohibition. The *Standard Encyclopedia of the Alcohol Problem* listed the LWV as one of several organizations with "strong stands on law enforcement, which aline them with" the WNCLE. (Other organizations with this informal affiliation included the Salvation Army and the American Association of University Women.) At the 1924 LWV national convention, delegates voted unanimously to call on "the President, Congress, and the Governors of all States to enforce the law, and particularly the Eighteenth Amendment to the Constitution." The resolution passed without incident, although a motion to include birth control in the 1924 platform failed after heated debate.[13]

Two years later, however, Prohibition nearly split the women's group. The 1926 convention voted against declaring the national League of Women Voters in favor of enforcing Prohibition because of "the policy of national officers to avoid so far as possible controversial matters." Speakers explained that they personally supported enforcement but worried that the league, in endorsing the resolution hastily, would look "hysterical." Nonetheless, several state delegations and Catt campaigned hard for endorsement, Catt telegraphing that "this crisis demands grave deeds." The incident illustrates Prohibition's changing status: an organization that in 1924 found the Eighteenth Amendment far less incendiary than birth control two years later described it as controversial and hysterical. In 1927 the national LWV executive committee, in a clear attempt to heal divisions within the league, declared that it would undertake a three-year, $500,000 "survey of the prohibition question." Until the survey was completed, the committee declared, the national LWV would "take no stand on the prohibition issue." Perhaps in reaction, state leagues began to express more fervently dry viewpoints. The New York LWV, after some debate, passed its first resolution in support of the Eighteenth Amendment that December. The following year, efforts to keep Prohibition from the state league's formal study program alienated both sides. The league finally demoted its pro-Prohibition sentiment from "active" to "endorsed," pleasing few. Other state leagues were only somewhat less contentious. Pennsylvania, which for years had sponsored dry proposals at the national convention, remained united, as did North Carolina.[14]

During the 1928 presidential campaign, the *Woman's Journal,* a monthly magazine with close ties to the national LWV, sponsored a series of columns on the candidates. Sally (Mrs. Alvin T.) Hert, director of the Woman's Division of the Hoover campaign, took care not to mention the actual word "prohibition." But she continually stressed Hoover's support for the home and home issues—synonyms for Prohibition. She even referred obliquely to the NWDLEL, the "women outside our party, women who insisted upon working for the Republican ticket because they know and love its leader, Herbert Hoover." In writing for the *Woman's Journal* about the Democrats, Nellie Tayloe Ross, former governor of Wyoming and vice chair of the Democratic National Committee, had the more delicate task of explaining Al Smith. She acknowledged that Democrats held a variety of opinions about dry legislation, and she pointed out that Prohibition was not as successful as its supporters had hoped. Thus, even women drys "must respect the views and acknowledge the sincerity of those who are seeking a solution to this baffling problem. We must respect also Governor Smith's frank assertion of his convictions." She then defined herself as dry and reiterated that Prohibition was "in no danger of repeal." Ross felt that the majority of *Woman's Journal* readers supported the Eighteenth Amendment; Smith needed to be presented as suitable in spite of his attitudes on Prohibition. While the LWV after 1927 did not endorse Prohibition publicly, the editors' opinions remained clear. The *Woman's Journal* in 1930 ran articles by Catt and journalist Ida M. Tarbell endorsing dry and wet viewpoints respectively. Several dry readers canceled their subscriptions. The editors hastily explained that "'dry' though we are, we admit there is another side, sincerely held by many people, and we believe no good cause is hurt by arguments in opposition."[15]

Other women's groups such as the Women's Joint Congressional Committee faced similar friction and misunderstanding. Following passage of woman suffrage, the national LWV, the WCTU, and eight other women's groups joined in organizing the WJCC to lobby Congress on issues considered important to women. The WJCC established committees on law enforcement to lobby in favor of stringent dry legislation. In 1923 it warned politicians that were they to weaken enforcement efforts they would face "feminine anger." Beginning in 1925, conservative women's groups such as the Daughters of the American Revolution criticized the WJCC for supporting such controversial measures as the child labor amendment. Disturbed by these accusations of radicalism and frustrated with flagging enforcement, the WCTU resigned from the WJCC in August 1927. Over the next five years numerous congressional efforts to modify or repeal the Eighteenth Amendment would be made, concluding in 1933 with legalization of 3.2 beer and ratification of the Twenty-first Amendment, repealing prohibition. In these five years WJCC committees scrupulously listed all congressional bills relating to education, peace, maternal and infant hygiene, the World Court, and unemployment relief.

Yet after 1928 the WJCC, according to minutes from its monthly meetings, did not ever mention Prohibition again. The obvious explanation is that the WJCC did not care about Prohibition—the Eighteenth Amendment did not matter enough to women to affect their lobbying. But countless sources indicate that Prohibition remained foremost in the agenda of WJCC member organizations such as the League of Women Voters, the General Federation of Women's Clubs, and the Council of Women for Home Missions.[16] The WJCC avoided discussion of Prohibition not because women did not care but because they cared too much. Newspaper reports on other women's groups stressed the controversy that Prohibition sparked. Feelings about the Eighteenth Amendment, particularly anger over its failings, rendered discussion all but impossible. In the interest of harmony the WJCC chose instead to avoid the issue completely.

Prohibition left scores of activist women facing an impossible decision. Should they, like the NWDLEL, support the woman's issue of Prohibition and thereby alienate political supporters concerned with other matters? Or should they abandon Prohibition and with it the ideal and power of female unity? The New Jersey Women's Republican Club (NJWRC) sat on the horns of this dilemma in 1924 when it faced a wet, male party hierarchy determined to nominate candidates who opposed Prohibition. Lillian Feickert, prominent in the state party and the LWV, advised Republican women to vote against the Republican nominee because of his wet stance. Such treason did not sit well with loyal Republicans. Her gesture led to her removal from the state Republican committee and the subsequent decline of the NJWRC. Feickert's attempt to live up to her principles rendered her useless, even dangerous, to the Republican Party and resulted in her discharge. Other women faced similar travails. According to dry supporters, U.S. Attorney Annette Adams was removed from her San Francisco post for enforcing prohibition laws too vigorously. Bertha K. Landes, chair of Seattle's city council, made national headlines in 1924 for firing the corrupt chief of police and otherwise drying up the city during the mayor's five-day absence. Elected mayor herself in 1926 on a dry, law enforcement platform, she did "too well" enforcing Prohibition. Particularly embarrassing were a series of raids carried out by the police near the University of Washington, where her husband taught. Landes ended up apologizing to neighbors for police behavior she had encouraged, and she lost the 1928 election. It is not surprising that party regulars criticized some women's "excessive moral stance on picayune matters."[17]

But—and here the horns of the dilemma were especially keen—women also faced criticism for not being moral enough. Charles Edward Russell, in the 1924 article "Is Woman-Suffrage a Failure?," stressed how women, by compromising their moral position, lost their political effectiveness. He presented as an example the Washington Conference for the Limitation of Armaments. The conference, instigated by women to eliminate armaments, ultimately only reduced some stockpiles. "When these results, so halting and ludicrous compared with the original conception, were accepted without protest by the women, the politicians must have hugged themselves with joy." Russell, it seems, would be just as critical of women's concessions on Prohibition. Women's compromises met much public and private scrutiny. As late as 1930, New Jersey Republican National Committeewoman Geraldine Livingston Thompson struggled over whether to endorse the party's nominated candidate, who was wet. She finally concluded that Dwight Morrow had "the best chance of winning in November. . . . Therefore, I am prepared to subordinate in this one primary election the issue of [Prohibition] to a position of secondary importance."[18]

Lillian Feickert, Bertha Landes, and Geraldine Thompson were not the only American women bruised by Prohibition controversy. Assistant Attorney General Mabel Walker Willebrandt found her career almost destroyed by it. Appointed to the Justice Department in 1921 in a Republican nod to new women voters, Willebrandt oversaw enforcement of the new Eighteenth and Sixteenth (income tax) Amendments. Within a few years, half the federal case load involved Prohibition, and Willebrandt built a staff of several hundred. Although she admitted to drinking before Prohibition, as a loyal Republican and public servant she gave the law her full support. A woman and the highest-ranking enforcement official in the Justice Department, Willebrandt was "the embodiment of Prohibition."[19]

Writing on the dry law in 1929, Willebrandt presented one of the decade's more coherent, evenhanded summaries of the issue. She agreed immediately that "Prohibition does not prohibit," pointing out that it never did: those desiring drink always had been and would be able to acquire it. She also felt that Americans would not support "an army of officers of the Federal Government" policing local communities. She blamed both sides equally. Wets weakened public support by disseminating stories of law breaking, while the dry faction refused to acknowledge or address weaknesses in the law. Drys also harmed Prohibition by stopping successful temperance education programs. Asserting that repeal and modification were impossible, Willebrandt concluded that better-written (not more) laws, better education, and a more committed citizenry would make Prohibition work.[20] Unfortunately, *The Inside of Prohibition* received a lukewarm reception. By the time the book appeared Willebrandt had managed to alienate dry supporters as well as wet opponents.

Willebrandt enjoyed political battles, but her honesty—what some might term her tactlessness—left her open to attack. In 1924 she responded to criticism from the Philadelphia Law Enforcement League by asserting that corrupt district attorneys, senators, and local officials made her task impossible. To her horror, the league published her letter. Willebrandt explained that she had meant officers were only "straddling on the prohibition question," but this indictment from the one of the nation's top drys cheered Prohibition's opponents, who enjoyed hearing Prohibition described as unenforceable. In the 1928 presidential campaign, Republican leaders considered Willebrandt an ideal campaigner among both drys and women. Speaking before the Ohio conference of the Methodist Episcopal Church, Willebrandt fiercely attacked Al Smith, mentioning his religion and criticizing his failure to support Prohibition. Although Willebrandt did not state specifically that Smith should be fought because he was Catholic, the combination of issues and audience made the distinction moot. Smith lashed back, and political observers castigated Willebrandt's tactics. The fact that Prohibition agents raided several prominent New York speakeasies during the Democratic National Convention in Houston made Willebrandt appear all the more willing to use her office as a soap box. Emily Newall Blair, of the Democratic National Committee, defended Willebrandt, in a manner of speaking: "I said that not until a woman in politics was criticized, aye, and hated, would women really have arrived in politics."[21] But most agreed the incident demeaned all involved.

In acknowledgement of traditional American customs, the 1919 prohibition law permitted domestic production of wine and hard cider. The California grape industry soon latched onto this as a solution to overproduction and began marketing naturally fermenting wine grapes and "grape concentrates." Willebrandt herself was a California native. After leaving federal office in 1929 she became counsel to Fruit Industries, Ltd., a California grape-growing consortium that produced Vine-Glo, a grape concentrate sold in such flavors as port, muscatel, burgundy, and Riesling. She also helped secure $20,000,000 in Federal Farm Board loans for the grape industry. Democrats accused the administration of "repaying" Willebrandt for her 1928 campaign work by leaving Vine-Glo "unmolested." Clarence True Wilson, of the Methodist Board of Temperance and Public Morals, conceded that grape concentrate "may be within the letter of the law" but felt that it "violates the intent of prohibition."[22]

Wilson spoke accurately. Willebrandt was technically defending a legal product, just as she had technically criticized only Smith's wet position in the 1928 campaign. But public perception damned her. Lucy Peabody, of the WNCLE, wrote privately that "Mrs. Willebrandt's whole performance is perfectly dreadful . . . She [is] a liability, not an asset." By 1931 Willebrandt had become something of a joke. An article on the Women's Organization for National Prohibition Reform, a women's repeal organization, praised the group: "They are not acting as stalking horses for the beer industry, as Mabel Walker Willebrandt is for the California vintners." When prohibition agents raided Fruit Industries, Ltd., headlines read, "Plant of Mrs. Willebrandt's Client Is Raided."[23] The media could not emphasize enough the irony of the situation. Willebrandt had entered the national spotlight as a "woman prohibitionist"—words that in 1921 were nearly synonymous. When she attempted to leave this association, to practice as an attorney free of gender and Prohibition associations, she found she could not. The political association between women and Prohibition was too strong. But Americans by 1930 were tiring of the issue of Prohibition. As Willebrandt discovered, those who had ridden the Prohibition wave to power now faced an abrupt and shattering beaching.

THE EMOTIONAL BATTLE BETWEEN WETS AND DRYS

Prohibitionists, in part to get the Eighteenth Amendment ratified and in part because they really believed it, had predicted a millennium for dry America. The liquor evils they fought were so blatantly evil, and the benefits of abstinence so patently clear, that few supporters of the Eighteenth Amendment paused to consider the management that victory would need. Prohibitionists failed to produce substitutes for alcohol or the saloon, despite warnings that people would continue to crave the companionship these afforded. With the amendment in place, donations to dry organizations dried up. Scandals in the late 1920s involving several prominent drys worsened the financial situation of the Anti-Saloon League and other dry groups, as did the Great Depression. Drys, moreover, began to appear less benevolent than vindictive, triumphant in their victory and dis-

missive of flaws in the system they had built. Dry leaders advised supporters not to participate in a 1926 New York State referendum polling public
opinion on Prohibition. They then claimed that the referendum, which
reported four-to-one wet support, did not truly reflect temperance sentiment. Supporters of the referendum accused drys of abandoning American democracy. To make matters worse, the urban-rural coalition that
had fueled many Progressive reforms fractured in the 1920s. Prohibition,
always a rural issue, now became associated with the worst of rural politics. Although the WCTU and the ASL sought to differentiate themselves
from the Ku Klux Klan, many causes—nativism, patriotism, Protestantism,
Prohibition—overlapped. In the Midwest, women with years of activism in
the WCTU joined and led the Women of the Ku Klux Klan.[24]

The WCTU and its goals had never been supported by all Americans.
From the early years of the temperance movement opponents mocked
drys as puritanical and joyless. Rip Van Winkle's shrewish wife Gretchen
drove him to drink. The 1882 *Story of a Country Town* features a "meddle-
some hypocrite" who demands abstinence from everyone and ends up in a
tryst with the local minister. Short silent movies produced in the early
twentieth century depict woman drys as snoops and killjoys who inevitably
become tipsy from spiked drinks or as Carry Nation figures wet with
whiskey from the saloons they've smashed. Negative stereotypes of the
WCTU increased as the 1920s progressed. Congresswoman Ruth Hanna
McCormick dressed so severely "she might be mistaken for a member of
the W.C.T.U." (The WCTU was so well known the journalist did not need
to spell out its name.)[25] A political cartoon reprinted in the June 1928
North American Review shows Al Smith pumping a cocktail shaker while
glancing nervously at one of his guests, a battle-ax in spectacles and antebellum curls (figure 5.2). As the 1928 election approached, this cartoon
suggests, women drys were wearing the patience of wet politicians.

Women who had led the nation's progressive reforms now found themselves overwhelmed, if not horrified, by the cultural metamorphosis—the
cocktail metamorphosis, one could say—of the 1920s. These women continued to emphasize social betterment and criticize what they perceived as
selfishness on the part of the drinker. Carrie Chapman Catt wrote in 1928
that contrary to arguments then popular, drinking was not a matter of personal liberty. To her mind, drinking affected the health of all citizens when
automobiles were involved and the taxes of all citizens when court costs
rose because of arrests. "The vital question then is, shall the few who
allow their appetites and habits to master their behavior, enjoy indulgence

at the expense of other people; or shall 'Thou shalt not' be enforced until they develop morals enough to master their appetites?" Another woman stated, "Here, precisely, seems to some of us to lie the cleavage between those who are individually minded and those who are socially minded," linking abstention from alcohol to voluntary gasoline conservation during World War I. Willebrandt compared personal liberty to arguments for sweatshops and child labor. Alice Stone Blackwell opposed repeal "because most of the drinkers care only for their pleasure and most of the dealers care only for their profits."[26]

129
○ ○ ○
*Prohibition
and Woman's
Public Sphere
in the 1920s*

Such sentiments affected the highest levels of politics in the United States. The most famous woman politician of the era cared deeply about Prohibition, publicly endorsing dry laws and abstaining herself. Eleanor Roosevelt encouraged women to respect Prohibition law and endorsed Hoover's law enforcement stance. But as one of the nation's leading

Figure 5.2 "The Host's Dilemma"

Presidential candidate Al Smith shakes up a pitcher of sidecars while keeping an eye on the woman voter, ridiculously old-fashioned and as uninterested in wet politics as she is in wet weather. Reprinted in North American Review 149 (13 June 1928): 247. From the New York Herald Tribune, 1928;
©*1928, New York Herald Tribune, Inc.*

woman Democrats, Roosevelt at other times faced the controversial task of campaigning for wet Democratic candidates. In the 1926 New York gubernatorial election, Al Smith ran against wealthy Republican Ogden Mills, a moderate scrupulously concerned with keeping Prohibition out of the campaign. In order to avoid criticism from dry Republican upstate districts, Mills focused attention away from liquor toward the quality of the state's milk. In a great political irony, Eleanor Roosevelt thus campaigned in country districts on Smith's milk, not booze, record. It appears that all beverages, temperate or non, seeped into 1920s politics.

Far more delicate was the battle between Roosevelt and the National Woman's Democratic Law Enforcement League. The NWDLEL, it may be recalled, began as an effort to force a dry plank and candidate on the Democratic Party. By January 1928, many believed that women were leading the fight against Smith's nomination. Roosevelt, invited to attend an NWDLEL meeting, chose the occasion to criticize the league. "I happen to be personally absolutely dry and to believe in the Eighteenth Amendment and the strict living up to the spirit of the law," she stated, "but I disagree with those who consider this question the question of vital importance today and I also think that there is a great deal of muddled thinking, especially on the part of certain groups of women, as to the manner in which to obtain temperance and enforcement of the Eighteenth Amendment." She asked why the women of the Law Enforcement League, so concerned with lagging enforcement of the Eighteenth Amendment, were not equally concerned with enforcement of the Fourteenth and Fifteenth Amendments guaranteeing citizenship to blacks. (Dry southern Democrats often faced this criticism.) As the campaign intensified, Roosevelt intensified her criticism of the NWDLEL. The NWDLEL replied with questions on Smith's corruption and insinuations about his support of racial equality.[27]

Surveying the fracas, the *New York Times* concluded, "the debate may now proceed on its merits. . . . It is politically safe. The greatest hazard of the [woman suffrage] Amendment has been passed." Eleanor Roosevelt's attack on the NWDLEL and her pragmatic loyalty to the Democratic Party seem today the pinnacle of reason and justice. But to the *Times,* the "greatest hazard" of woman suffrage amendment was the potential of women's unity as captured in the paradigm of Prohibition. In supporting party instead of principles, Roosevelt divorced women from one of their most powerful political weapons. When 3.2 percent beer was legalized in April 1933, the press reported that "it will be provided at the White House for any one who wants it, the personal views and tastes of the first lady to the contrary notwithstanding." Eleanor Roosevelt affirmed that "no matter what the legislation, I myself do not drink anything with alcoholic content, but that is purely an individual thing. I should not dream of imposing my own convictions on other people as long as they live up to the law of the land." Roosevelt was painting herself in opposition to the WCTU, the NWDLEL, and other moralists who had fought in vain for retention of the Eighteenth Amendment. The most powerful woman in America would not dream of imposing her own convictions. Roosevelt had bowed to modern arguments for civil liberties and American individuality.[28] In placing party loyalty and individualism before her support of the Eighteenth Amendment, however, Roosevelt contributed to the dismantlement of womanhood as a public and political force.

PROHIBITION AND THE DECLINE OF THE WOMAN MOVEMENT

Women's first decade of full political participation produced numerous divisive political decisions. Should women voters join the two major parties and reform politics as they climbed to positions of party authority? Or should they avoid the compromising and corruption that party politics fostered and attempt reform as outsiders? Debate over the equal rights amendment further divided women. Supporters felt the amendment took precedence over other women's issues, while well-meaning opponents worried that several decades of protective legislation would be lost in the name of equality. No subject portrays the dilemmas facing women in the 1920s as clearly as Prohibition. Because it was closely associated with women's political activism and history, controversy over Prohibition more than any other cause destroyed the image of women as a virtuous and unified voting bloc. It should not be surprising that many women who came of age politically in the first two decades of the twentieth century would continue to see liquor as the enemy of their sex and continue to believe that women would unite to effect its eradication. But here they faced the dilemma of women's political participation. Women had argued for enfranchisement in the belief that they were more moral than men and thus would cleanse politics. Not all suffragists used this argument, but a significant portion did, particularly women interested in reforms such as Prohibition. After enfranchisement, however, women such as Lillian Feickert of New Jersey faced the difficulty of retaining their moral superiority in the amoral world of 1920s politics. The New Jersey Republican Party ultimately dismissed Feickert because of her adamant dry stance.[29] She and other dry women were overtly and maliciously excluded from partisan authority because of their unyielding dry support.

Public rejection of Prohibition in the early 1930s indicated a covert dismissal of women, of the distinctiveness women traditionally brought to the political discourse. Indeed, it is probable that Prohibition not only reflected this process but triggered it. Historians today praise the General Federation of Women's Clubs (GFWC) for involving itself more in politics in the 1920s than it ever had or would again. But they fail to identify why so many women in the GFWC and other organizations left politics at the end of the decade. A crucial relation exists between women's withdrawal from politics and the failure of Prohibition. Many women, in endorsing and fighting for Prohibition, backed the wrong horse. Dissent over Prohibition disturbed many in the WJCC, the GFWC, and the LWV. As the issue became increasingly contentious, women responded by leaving a political realm that no longer appeared to respect their interests. The GFWC, the last major women's organization outside of temperance groups to endorse Prohibition, finally abandoned the issue in 1932. At the insistence of state organizations, the federation returned to "its original specialty of cultural uplift."[30] Politics, many women felt, no longer offered a milieu in which they could effectively operate.

Elizabeth Tilton, a member of the WNCLE and other dry organizations, had worked since the early 1910s for woman suffrage, international peace, public health, and education and welfare reform in Massachusetts. At the end of the decade, she wrote and published the small pamphlet, *Which? A Story. Which?* describes Mrs. Lina Carter, a widow active for many years in public causes, now engaged to a prominent and wealthy doctor. Tilton here outlined the classic gender divisions of the temperance movement. Dr. Yost drinks at his men's club, where members voted "unanimously wet." Lina, on the other hand, cares about society, "the Race" as she phrases it. She intends "to head a committee to elect a dry who will bring ever increasing benefits to women and little children." Lina focuses not on drying out Yost and other male drinkers, who appear past redemption, but rather on helping millions of unfortunate women and their offspring.

Tilton in *Which?* conflates Prohibition with other reform causes and with female independence. Dr. Yost has little respect for Lina's interests, expecting her to work only on issues within his psychiatric hospital. Lina finds herself hiding her concerns from him. "Especially great was the strain at dinner parties. Subjects would arise, such as Prohibition, Prison-Reform, the League of Nations. Lina felt like a coward when she did not speak up, and yet somehow the words would die on her lips." Driving to his country house one morning, he tells her

133

o o o

*Prohibition
and Woman's
Public Sphere
in the 1920s*

"We must keep you fit—nerves make bad companions. They corrupt good thinking."

"He means," said Lina to herself, "that to be against war and liquor is to have Nerves. Reforms are nerves." . . .

Dr. Yost turned to her with a look of meaning business. "You know, Lina," he said, "you have got to get over this damned nonsense about Prohibition. You've led too lonely a life. Your nerves have got going. You need diversion. That will normalize you." He patted her knee. "Normalize you, my girl," he repeated.[31]

To Lina, capitulating on the issue of Prohibition—supporting actions she considers "disgusting"—means conceding not only to a wet position but to a male position as well. Dr. Yost expects to "normalize" his future wife, which in her eyes entails losing her identity as a reformer and as a woman. The passage provokes chilling images of docile Stepford wives drugged past caring. Tilton considered Prohibition integral to women's political and emotional freedom.

Which? explains the emotional reaction of women drys to their opposites who worked for repeal. For dry women, the Women's Organization for National Prohibition Reform and other such groups were not only campaigning to bring liquor—Demon Rum—back to the street corners and parlors of America. They were also betraying their sex. This public opposition to Prohibition demonstrated that women no longer united on the era's definitive moral issue. Thus, drys felt, women no longer had a separate and respectable political voice. The best that could come from such repeal-oriented activity was the return of the legal liquor traffic. But the worst was guarantee of permanent masculine political hegemony. Small wonder that one dry woman wrote the WONPR's founder that "every night I get down on my knees and pray to God to damn your soul."[32]

THE MORAL AUTHORITY OF THE WOMEN'S ORGANIZATION FOR NATIONAL PROHIBITION REFORM

"It appears that the women of this country are no longer a unit on this question" of Prohibition, wrote the *Literary Digest* in 1932.[1] Such understatement hardly seems merited considering the omnipresence that year of the Women's Organization for National Prohibition Reform. Founded by one of the most adept political women of the era, the WONPR surpassed in influence and membership all other men's and women's repeal groups. In arguing for repeal, the WONPR emphasized both domesticity and states' rights, civil liberties and the horrors of women's drinking. No other organization so cleverly utilized the gender ambiguities that Prohibition had produced. Most importantly, no other women's organization of the late 1920s so thoroughly—some might say so brutally—used women's imagery to advance itself in the political discourse.

Women had been associated with temperance legislation since the 1850s. The Woman's Christian Temperance Union began in 1874 with the belief that women as a sex opposed liquor. The WCTU and other dry organizations simply could not accept the idea that large numbers of women would voluntarily work for Prohibition's repeal. And, one might ask, what woman would? As one writer noted in 1933, "Even women who distrusted or disliked prohibition hesitated to enter the lists for an institution that had gathered into focus every corrupt element in the commonwealth."[2] Women had consumed alcohol before Prohibition; the Eighteenth Amendment as it was written affected them no more or less than it did men. But private drinking differed profoundly from public politicking, particularly when all wet activists faced being cursed as a tool of the liquor interests.

The WONPR pointedly and permanently dismantled the association between women and Prohibition, thus freeing politicians to vote wet without fear of feminine reprisal. With the WONPR, women's last claim to moral superiority and political unity was eliminated. Individualism and acrimony overwhelmed the gendered collectivity that defined women's politics in the second decade of the twentieth century. By the Great Depression, the edifice of true womanhood and "home protection" lay in ruins. To younger generations, the "woman politics" that separate spheres permitted now seemed as old-fashioned and ill-conceived as the Prohibition movement itself—and one can easily see how one may have weakened the other.

135

o o o

*The Women's
Organization
for National
Prohibition
Reform*

ORGANIZING AGAINST PROHIBITION

Wet responses to Prohibition took several forms. Repeal was out of the question. No amendment had ever been repealed. A constitutional amendment required support of two-thirds of the Congress and three-fourths of the state legislatures. The Eighteenth Amendment had passed with striking enthusiasm and speed; a handful of senators or thirteen states could hold back a repealing amendment.

The most popular proposal in Prohibition's first years was thus modification. The Eighteenth Amendment, wets proposed, would continue to prohibit "spirituous liquors," but the definition of spirituous liquor would be modified to allow sale of beverages with more than 0.5 percent alcohol. In the middle of the decade, Walter Lippmann and others argued for nullification. Stating that Prohibition could be neither repealed nor enforced, Lippmann recommended that the law simply be ignored, as amendments guaranteeing African American enfranchisement were ignored in the South. Lippmann felt, and others then and since have agreed, that the level of Prohibition violation was simply unacceptable. Even if it could be proved that 51 percent of the populace observed the law, the wet minority in its disregard rendered the amendment useless.[3]

Throughout the decade, wets argued that Prohibition increased crime, weakened personal liberties and the Constitution, and raised instead of reducing alcohol consumption. Worst, enforcement cost the government millions of dollars, rather than providing millions in legal liquor taxes. The Association Against the Prohibition Amendment (AAPA) began in 1919 as a last-ditch effort to prevent state ratification of the Eighteenth Amendment. It reorganized in December 1920 as a repeal organization. Sensitive to dry accusations that it was only a front for the liquor interests, the AAPA focused on attracting "individuals of irreproachable reputation." By the mid-1920s members included John Raskob, treasurer of the Du Pont Company, the du Pont brothers themselves, and several New York leaders of finance. By 1930 the association claimed 150,000 members and a $450,000 yearly income—still a far cry from the Anti-Saloon League's $2.5 million annual budget in the 1910s. In its first years, AAPA activity focused on publication of anti-prohibition literature. Early attempts to pressure Congress failed spectacularly. Representatives identified as wet by the AAPA lost reelection. From 1920 to 1928 the United States Congress increased its proportion of dry representatives with each election; in 1928, forty-three of the nation's forty-eight state governors considered themselves dry.[4] The AAPA did not single-handedly produce this result, of course. But widespread public support for dry candidates increased the perception of Prohibition as immutable. The AAPA had set itself an impossible task.

Numerous other wet organizations rose and fell in the decade. Early groups such as the Association Opposed to National Prohibition and the American Liberties League had visible connections to liquor-related businesses such as hotels and commercial real-estate firms. State Moderation Leagues, which lobbied to modify the prohibition law, attracted few members. The Crusaders, begun in May 1929 to organize repeal sentiment among young adults, included sons of some AAPA members but petered out before repeal. More significant was the Voluntary Committee of Lawyers (VCL), begun in 1927, which attracted some of the most powerful lawyers in New York and the nation.[5] The VCL would play a critical role in organizing the legal machinery of the repeal process.

The AAPA from its beginnings sought the support of women. In the grand tradition of the Freemasons, the Sons of Temperance, and the Ku Klux Klan, it organized a women's auxiliary, the Molly Pitcher Club, in 1922. Based mainly in New York and Philadelphia, Molly Pitcher Clubs never attained more than a few hundred members. This stemmed in part from their pointed association with the AAPA but mainly from the irascibility of their leader, M. Louise Gross. A lawyer with profound concern for personal liberties, Gross went on to found a series of wet women's groups unaffiliated with the AAPA. The Women's Committee for Modification of the Volstead Act, the Women's Committee for Repeal of the Eighteenth Amendment, and the Women's Modification Union (WMU) overlapped on members, addresses, and issues. Gross organized anti-Prohibition rallies at the 1924 Democratic National Convention and testified against Prohibition in Congress in 1930 and 1932, stressing there her libertarian sympathies. The slogan of the WMU, "Repeal or Rebellion," seemed designed to alienate all sides. The National Voluntary Committee of Women of the AAPA, which rose and faded in 1926, was even less effective. Members of Gross's organizations and the Voluntary Committee of Women would show up later, however, in the Women's Organization for National Prohibition Reform.[6]

137

o o o

*The Women's
Organization
for National
Prohibition
Reform*

Other female murmurings of protest were heard throughout the 1920s. Mrs. John D. Rockefeller Jr., as early as 1924, asked, "Have [we] not come to the time when we must honestly enforce our prohibition law or honestly try to change it?" In 1929, the feminist journalist Rheta Childe Dorr published *Drink: Coercion or Control?* endorsing government regulation of liquor sales (fig. 5.1). She contrasted the lawlessness and discord of the American system with rational Scandinavian government controls. Two congresswomen, Florence P. Kahn of San Francisco and Mary Norton of Newark, New Jersey, opposed Prohibition publicly throughout their tenures. (It should be noted that their districts were both solidly wet.) Edith Dolan Riley, a Washington state Democratic Party regular committed to Roosevelt and to repeal, in 1930 led a squadron of similarly minded women to the state party convention: "During a long evening in June, the convention was held in suspense by the delaying tactics of the drys who hoped that Mrs. Riley's ladies would sooner or later go home to cook for their families. . . . But at six o'clock, there were still 105 hungry and wet women voting against only fifty-five dry and hungry defenders of prohibition. While husbands and children waited, the wets won Spokane County for repeal and guaranteed a wet Democratic platform at the state convention."[7]

The dry forces of the Anti-Saloon League and the WCTU lost no time in criticizing these women opponents. "Now in these degenerate days some . . . women in their effort to aid the outlawed liquor traffic and nullify the Constitution have organized a Molly Pitcher Club. [Molly Pitcher] would turn over in her grave if she knew what these so-called respectables were doing in her name," stated the ASL's newspaper, *American Issue,* in early 1923. The *Union Signal,* official organ of the national WCTU, wrote in 1929 that the Women's Modification Union did not understand Prohibition's benefits and in any case was backed secretly by bootleggers. "We feel certain it will not find [members] in our churches, . . . in the women's clubs, the Parent-Teacher Association, the League of Women Voters, or the big patriotic organizations."[8] Ultimately, however, the WCTU's single-minded faith in dry women would prove its undoing. The WCTU was unequipped to battle female repeal activists for the moral high ground in the Prohibition repeal debates. Moreover, its arrogant belief in women's innate dryness inspired the formation of its most formidable enemy.

As *Time* magazine told the story in 1932, Pauline Morton Sabin decided to found the Women's Organization for National Prohibition Reform at a 1928 congressional hearing at which Ella Boole declared, "I represent the women of America!" Pauline Sabin reportedly whispered to herself, "Well, lady, here's one woman you don't represent." Journalists throughout the country repeated the anecdote. It appears in every history of the WONPR, and for good reason.[9] It captures—from the wet viewpoint, which is significant—the wet-dry controversy between women in the late 1920s. The WONPR comes across as a mass movement arising spontaneously from wet indignation with dry hypocrisy. Sabin, it appears in this telling, supported Prohibition up to the day, even to the moment, Boole spoke. Her explanation of her epiphany is delightful. It is also untrue.

In the first place, the reader should wonder what exactly Pauline Morton Sabin, heir to the Morton Salt fortunes, wife of the president of the Guaranty Trust Corporation, charity activist, and Republican fund-raiser, was doing in the congressional galleries during Boole's testimony. A meticulous scholar might then notice that no major hearings on Prohibition took place in 1928 and that Boole did not testify in Congress that year. When she did testify in the Senate, in 1926, Boole described herself as representing only the national WCTU, not "the women of America."[10] WONPR scholars, perhaps because journalists so described her at the time, have been quick to paint Sabin as a socialite, a chic Republican enthusiast who just happened to organize a million and half women to topple a president and rewrite the Constitution. This anecdote reinforces that image. By reading between the lines, however, we come to understand how Sabin used an image of political naiveté to extraordinary political advantage.

Sabin was by all accounts a political insider with great authority in the Republican Party. She was a delegate to the 1920, 1924, and 1928 Republican National Conventions and served on the Republican National Committee from 1924 to 1928 as part of the party's effort to represent equally men and women. In 1921, Sabin founded and presided over the wealthy and exclusive Women's National Republican Club. A biographer in *McCall's* in 1930 described her as "the best money-raiser and membership-getter in the Republican party in her state." As New York's most prestigious Republican woman, Sabin met Eleanor Roosevelt, then a member of the state Democratic Committee, in a 1927 radio debate on state election reform. The radio station structured the debate as a contest to be gauged by listener response. Both accused the other's supporters of stuffing the ballot box with telephone calls and telegrams. Sabin won.[11]

In point of fact, comparison between Roosevelt and Sabin highlights Sabin's position in the 1920s. Both women came from wealthy families with a history of political involvement, and both women created political careers distinct from those of their husbands. Both rose to prominence within the country's most populous and powerful state, then used allegiances built in New York as a stepping-stone to national prominence. Sabin in 1929 was forty-two, Roosevelt only forty-five. A 1928 article on women in politics described "a new type of woman leader—the woman of maturity and leisure, often of wealth, whose children are grown and who now turns to politics as in former generations she might have turned to philanthropy or the woman's club as an outlet for her civic energies." Roosevelt was cited as an example; Sabin was not, but could have been.[12]

Eleanor Roosevelt's complex relationship with Prohibition has been examined in an earlier chapter. Sabin was similarly challenged. As the 1920s progressed, the Republican Party became increasingly identified with Prohibition. Sabin would have ample opportunity to witness Prohibition's effect on the party and the country at large. She never mentioned the impact her political experiences had on her anti-Prohibition consciousness, which seems due to her need to present the WONPR as a spontaneous mass movement. Nevertheless, Sabin participated in several of the most brutal political campaigns of the decade, campaigns that revolved on the single issue of Prohibition.

James W. Wadsworth Jr. had served in the U.S. Senate for twelve years prior to the 1926 election and there distinguished himself as a conservative spokesman and leader. A patrician farmer, he opposed both the prohibition and woman suffrage amendments on the grounds of states' rights. (Ella Boole ran against Wadsworth in 1920, first in the Republican primary and then as a Prohibition Party candidate, and attracted 160,000 votes.) In 1926 many believed that a Senate victory would put Wadsworth in the running for the Republican presidential nomination in 1928. Drys agreed he must be stopped at any cost. On November 3, with two million New Yorkers voting, Wadsworth lost the election by 116,000 votes. Frank Christman, an independent candidate fielded by the drys, garnered 231,000, thereby keeping Wadsworth out of office. Ironically, Christman's siphoning of dry Republican votes ensured the election of wet Tammany Democrat Robert Wagner. But both sides agreed that drys had won a victory, however Pyrrhic.[13]

Sabin witnessed prohibitionists' efforts firsthand. A friend of the Wadsworths, she served as vice chair of Wadsworth's 1920 and 1926 campaigns. In late 1926 an upstate woman wrote Sabin, "You can[']t imagine what a nasty fight it was. It revolved itself entirely into a wet and dry campaign. They went from house to house telling stories. . . . Can you imagine so-called Christians playing such dirty politics. You, in the city, cannot have any realization of what we are up against here." The Wadsworth campaign drove home Prohibition's destructive force in politics. Moreover, women were widely regarded as determining the election's outcome. One male supporter wrote to Wadsworth the week before the election that "we are going to beat these 'Fool Women' good." An anonymous telegram sent to Wadsworth the day after he lost stated only "the women of New York did not forget."[14] Sabin may not have mentioned these experiences later in her career. But the 1926 election should have left a deep impression.

A devoted Republican, Sabin was most affected by the role women's organizations played in unseating Wadsworth. The New York League of Women Voters took no official position on the 1926 Senate campaign, though many members opposed Wadsworth personally. (His loss "was undoubtedly the political highlight of the 1920s" for Carrie Chapman Catt, according to her biographer.) Three days after the election, Sabin publicly resigned from the League of Women Voters, claiming the state league's weekly bulletin had insulted Wadsworth's wife. By March of the following year, Sabin was criticizing "feminine blocs" in politics for focusing only on "measures pertaining to women and children" and not "cooperating with the men" on party issues.[15]

Five months before the 1928 presidential election, while still a member of the Republican National Committee and an active campaigner for Herbert Hoover, Sabin set her wet sentiments in print. "I Change My Mind on Prohibition" appeared in the progressive journal *Outlook* with the subtitle, "a former advocate of Prohibition finds that she made a mistake and has the rare courage to admit it." Sabin stated that she worried in particular about Prohibition's effect on "the coming generation." She described a poll earlier that year that revealed 85 percent of Women's National Republican Club members did not support Prohibition. The poll, she stated, surprised people accustomed only to members of the WCTU and National Woman's Democratic Law Enforcement League, who "appear before hearings of the various legislatures and Congress and do not hesitate to state that 'they speak for the women of America.'" She accused such women of having "one-plank minds" and particularly resented that they voted for dry candidates whom they knew to drink privately. This situation, she felt, demanded the same political unity by wet women as that enjoyed by their dry opponents. "In my opinion, as soon as the women who are opposed to prohibition organize and become articulate they will be able to do more towards bringing about a change in the conditions which exist today than any organization composed solely of men."[16] "I Change My Mind on Prohibition" merits close examination in light of Sabin's anecdote about the spontaneous formation of the WONPR. Sabin, who had been so critical of feminine blocs, appeared ready to fight fire with fire.

Sabin was by now a national figure. Although she had opposed Herbert Hoover at the 1928 Republican convention, she directed the campaign among women in the East and raised $240,000 for his election. Her support stemmed in part from Hoover's campaign promise to investigate Prohibition laws once in office. By early 1929, however, it was clear that Hoover would be dryer personally and politically than his two Republican predecessors; his Prohibition commission now studied law-breaking generally. At his inauguration Hoover endorsed the amendment: "Our country has deliberately undertaken a great social and economic experiment, noble in motive and far reaching in purpose. It must be worked out constructively." The press soon abbreviated his statement to "noble experiment," the classic epithet for national Prohibition.[17]

Two days after Hoover's inauguration Sabin resigned from the Republican National Committee. At a testimonial luncheon in her honor hosted by the Women's National Republican Club, Sabin called on women to organize for repeal. Meeting two months later in Chicago with forty-nine other women, Sabin formally inaugurated the Women's Organization for National Prohibition Reform. "This organization is a result of a demand from women, all over the country, that an aggressive effort be made for the protection of the American home," she stated at the time. (Two other repeal organizations also appeared in May 1929, and the AAPA probably had some role in the formation of all three.)[18]

Sabin, now officially chairman of the WONPR, formed a national advisory board at the Chicago meeting and encouraged organization at the state level. Not surprisingly, she tapped her own social and political circles for leadership positions, turning to fellow members of the Women's National Republican Club and to well-known women in the Democratic Party. This focus was more than snobbery on the part of the wets. The WONPR,

like the AAPA, required "unimpeachable leadership" to deflect association with corruption and the liquor interests. The organization did not require dues, surviving solely on donations. It never suffered from lack of
income.[19]

Beyond respectability, the WONPR required a large enough membership to be taken seriously as a pressure group. For this reason, WONPR
publicists frequently reported membership numbers to newspapers. In December 1930, Sabin announced that the nineteen-month-old organization
had more than four hundred thousand members, matching the WCTU.
She stressed recent growth "in the so-called 'dry' districts" and the fact
that "ten of the State divisions . . . have already outstripped the State
branches of the Women's [sic] Christian Temperance Union." She continued, "I know of nothing since the days of the campaign for woman's suffrage to equal the campaign which women are now conducting for repeal
of the Eighteenth Amendment." By the 1932 presidential elections, the
WONPR claimed 1.1 million women members, and 1.5 million at the
ratification of the Repeal Amendment in December 1933. Although drys
painted the WONPR as an elite organization, the bulk of its membership
reflected the diversity of American womanhood. In Delaware, almost two-
thirds of WONPR members categorized themselves as mothers or housewives.[20]

RHETORIC OF THE WONPR

Domesticity had always been a persuasive argument for temperance.
From the earliest years of the temperance movement, drys juxtaposed
male drunkenness against the joyous temperate home, devoted wife, and
delightful children. Such imagery was a mainstay of the WCTU through
the 1930s. But women did not monopolize domesticity and home protection. Dry men praised prohibition laws for increasing family income, improving the morals of children, and decreasing brutality in the home. A
Kansan stated he had "seven reasons for supporting this law—four sons
and three daughters." As the repeal movement developed in the 1920s,
both men and women repealists capitalized on these themes. Male wets
were as quick as male drys to discuss women, children, and the home, but
as harmed, rather than helped, by Prohibition. In 1926 the AAPA argued
that women and young people suffered most from the "evils of liquor,"
which were more prevalent than ever under federal prohibition. Fred G.
Clark, founder of the Crusaders, felt even drys would support his move-

ment, since his motives were "practically the same code of principles the W.C.T.U. adopted when present-day grey-haired mothers were children in short dresses." Drys dismissed such "sob stuff . . . being put over by men." But wet men, regardless of how they felt personally about the "sob stuff," on a political level were eminently practical. Emotional arguments and personal anecdotes produced cash and converts.[21]

The WONPR did not delay in entering this discussion. Pauline Sabin voiced her concerns about "the coming generation" in her 1928 *Outlook* article and returned to this theme through the 1930s. Jeanie Rumsey (Mrs. John S.) Sheppard, vice chair of the New York State Branch of the WONPR, stressed to the House Judiciary Committee in late 1930 that drunkenness among the young was increasing. Prohibition, instead of protecting children, had produced "a generation oblivious to the evils of liquor," because illegal speakeasies glamorized drink. A sympathetic journalist in *Liberty* magazine pointed out that many WONPR members were "too young to remember the old saloon. . . . But they are working for repeal because they don't want their babies to grow up in the hip-flask, speakeasy atmosphere that has polluted their own youth." WONPR members discussed women's drinking with the same shocked tone used by drys. Many stressed they were "personally dry." They "believe[d] in temperance" and considered themselves the modern "temperance party" out to eliminate the alcohol abuse that Prohibition apparently fostered. The WONPR strove to depict itself as a conservative organization opposed to drinking (particularly youth and immoderate drinking) and to female impropriety.[22]

In comparison with the WCTU and other dry organizations, however, the WONPR used a broad range of arguments unrelated to home protection. Members worried just as much about civil-liberties violations, corruption, crime, and the expense and disrespect that Prohibition fostered. Indeed, women in the WONPR can best be compared to suffragists for the skill with which they matched audience to argument, using constitutional law or dire predictions of lost elections in addition to the threat to the home. One constant theme of the WONPR was hypocrisy. While drys campaigning in the 1910s had stressed how liquor corrupted politicians, wets now asserted that Prohibition rendered politicians frauds. A political cartoon in the *Cleveland Press* depicted a slim young WONPR member revealing the hip flask of a portly, self-righteous legislator (figure 6.1). (Compare this depiction of women wets to the woman dry in figure 5.2.) Sabin described legislators who voted for harsh enforcement laws but drank personally as "unfit for any public trust." She criticized further prohibitionists who knowingly campaigned for and elected men who "vote dry and drink wet." Judging by the number of times Sabin raised the topic—from her first wet statements in 1928 through 1932—she considered hypocrisy a primary concern. WONPR members often combined home-protection, hypocrisy, political, and other arguments in the same document or speech.[23]

As repeal grew closer, members examined liquor control systems in other countries and published a survey of thirty-seven possible foreign models for the United States. State branches researched state prohibition laws that had been passed before 1920 and were still in place. They then publicized these to reassure voters and lawmakers that repeal would not lead to anarchy. The WONPR reported on the 1931 prohibition election in Finland, Europe's last dry country, in which women had voted more than two to one for repeal. WONPR pamphlets included "For Your Children's Sake" but also "National Prohibition versus States' Rights" and "A Primer of Prohibition History in the United States."[24]

Figure 6.1   A slim and stylish WONPR member exposes a portly Southern legislator.

The women of the Women's Organi-
zation for National Prohibition Re-
form played upon both their own
fashionability and drys' political
hypocrisy in their successful cam-
paign to repeal federal prohibition.
Reprinted in Grace Root, Women
and Repeal *(New York: Harper and*
Brothers, 1934), frontispiece. Origi-
nally printed in the Cleveland
Press, *a Scripps Howard paper.*

AND HE VOTED DRY !

These images and arguments reveal the pervasive modernism of the WONPR. The organization's 1934 corporate history, *Women and Repeal,* continually stressed its modernity in comparison with the WCTU. The WCTU appealed to emotions and to prejudice, the WONPR to reason. WCTU members "nearly knocked down" repeal women. They cried at congressional hearings and took criticism personally. Ella Boole spoke on fruit juice, whereas Pauline Sabin spoke on details of constitutional law. Sabin "and her followers . . . dealt in facts and not fancies, . . . often to the consternation of the committeemen before whom they spoke." An article in the magazine *Outlook and Independent* described how "such leaders of the old school as Ella Boole and Mrs. [Lucy] Peabody made the argument [that] . . . no matter what happened, . . . women would always be dry. Women, in short, were not people, they were merely a sex; which voted according to its emotional prejudices." The WONPR, so the title went, let "women become people." WONPR members even praised themselves for supporting wet candidates over women candidates—evidence that they were swayed by logic, not by sex-specific arguments.[25] A women's organization, the WONPR nonetheless prided itself on avoiding what it perceived as traditional weaknesses in women and women's politics.

Repeal supporters capitalized on the image of repeal as more contemporary, more realistic, than dry beliefs. Wet congresswoman Florence Kahn stated that it was "absurd to talk about the return of the saloon. The saloon is as much out of the picture as the horse-drawn carriage." A journalist similarly equated the saloon with long skirts. Sabin associated Prohibition with other archaic practices, describing how Americans in 1920 "gave ourselves over to Dr. Fanatic to be bled." Others within the media attacked women drys with the deadliest of weapons: humor. *Time, Vogue, McCall's, Smart Set,* and the *New Yorker* snickered about the women of the WCTU and other women's reform groups, "recruited, most of them, from the ranks of the British Grenadiers. Portly and important, stuffy with causes and sententiousness, their passing-in-review has been a pretty saddening spectacle." Jefferson Chase in *Vanity Fair* mused that the "Sabin women" were now finally reversing the rape of the Sabine women. Instead of dragging women away from Roman senators, they were dragging American senators away from *their* women, the WCTU. The *Wilmington (Delaware) Star* wrote that Sabin was "hacking away at that amendment with a hatchet as biting as Carry Nation's bar-smasher—the tongue of a liberated and thoroughly civilized woman." Journalists stressed the beauty and youth of WONPR members, repeating the story of a minor politician who on seeing

Sabin praised God for "a pretty woman in politics at last!"[26] Women drys found their most cherished weapons—femininity, domestic imagery, appeals to womanhood—laughingly dismissed.

o o o

THE WONPR'S BATTLES WITH WOMEN DRYS

The WONPR applied the same smooth rationality to its confrontations—closely followed in the media—with women drys. Wet women challenged dry claims that the 2.8 million members of the General Federation of Women's Clubs supported Prohibition. If the GFWC claimed to be nonpartisan and nonpolitical, the WONPR argued, it should take no stand on the Prohibition issue. The president of the GFWC conceded in 1932 that since Prohibition had passed from the moral into the political realm, it was now "a matter outside of our rights as an organization."[27]

Sabin scheduled WONPR meetings, which were then publicized, in cities hosting dry women's conventions. She challenged the WCTU to provide the names of one thousand people who had drunk to excess before Prohibition but were now saved. She invited leading women drys such as Boole and Molly Nicholson, of the National Woman's Democratic Law Enforcement League, to join her national advisory council to help formulate an alcohol control policy to curb "unseemly hilarity" after repeal. The women refused, accusing Sabin of opposing Prohibition for "pecuniary motives" and, more accurately, of inviting them for publicity purposes.[28]

Sabin met Mamie (Mrs. D. Leigh) Colvin, president of the New York WCTU, in several debates. Sabin argued, as usual, that Prohibition increased drinking and drunkenness, promoted hypocrisy, and violated states' rights and individual liberties. Colvin, on the other hand, praised Prohibition's benefits and accused wets, most of whom she considered to be fronting for the liquor interests, of spreading anti-Prohibition propaganda. Wets were like babies, "kicking and screaming when their bottles were taken away." Sabin controlled the debate; the *New York Times* reported that "it was necessary for the chair to ask that hissing be discontinued during Mrs. Colvin's speech." Because of the "considerable ill treatment" Mrs. Colvin received, Ella Boole instructed WCTU officers not to participate in such debates unless only the dry position were offered.[29]

Other women's dry organizations suffered even more in battles with women wets. The Woman's National Committee for Law Enforcement had been founded solely as an enforcement organization. WNCLE members were especially critical of repeal efforts. Lucy Peabody, WNCLE chairman, in her private writings did not refer to the WONPR but only to the "Sabin forces." She emphasized the liquor interests backing the group and the meager membership of the WONPR compared with the associations affiliated with the WNCLE. While the WCTU might encourage its members to treat the WONPR civilly, the WNCLE had no such qualms. "Show me a woman who wants to bring liquor back and I'll show you a woman who is either abnormal or subnormal," Peabody wrote President Hoover in 1931.[30]

The fundamental difference between women wets and the WCTU and WNCLE, a difference that cannot be emphasized enough, is that dry women considered alcohol inherently pathological. Wet women, on the other hand, did not see alcohol as dangerous in and of itself, or at least not dangerous enough to warrant federal prohibition. When Sabin wrote Boole in 1933 asking for her assistance in promoting moderation, Boole had no interest. "If you sincerely want to get rid of the evils of alcohol we challenge you to inaugurate a campaign for total abstinence as the only safe method." The WCTU and other dry women thus could not discuss any solution to the prohibition dilemma other than total abstinence, voluntary or enforced. Drys saw no moral distinction between selling liquor, which was illegal, and purchasing and consuming it, which were not.[31] They did not drink; they did not want to drink; they knew drink harmed others and was addictive enough to kill many. Why, therefore, continue the discussion?

Prohibitionists' second fatal weakness involved their faith in the dryness of American women. The belief that women supported Prohibition pervaded public discourse in the 1920s. Sabin founded the WONPR specifically to dispute this notion. But even as membership in the WONPR rose and wet women became bolder in the press and in public, women drys continued to view them as anomalous. Ella Boole testified in Congress in 1930 that polls of repeal support reflected men's sentiments, not women's. "Women with the ballot will continue to be the implacable foes of the liquor traffic."[32]

Dry women continued to view their wet enemies in decidedly gendered terms. The front page of a 1930 *Union Signal* depicted a massive "American Woman" defending American suburbia from "Liquor & Co. Expert Home Wreckers," all male. In 1932 the *Union Signal* published the short story "The Anchor."[33] The hero, Geoffrey Kelland, has a close relationship with his mother reminiscent of that between Mary and Willy Hammond in the classic 1854 temperance novel, *Ten Nights in a Bar-room.* Mrs. Kelland, like Mary Hammond, begs her son not to drink. Geoff's father, the story's antagonist, insists that Geoff drink, accusing his wife of turning their son into a "mollycoddle." Geoff's father also criticizes Geoff's girlfriend because she won't use makeup and is otherwise old-fashioned. The story, serialized over five issues, includes a Harvard crew race, plotting college roommates, and a final debate club scene in which Geoff endorses the temperance arguments in the *Union Signal* and pleads for subscribers. The story encapsulates the gender divisions of drink as seen through dry eyes. Moral suasion is alive and well in "The Anchor"—Mrs. Hammond cannot even control her husband's drinking and must wait three issues for a temperance pledge from her son. The affection between mother and son, while acceptable and desired in nineteenth-century society, would be labeled Oedipal by 1930s readers familiar with Freudian analysis. Dry principles are presented here as old-fashioned, like Geoff's girlfriend, and therefore subject to question. Temperance pledges produce mollycoddles.

WCTU members took particular offense at the WONPR's appropriation of woman-centered imagery. The *Union Signal* reported with shock on the WONPR's repeal poster, which depicted a mother with two towheaded children (figure 6.2). The newspaper then described a retaliatory dry poster of a mother and child in prayer. When the WONPR pointed out the failures of Prohibition, women drys had a simple and well-argued response.

> You and your associates may think that we of the Woman's Christian Temperance Union are women of one idea—prohibition. I hope you will believe me when I say that this is not so—we have supported every idea which gave promise of limiting or preventing the legal manufacture and sale of this drug.
>
> We have tried moral suasion, going even to the extreme of visiting the saloons and pleading with the saloon keepers on our knees to cease this deadly traffic. We have supported high license and low license. We have tried local option, county option, State prohibition, and in the case of one State, government control. All were futile because the liquor traffic was corrupt, ruthless, and law-breaking.
>
> We came to support national prohibition as the best method yet devised for controlling the liquor traffic. We recognize that the plan has not worked perfectly, and we say, in all kindness, that we are con-

vinced that you and your associates, in constantly criticizing instead of
supporting the law, have done much to make it ineffective.

149

∘ ∘ ∘

*The Women's
Organization
for National
Prohibition
Reform*

Mamie Colvin's response is tragic. By 1933, she and her compatriots had
indeed witnessed every American alcohol control measure to date.
Women drys spent their adult lives fighting the liquor interests and
Demon Rum: in 1933, Boole was seventy-five, Catt seventy-four, Peabody
seventy-two. Colvin, who would serve as president of the National WCTU
in the 1940s, was a youthful forty-five.[34]

In their well-meaning excess, these women and men equated "dry" with
bone-dry, toe-the-line support of the Eighteenth Amendment at any cost.
"Wet" came to define anyone questioning absolute observance of the law,
including those arguing that modification of the Constitution was an in-

Figure 6.2 "Their Security
Demands You Vote Repeal"

*The Women's Organization for
National Prohibition Reform
released thousands of copies of
this poster during its May
1932 "Repeal Week" cam-
paign. Temperance women
had always used images of children, maternity, and America
to promote their cause. Now, to
their great chagrin, they found
wets doing the same. On the
other hand, the WONPR's conservative Republican leadership was equally chagrined to
realize that "vote repeal"
meant supporting Democratic
candidate Franklin D.
Roosevelt. Original poster
in author's possession.*

herent right of democracy or that harsh dry laws violated civil liberties and exposed citizens to terrible and unnecessary danger. "Wet" now meant support of other forms of temperance legislation and of personal abstinence beyond the confines of the Eighteenth Amendment. Drys in their single-mindedness ceded to their opponents—or were forced to abandon—the entire middle ground of the debate. To their credit, drys had already tilled this middle ground, but in an earlier, more contentious era. Colvin and Boole could not debate wets on alcohol policy because of their perception that all other options had been proved wrong. Instead, they criticized the integrity of wet speakers.

Temperance men and women had a long history of labeling opponents as coming from a different, tainted social class. In some respects their labeling was true. Most upper-class supporters left the temperance movement in the 1830s, when total abstinence replaced moderation. Drys in the nineteenth century discussed upper-class drinking frequently, emphasizing how inebriety affected all levels of society as well as criticizing the bad example that so-called respectable women and men set. The reverse snobbery of women drys reached new depths in the late 1920s and early 1930s. In a 1929 address to the New York WCTU convention, Mamie Colvin described WONPR supporters as "women known chiefly because of their position in smart society and the financial standing of their husbands." The dry *American Independent* of Kentucky described repeal supporters as either immoral or connected to the liquor industry, "no more than the scum of the earth, parading around in skirts, and possibly late at night flirting with other women's husbands at drunken and fashionable resorts." Drys referred to "wine-drinking society women," country clubs, and the "privileged" children "accustomed to associate stimulants with their parents, with their Mother and her friends." Fletcher Dobyns in his 1940 dry history, *The Amazing Story of Repeal,* rechristened the WONPR the "Women's Organization to Bring Back the Liquor Traffic and the Saloon and Save Our Husbands' Profits." When Eleanor Roosevelt, abstemious though she was, in 1933 discussed the increase in girls' drinking, Republican minister Norman Vincent Peale questioned "this statement by this child of the rich who doesn't understand anything about American life." Many other themes found in nineteenth-century discussions of women's drinking reappear in this dry criticism: the failure of drinking mothers, the dangers of heredity. An article entitled "Privileged People Dissent," in the 1931 *Report of the Women's National Commission for Law Enforcement and Law Ob-*

servance, described the women drinkers in country clubs, "vivid minorities given much newspaper publicity, . . . groups which must spend a great deal in the repair-shops of doctors' offices; who must, after marriage, haunt the classes for over-nervous children."[35]

The *Woman's Journal* of the League of Women Voters repeated dry classism more tactfully. Editorials and articles stressed the temperance found in the "thousands of homes . . . in between these classes" of rich and poor. Carrie Catt felt that behavior of the wealthy was no measure of public sentiment. Assistant Attorney General Mabel Walker Willebrandt, who admitted that "wealth and family and social position make me shudder," particularly criticized upper-class women. "The predominating dry sentiment among the women of the country is not so noticeable, of course, among those who congregate in country clubs and who have plenty of leisure and very little work," she stated in 1929. Impartial observers pointed out that the WONPR faced most opposition from suspicious and envious rural women.[36]

The WONPR also provided class-based arguments. Members pointed out that Prohibition allowed the rich bootleg liquor while paternalistically keeping it from workingmen. For the most part, however, the WONPR consciously avoided class discussion as part of its campaign to appear modern and rational. For example, a wealthy dry woman asked New York society women to set a positive example by not serving cocktails. Sabin replied that she did not join groups "based solely on social standing" and instead was cooperating with women "from every walk of life" on repeal. Other WONPR members pointed out the hypocrisy of drys who criticized wet "society women" but praised dry "socially prominent" women. Such sentiment reflects the lack of class consciousness or "class appeal" in repeal literature generally, particularly when compared with earlier dry pleas to the middle class.[37]

Women of the WONPR used every conceivable argument for repeal. They opposed Prohibition because it reduced control of children but controlled adults too much. They rejected the association of women with Prohibition while celebrating their association with temperance. They were conservative and traditional and at the same time chic and modern. They abstained from alcohol but voted wet; they castigated those who drank but voted dry. They used constitutional law, civil liberties, and economic arguments in the same breath as home protection and mothers' love. They were both fashionable and classless, feminine yet above female rhetoric.

Horrified, they published dry criticism and then responded to this criticism with devastating equanimity. These were not easy enemies for dry women to face.

○ ○ ○

REPEAL OF THE EIGHTEENTH AMENDMENT

Dry women, however, could not avoid them. Prohibition continued to dominate political discourse in the United States. It was a central element in the 1932 presidential campaign. Prohibition may strike readers as a superfluous issue in light of the state of the economy at the time. In such hopelessness, however, debate over the amendment "was almost a welcomed diversion." It was also one of the few campaign issues on which the parties took definite and contrasting stands. John Raskob, Democratic Party chair, had long associated with the AAPA and considered repeal of the Eighteenth Amendment paramount. Because the Republican Party and President Hoover were so closely linked to Prohibition, Democrats began the campaign with a distinct advantage in repeal discussions. Just as Hoover's election in 1928 had been interpreted as an endorsement of Prohibition, so, too, would a Democratic victory be seen by both sides as a call for repeal.[38]

Numerous factors played into wet hands. More than a third of America's voters in 1932 had come of age after 1919. Propaganda against saloons and the liquor interests carried less weight with this younger generation. Congressional voting districts were finally reapportioned, now reflecting the urbanization of America and the decreasing voting power of dry rural districts. Such powerful organizations as the American Federation of Labor, the American Legion, and the Veterans of Foreign Wars publicly endorsed repeal. A 1931 federal study of Prohibition in its fine print recommended modification or repeal. Most important was the Depression. Arguments that dry workers helped productivity no longer carried weight. Wets could now argue that repeal would increase local, state, and federal tax revenues and put thousands of men to work in legalized positions.[39] If Prohibition had been a simplistic solution to alcoholism and political corruption, repeal was just as simplistic a solution to the gravest economic crisis of the century.

From its beginnings, the WONPR had worked to ensure election of wet candidates. With the presidential election looming in early 1932, the organization declared it would endorse the candidate of any party with a platform for repeal. WONPR leaders hoped that both parties would endorse outright repeal and thereby preclude any need for endorsement. With leadership culled from the Women's National Republican Club, the WONPR faced the extra challenge of overcoming the partisan sympathies of its most prestigious members. It joined other wet groups in lobbying for repeal at both party conventions. The Democrats, with minimal contention, developed a wet position. At their June convention, however, Republicans formulated an ambiguous policy soon labeled the "dry-moist-wet" platform because it attempted to placate all sides. The WONPR Executive Committee, therefore, took a deep breath and "urge[d] the members of this Organization, because they are committed to the cause of Repeal, whether they be Republicans or whether they be Democrats, to give their support to the nominee of that party which favors the Repeal of the Eighteenth Amendment, Franklin Delano Roosevelt." The WONPR action attracted much attention. Its backing of Roosevelt made the cover of *Time* and was generally praised by the press. The organization boasted their endorsement cost them "150 resignations and . . . 137,000 new members." Prominent Republican members spoke publicly about the two parties' platforms, endorsing Roosevelt and the Democrats. The WONPR released billboard advertisements of a woman shielding a child from the clouds of violence and corruption. The billboard read: "Prohibition failed! . . . Vote the Straight Democratic Ticket."[40]

As it emerged, the WONPR was not the first repeal organization to endorse FDR, it was the only major one to do so. Neither the AAPA nor the Women's Committee for Repeal of the Eighteenth Amendment could sway Republican members to leave their party. Republicans such as James Wadsworth held a special aversion to FDR. At the Republican convention Wadsworth predicted gloomily that because the Republicans remained dry, FDR "will get in, and if he does we won't get rid of him until he dies. And thrift will never be heard of again."[41]

Roosevelt's victory in November 1932 was considered a mandate for repeal. The lame-duck Congress that winter passed a repeal amendment on February 21. Thirty-six states approved the amendment over the next nine and a half months, and final ratification of the amendment was achieved in early December 1933. In addition to repealing the Eighteenth Amendment, the Twenty-first Amendment banned smuggling liquor into dry states. But for all intents and purposes, the noble experiment of federal alcohol prohibition was finished.[42]

The extraordinary speed of repeal should be credited not so much to public sympathy as to the well-laid plans of wet organizations, particularly the Voluntary Committee of Lawyers. Many wets believed that the Anti-Saloon League had whisked the Eighteenth Amendment through docile state legislatures. The WONPR, the VCL, and the AAPA, therefore, proposed amending the Constitution through special state conventions decided by voters, not legislators. Although this method was constitutional, it had been unused since ratification of the Constitution itself in the late eighteenth century. With Congress still debating the amendment, the VCL sent all forty-eight states its recommendations on the convention process. State legislators, more than happy to have others finally decide this issue, complied.[43]

The system required each state to hold elections in which voters chose convention delegates for either their proratification (wet) or antiratification (dry) platform. These state conventions required much human labor. Dry and wet convention candidates needed to be selected and their positions publicized. Voters had to be alerted to the special elections held in various states throughout the spring, summer, and fall of 1933. The conventions themselves required organization, with procedures to be established and officials selected. The WONPR carried out the bulk of the organizing. State WONPR organizations prepared motorcades, parades, rallies, and literature. They released repeal license plates and repeal lapel pins (in the shape of the Liberty Bell) and campaigned door-to-door for members and voters. Sample ballots explained when and how to vote while listing again the reasons for repeal.[44]

In thirty-seven state elections held between April 14 and December 5, 73 percent of voting Americans chose repeal delegates. At the subsequent conventions, only South Carolina voted against the Twenty-first Amendment; delegates in several states endorsed it unanimously. WONPR members served as president or secretary in seven conventions and as delegates in twenty-one others. Because the election of delegates almost guaranteed the outcome of the convention, most conventions proceeded smoothly, even gaily—a welcomed respite (if one were wet) from the Depression. The governor of New York hosted a beer party for that state's convention-goers, who included Pauline Sabin and Ione Nicoll.[45]

At its December 1933 victory dinner, the WONPR formally dissolved itself, its budget surplus going into a graduate fellowship in political science at Barnard College. The abruptness of this dissolution is particularly striking in light of Sabin's earlier statements that the WONPR would help frame state liquor laws and institute a "campaign of temperance education." In point of fact, former WONPR members played prominent roles in developing states' postrepeal alcohol policy. Jeanie Sheppard of New York, for example, was active through the 1930s and early 1940s in the State Liquor Authority and the Alcoholic Beverage Commission.[46]

WONPR leadership worried, however, that its continued existence would provide drys a scapegoat for postrepeal policy failures. Sabin wrote Alice du Pont that the WONPR must not allow its reputation to be tarnished by subsequent nonpartisan organizations, as the National American Woman Suffrage Association had been by the League of Women Voters. Granted, Sabin's feelings about the LWV were fairly strong. But she was, first and last, a partisan creature and, like many party regulars who had endorsed repeal as a nonpartisan issue, found herself burned by the final outcome. Conservative wets were none too pleased with the man they had helped put in office and by late 1933 were organizing against the New Deal. The anti-Roosevelt American Liberty League contained many former members of the AAPA, the Crusaders, and WONPR. Sabin served for a time on its executive committee. But public support for the Liberty League never came close to that for repeal. While repeal leaders desired personal liberty and states' rights, the mass of American voters wanted only repeal itself and did not join these organizational spin-offs. Sabin campaigned for Alf Landon in 1936 but remained outside the Republican power structure; one can understand how party leaders would hesitate to welcome her back with open arms. In 1945 she resigned from the American Red Cross in a dispute with its chair's liberal policies. She would die of pneumonia in 1955, at the age of sixty-eight.[47]

Sabin, like many of her conservative associates, found repeal anticlimactic. But wet disappointment was no match to the emotions of drys. Funding for the ASL and the WCTU, never extensive in the 1920s, almost disappeared after 1929. In the South especially, the WCTU lost members over its partisan endorsement of Hoover in 1928. At the end of the decade it claimed six hundred thousand members, though actual figures came closer to half this. The union complained about the difficulty of attracting new members at the same time that it criticized the judgment of younger generations. In 1931, Boole reassured members that five hundred thousand youths pledged to abstain from drink, "concrete evidence that all young people are not going bad." The WCTU slogan of 1932 was "Advance, Not Retreat." A *Union Signal* article on the WONPR began, "They are Working. Are You?" Elizabeth Tilton, WNCLE member and chair of the

Women's Committee for Education Against Alcohol, called for "a convention of the forgotten woman of the 1932 election," and Boole even suggested a third party. But compared with 1928, dry women's participation
in the 1932 presidential campaign was dispirited and meager. As far as
Prohibition went, the Republicans were traitorous and the Democrats,
with their "cocktail president," just plain hopeless. Five days before the
election, Ella Boole announced formally that the WCTU endorsed neither
candidate, because "one is as wet as the other." With profound understatement, she advised dry women to vote in any case, because "there are many
other vital issues in the campaign."[48]

The repeal campaign of 1933 approached a nightmare. More reasoned
prohibitionists questioned the morality of repeal: removing legislation
to satisfy the wishes of those who already violated it did not seem the
best way to increase respect for the law. Irrationally, many drys considered
repeal by convention unconstitutional. Moreover, they argued, "wet
influences" controlled the "big-city vote" that made repeal possible. With
no acknowledgement of earlier ASL power, they accused the AAPA of ma-
nipulating Congress. Drys also felt wets supported repeal only to lower
their own income taxes. By the end of Prohibition, the *Union Signal* was
asking WCTU members to donate jewelry and silverware to the antirepeal
cause. Boole developed the astounding slogan, "No Quarter for Repeal but
Thousands of Quarters to Retain the Eighteenth Amendment." Following
repeal, Boole left the national WCTU to lead the World WCTU. Her successor vowed to continue temperance education and to battle the liquor
interests, obscenity in film, and other traditional WCTU concerns. The
union even prepared an educational film, "The Beneficent Reprobate," on
alcohol's benefits in industry and its danger in beverages.[49]

The WCTU criticized FDR as much as women wets did, blaming him for
the "social evils that have come upon us in recent years." It had little patience for research organizations begun in the 1930s, such as the Yale
Center for Alcohol Studies, because social scientists refused to condemn
beverage alcohol as a substance. Members during World War II campaigned far less successfully than had a generation earlier against beer
and liquor on military bases. In 1951 more than a quarter of a million
women belonged, more members than at any point in the organization's
history prior to 1920. The WCTU today still concerns itself with alcohol,
tobacco, and illegal drug use, particularly as they affect children; as such,
it sounds remarkably contemporary.[50]

The study of women's role in the history of Prohibition reveals the dilemma of feminism, the difficulty of expecting both personal independence and group solidarity among women. The Woman's Christian Temperance Union and other dry women considered Prohibition integral to their social activism and political independence. In such light, repeal was more than an opposing viewpoint. For women drys, the WONPR and other wet groups fundamentally challenged their definition of womanhood. The Women's Organization for National Prohibition Reform, on the other hand, illustrates the effort by women to create a new model of women's political participation based not on gender or morality but on political interest. By the end of the decade it was possible for women who advocated return of the legal liquor traffic to mouth home-protection arguments back at their helpless opponents. Women who in the nineteenth century had mobilized around the issues of motherhood and home protection were simply too diverse by the late 1920s for the uniform arguments of the WCTU. The debate was becoming meaningless.

In its efforts to create a new model of female political participation, the WONPR might best be compared to later women's nonpartisan reform organizations. Women Strike for Peace (WSP), for example, campaigned against nuclear weapons testing during the anticommunist 1960s. These peace activists utilized female imagery and traditional roles—motherhood, home protection, even "absent-mindedness" and "disorganization"—to unglue their critics and make their case. Such behavior was both self-conscious and calculated. WSP members were ultimately more successful than male peers because of their pragmatic use of their femininity.

For the women of the WSP and the WONPR, feminine behavior and feminine rhetoric cloaked the extent of their effectiveness within male-dominated politics. They utilized, in Joan Rivière's words, "womanliness as a masquerade." A Freudian analyst in the 1920s, Rivière applied the concept of masquerade to a patient who disguised her "masculine" assertiveness and management skills by adopting feminine manner and dress. Such behavior can be seen in both the corporate philosophy of and the many individuals within the WONPR.[51] Members treated cosmetics, fashion, and graciousness as window dressing facilitating resolution of the prohibition issue.

We have discussed how the WONPR viewed itself as more modern and rational than the WCTU. The organization historian Grace Root proudly

157

∘ ∘ ∘

*The Women's
Organization
for National
Prohibition
Reform*

related how members after 1933 joined state alcohol commissions. They have "come to look realistically upon the problem of regulation which a generation before their maiden aunts had regarded only with romantic fear and horror. The failure of prohibition has taught the women of today to make a calm, clear-eyed appraisal of liquor's proper role in American life."[52] This passage contrasts strongly with the writings of dry women. For wets such as Root and male Dr. Yost of Elizabeth Tilton's fictional *Which?*, dry women *did* appear nervous, in need of "normalization." Dry women, in the eyes of these wets, brought to political discussion archaic and unnecessary female emotions. Gender thus was removed from the prohibition discourse because gender no longer had a definable role in politics.

On a deeper level, however, the relationship between gender and Prohibition faced an even greater threat. Wet women argued that the all-male saloon was as obsolete as the horse-drawn carriage and the female hoop skirt. While they, for the most part, did not discuss their own drinking, they did not demur when others did. Granted, some wet women expressed the same shock over women's drinking as did their dry opponents. But the fact that they could even speak in favor of alcohol is much more significant. By the end of the 1920s, gender was no longer essential to politics. More importantly, however, it was no longer essential, or even significant, to alcohol use itself.

The association of men with alcohol and women with abstinence—an association tapped in the story *Which?*—no longer carried the same effectiveness. Women now drank, in public, with men. During the time of the WCTU and the WONPR, and of the Eighteenth and Twenty-First Amendments, a massive social transformation had taken place in the manner and atmosphere in which men and women interacted. This cultural evolution sparked both Prohibition and its repeal, affecting the structure of the Constitution and the lives of millions of Americans. Dry women argued that alcohol rendered men ungovernable, that the substance was in and of itself beyond control. At the same time, however, other women domesticated drink.

THE DOMESTICATION
OF DRINK

*I have always been afraid of a drunken man. I will change my
seat in a car any time to avoid sitting next to one, or will cross
a street rather than pass a man staggering along the sidewalk.
And I cannot help but think, with large sympathy, of the
woman whose husband in those days came home drunk, locked
the door—his house being his castle—who claimed the right to
treat his wife as he pleased, and in his drunkenness considered
her his property.*

—Ella Boole

The debates surrounding the prohibition, woman suffrage,
and repeal amendments reflect deep anxiety over gender
roles in the first third of the twentieth century. Prohibitionists and suffragists, often one and the same, sought to eliminate male excess—abusive
drinking, political corruption, domestic violence—through Prohibition
and suffrage reforms. Women antisuffragists, who often supported Prohibition, worried that women's gendered unity would be destroyed by enfranchisement. Yet at the same time that female reformers sought to eliminate Demon Rum, millions of women, in what appears to be a contradiction
or at best a massive misunderstanding, continued to drink. Women from
many classes and regions drank wines, beer, and hard liquor at formal dinners and celebrations such as weddings and christenings, in respectable
public spaces such as beer gardens, and at women-only gatherings. Beyond this, alcohol was a medicine, a preservative, and an integral ingredi-
ent in cooking. After the turn of the century, opportunities for and acceptance of this drinking only grew. Public entertainment venues such as
dance halls, cabarets, restaurants, and cafés increasingly attracted respectable women, who drank with their male companions.

At the same time, growing numbers of these drinkers, disgusted with
the corruption and evils of the liquor interests, supported Prohibition. The
Progressive enthusiasm for reform through legislation increased the ac-

ceptability of dry laws. Prohibition's supporters benefited as well from World War I. Food conservation efforts and ill-timed brewer support of Germany rendered dry laws even more palatable to legislators and voters. It must be stressed again, however, that the Eighteenth Amendment and most state prohibition laws controlled distribution but did not attempt to monitor at-home drinking. Americans male and female could support federal prohibition while continuing to drink privately without moral qualms. Two kinds of prohibitionists existed in the United States: those, whom we might dub moderate, who opposed the saloon and liquor interests, and those who considered alcohol in and of itself evil—the radicals.

The radical drys who escorted Prohibition through Congress hoped that it would lead to national abstinence. Organizations such as the Woman's Christian Temperance Union insisted upon personal abstinence, and well-known feminists such as Carrie Chapman Catt frowned upon any drinking in any setting. With the enticements of the alcohol distributors gone, many drys felt, citizens would lose their appetite for the toxin. Temperance supporters refused to integrate moderate home consumption into their Prohibition platform. They criticized not only brewers, saloon keepers, and bootleggers—standard villains—but also the average American drinker, who did not take kindly to the association. In speaking for abstinence—indeed, in campaigns for "law observance" demanding it—drys lost their audience.

Throughout the 1920s the wet opponents of Prohibition would argue for modification of federal prohibition laws. They pointed out that the definition of "intoxicating liquors" in the Volstead Act could be altered without affecting the prohibition amendment itself. But their pleas fell on deaf ears. Drys, secure within their dry Congress and well aware of the unlikelihood of repealing a constitutional amendment, had no interest in aligning dry law with behavior or public sentiment. Modification might very well have delayed or averted repeal, but the question remains theoretical.[1] As it was, dry and wet values continued to diverge. It is clear that men's abusive drinking diminished in the 1920s, thereby easing public support of Prohibition and abstinence. Sympathy for private drinking grew over the decade, as did acceptance of women's alcohol consumption within and beyond the home. Women drank before Prohibition, both at home and publicly. But elimination of alcohol's associations with brewers, saloon keepers, and abusive male drinking patterns allowed Americans of both sexes to consider the substance alcohol without its most negative trappings. By

1929 the gendered attributes of alcohol and temperance had faded to such a point that a Republican committeewoman could organize an anti-Prohibition women's group. The Women's Organization for National Prohibition Reform applied the rhetoric of motherhood and home protection to the repeal cause. Pauline Sabin and her supporters thus dismantled the last ostensibly woman's issue within American politics. The WONPR does not represent the final gasp of women's moral authority but rather the most practical, conniving use of it. Repeal encapsulates women's efforts to return to a woman-dominated model of moderation, to promote what the WONPR labeled "true temperance."

The rest of this chapter explores in more depth the repercussions of modern drinking practices. One could argue that younger women in the second and third decades of the twentieth century adopted drinking as a positive masculine attribute, much like paid employment or sports. At the same time, they continued to mold male drinking habits. Younger women's drinking, regardless of the accusations leveled against such behavior, constituted a rejection not so much of feminism as of its more old-fashioned, self-sacrificing aspects.

WOMEN'S DRINKING AND WOMEN'S RIGHTS

Since the 1960s, social scientists close to alcohol studies have agreed that drinking is "the prerogative of full citizenship in most cultures." For this reason, alcohol consumption and the women's rights movement may have a legitimate relationship. Although statistics on moderate consumption are often difficult to come by, some conclusions may be drawn. One 1960s study of drinking patterns within one community established that women who came of age during Prohibition drank much more than the cohort who came of age before 1922. Other studies from the 1940s revealed "a narrowing of the gap between the sexes in respect to drinking." A 1947 report ascribed this to "the general trend in our society toward less and less differentiation in the social behavior of men and women." These authors do not attribute the increase in women's drinking to Prohibition in and of itself. They also stress that men continue to drink and abuse alcohol more than women. Moreover, the increase in women's drinking had less to do with Prohibition than with employment, birth control, suffrage, divorce laws—all the elements of modern American womanhood. Male and female rebels and rebel aspirants settled upon drinking as a symbol of, a behavior reflecting, individuality and liberation.[2] Cocktails and mixed-sex drinking epitomize the social changes experienced by young America in the 1920s.

I have refrained from introducing the flapper before now because the term remains so hypnotic—even in print, "the flapper" tends to overwhelm rational discussion and analysis. The flapper came to American consciousness two decades after the educated, mobile, independently minded "New Woman." The New Woman concerned herself with public matters, with suffrage, appearing in "all the places she is needed." The flapper, a generation younger, took her position for granted, asserting her independence and heterosexuality in a manner disconcerting to her elders. Flappers' drinking, particularly in the 1920s, often appeared to snub older feminists' temperance goals. The irony of the situation was not lost on observers of the time. Many critics of the modern woman considered her the worst amalgam of traditional male behavior. "Woman, in doing man's work, in assuming man's duties and responsibilities, shows a tendency to adopt, for women, the man's viewpoint of men's chastity," a journalist sniffed in the 1915 *Forum*. An editorial on women's smoking in the 1920 *Union Signal* agreed. "A phase of present-day feminism demands every privilege for women that man claims for himself. Concerning the justice of this demand there can be no question. Concerning its expediency much can be said." Throughout the 1920s, WCTU members fretted that "the girls have adopted the boys' standards instead of raising them to their own."[3]

Commentators in the 1920s and 1930s emphasized (with varying degrees of enthusiasm) that personal acts of liberation such as drinking superseded the political autonomy that women had sought earlier. A psychoanalyst writing in 1919 felt that expanded opportunities in women's employment and women's rights explained their drinking. "The virile component of women is stirred today and this helps to explain woman's increased turning to alcohol," which had been "formerly reserved for men." A 1925 article on "petting and the campus" also merged discussion of alcohol and sexuality. Upperclassmen advised incoming students to practice temperance—by which they meant moderation—in both drinking and "petting." Thus, we see the intersection of gender, alcohol, sexuality, and modernity that marked the 1920s. Dorothy Dunbar Bromley's article "Feminist: New Style" (1927) described a generation who sought to refute the behavior and values of their "perfect lady" predecessors. "'Feminism' has become a term of opprobrium to the modern young woman. For the word suggests either the old school of fighting feminists who wore flat heels, or the current species who antagonize men with their constant clamor about maiden names, equal rights, woman's place in the world, and many another cause . . . *ad infinitum.*" Bromley's "new-style" feminist appears heterosocial and heterosexual, eager to assume male attributes and willing to reject any gender role that "cramps her style too much as an individual."[4]

In her 1933 history of American women, *Angels and Amazons,* Inez Haynes Irwin observed that recently, "masculine and feminine habits began to float toward a common focus." She applied this melding to smoking and also to drinking: "In few circles where conventionality grants alcohol to men does it deny the privilege to women. And impatience with the vices of the other sex, an unconscious spring of action with the old feminine temperance crusaders, [has] no more force." Irwin, in her implicit criticism of dry values, comes across very much as a "new-style" feminist. She went so far as to define the speakeasy as *dioecious,* a botanical term for male and female organs on separate plants, for plants that are, in effect, heterosexual. Banning, Irwin, and other social commentators continually described alcohol as modern. Pop historian Frederick Lewis Allen associated cocktails with Freud, scientific skepticism, and a general outspokenness: "It was better to be modern,—everybody wanted to be modern,—and sophisticated, and smart, to smash conventions and to be devastatingly frank. And with a cocktail glass in one's hand it was easy at least to be frank." When a WCTU member stated in the early 1960s that "we ladies who are against taking cocktails are a little queer," she was describing the decline of temperance support among the middle class or, rather, among the peers she defined as middle class. To abstain from alcohol meant in effect abstaining from modern heterosocial interaction.[5]

The cultural metamorphosis of drinking during Prohibition did not travel in one direction alone. Women did begin to drink, to take on male attributes that to their minds represented the best amalgam of femininity and masculine power. At the same time, they redefined male drinking habits. Much of the drinking that took place in respectable circles during and after Prohibition entailed a significant change from that preceding World War I. In the 1870s, Woman Temperance Crusaders had smashed saloons as a legitimate expression of their female role. So, too, did respectable women in the 1920s and 1930s pursue and tame male drinkers in the home and in public.

Etiquette writers demanded as much from American hostesses. Mrs. Alma Fullford Whitaker introduced her 1933 guide to polite drinking with a call to arms.

> It is enormously important that the Repeal of the Eighteenth Amendment should be a success. This can best be achieved if the women of the nation, and specifically the hostesses, take the matter in hand. If we are as fussy and fastidious about the quality, quantity, and service of our liquor and about the conduct of our guests as we are about the food, the table service, and the accouterments of our parties, all will be well. . . .
>
> The women of the United States are credited with being the most influential with their men of any country. *Voilà,* sisters, for pity's sake let us set a standard that is at least equal to that of the more civilized nations in this delicate matter of the cup that cheers but positively should not inebriate. It is up to us.

Whitaker expected both men and women to drink—indeed, she advises potential mates to see each other "unpleasantly drunk" before marrying.[6] Her prose illustrates the close and legitimate connection between women and alcohol-related sociability. Whitaker felt that women should simply exert the authority they already possess in order to make repeal successful.

During Prohibition, acceptance of women's home drinking facilitated development of new drinking rituals, in particular the cocktail party. The cocktail provided hard liquor, but softened—feminized enough to remove its most opprobrious male associations. Women who would never think of consuming straight gin could ask for a dry martini without fearing for their reputations. The cocktail provided a neatly packaged, suitably disguised, fashionably decorated shot of liquor. The cocktail gave alcohol a mystique; note the laudatory histories of the martini and other drinks. It was, moreover, an American invention, one that American drinkers took quite seriously. "American Bars"—what Americans would call cocktail bars—appeared abroad, complete with polished bar and brass rail. By the 1920s cocktail manuals were published in French, supplying both the American expatriate audience and interested foreigners with "boissons Americans."[7] These sources present an image of moderate group drinking as positive and ubiquitous.

If purchasing patterns are any guide, drink does appear to have been domesticated by Prohibition, by drinking rituals such as tea dances and cocktail parties, and by women. This may be seen not only in the reduction of beer consumption (beer being mainly a saloon beverage) during the 1920s but also in new postrepeal alcohol outlets. Before Prohibition, most of the alcohol sold in the United States was consumed at the site of sale in saloons, bars, and other public drinking establishments. After 1900, communities experimenting with alcohol regulation created "package stores" selling sealed bottles for consumption off premises—an attempt to restrict saloon excess while still providing alcohol to voters. In Boston and Chicago the number of package store licenses exploded in the years before World War I. These stores hint at the obsolescence of saloons and saloons' opponents. After repeal in 1933, state regulatory agencies encouraged this "privatization of drinking," and by 1941 most alcohol in the country was sold for off-premises consumption. State package stores, and grocery stores that sold bottled beer, legitimized domestic drinking and undercut the public drinking rituals of historically male spaces.[8] These new state alcohol regulations built upon and facilitated new cultural practices.

Drys objected wholeheartedly to this evolution. A 1935 editorial in the *American Issue,* the national newspaper of the Anti-Saloon League, asserted that "cocktail parties in thousands of homes are capturing large numbers of the women of America for permanent membership in the ranks of confirmed alcoholics. Distillers are appealing through alluring advertisements in women's magazines to the women to drink and serve drinks as 'good and perfect hostesses.'" Drys objected equally to the promotion of women's public drinking. The *American Issue* editorial continued, "Repeal has brought many innovations but none more alarming than women crowding men from the barrooms much to the dismay of bartenders."[9]

It is noteworthy that the writer considered bartenders "dismayed" by women's public drinking, which may very well have been the case. Diehard male wets found this "feminization" of drinking (as two 1930 writers dubbed it) as disconcerting as drys did. Men's clubs, so popular in Victorian America, now had trouble retaining members. One club member in 1923 mourned the "one-time meccas . . . deserted after nightfall." The corporate history of the Philadelphia Club reported in 1934 that "the blight of prohibition—for its blight in forms transmuted survives repeal—and various other factors, have changed the life of the Club—not only this Club, but clubdom in general." Some of the most interesting and most amusing descriptions of the evolving relation between alcohol and gender may be found in drink histories published in the 1930s. The newspaperman George Ade's memoir, *The Old-Time Saloon,* the humorist Don Marquis's *Her Foot Is on the Brass Rail,* collections of bar songs such as *My Pious Friends and Drunken Companions* (1927)—these sources reveal grudging male resignation over the loss of the male drinking culture. Don Marquis bemoaned the replacement of the "old saloon" by the "new barroom."

> But there is worse. Women come into this New Barroom. Not through a Family Entrance, but through the front door. They go right up to the bar. They put a foot on the brass railing. They order; they are served; they bend the elbow; they hoist; they toss down the feminine esophagus the brew that was really meant for men—stout and wicked men. . . .
>
> The last barrier is down; the citadel has been stormed and taken. There is no longer any escape, no hiding place, no hole or corner, no burrow nor catacomb, no nook amongst the ruins of civilization, where the hounded male may seek his fellow and strut his stuff, safe from the atmosphere and presence of femininity. A man might as well do his drinking at home, with his wife and daughters; and there never was any fun in that. It was merely—drinking! It was merely a satisfaction of the physical side of alcohol.

Her Foot Is on the Brass Rail even contains a James Thurber illustration of a man cursing a roomful of women at the "Sapphire Bar." A similar cartoon from a 1935 *New Yorker* has a bartender reprimanding the lone male patron for not removing his hat: "Try and remember where you are, will you!" As Frederick Lewis Allen summarized, "Under the new régime not only the drinks are mixed, but the company as well."[10]

Although these men continued to wax nostalgic on the passing of "the niceties of communal drinking," most put no conviction into their complaints. Exclusive homosocial drinking was presented in films and funny papers as laughable, not terrifying. For all Ade's hilarious anecdotes and gossipy commentary, he comes across in the end as relieved the saloon is gone and certain it will never return. Other male drinkers less accepting of the saloon's passing were equally impotent to change the situation. And psychoanalysts now discussed with equal concern the dangers of prohibitionist fervor and the repressed homosexuality inherent in the male-only saloon.[11] By the 1930s, it seems, American manhood was as domesticated as alcohol.

FEMINISM IN THE 1920S

In much women's history written in the past decades, the female-centered lives of Victorian women come across as a sort of golden age destroyed by the heterosociality of the 1920s. While freely acknowledging legal advancements such as divorce, birth control, and suffrage, scholars have been quick to emphasize how new sexual and social norms oppressed women. Advertisers and social scientists appropriated feminist themes of freedom and independence to promote motherhood, materialism, and conventional gender stereotypes. The single-sex environments created by women were now labeled old-fashioned and possibly lesbian.[12] Historians stress the generational divisions that developed between Progressive Era social reformers and younger women intent on heterosexual relationships and consumerism. But few historians recognize the relation between women's history and the decline of the prohibition movement.

Much of the conflict over feminism in the later 1920s and 1930s can best be seen through the lens of Prohibition. Support for Prohibition extended beyond dry groups to more broadly based women's political organizations: the League of Women Voters, the Women's Joint Congressional Committee, and female leaders within the major and minor political parties. This connection had begun in the earliest days of the temperance and woman movements. It may be seen in such extraordinary events as the concurrent ratification of the prohibition and woman suffrage amendments and in such small examples as the 1886 *Woman's Suffrage Cook Book,* which did not include a single recipe requiring alcohol. This cookbook stands almost alone in the plethora of nineteenth-century cookbooks and advice manuals—from Catharine Beecher to Fannie Farmer—that describe, even advocate, alcohol consumption.[13] Might the *Woman's Suffrage Cook Book* thus illustrate the radical, minority status of woman suffrage and women reformers in the nineteenth century?

Women's differences of opinion regarding Prohibition and moderate drinking continued in the twentieth century. Women drys during federal prohibition contrasted their peers' lack of law observance to earlier dry sympathies in the second decade of the twentieth century, to wartime gasoline conservation. Yet wartime rationing demands extraordinary personal sacrifices that the American public finds hard to maintain in peacetime. Dry support in the 1910s far exceeded the temperance enthusiasm of the preceding decades and even in this decade was marred by new public drinking rituals that undercut much of the gendered nature of alcohol consumption and of dry criticism.

Public support for Prohibition and the woman movement faded in tandem in the last years of the 1920s. Changes within American culture rendered the goals of the Victorian woman movement—morality, social improvement, suffrage, and temperance—obsolete. Feminism, as Nancy Cott has brilliantly argued, developed in the 1910s in part as a reaction to the strictures of the woman movement. Yet the tenets of feminism entailed contradictions that have yet to be resolved. In advising individual fulfillment, feminism refutes the concept of gender-based unity among all women. In advising self-gratification, feminism negates the notion of group solidarity essential to any movement.[14] Older activist women opposed to alcohol defined themselves as feminists at the same time that younger women drinkers did. The history of prohibition and repeal encapsulates feminism's uneasy balancing of group morality and private choice.

By the late 1920s, dry women appeared almost paralyzed by their reliance on obsolescent gendered attributes. Members of the WCTU and the Woman's National Committee for Law Enforcement were acutely aware of the feminine, moral nature of Prohibition. Dry women continued to refer to alcohol as "a masculine indulgence," to "the bondage of beer and the humiliation of the old Saturday night," and thus dated themselves by their rhetoric.[15] These women persisted in believing that temperance support was in some way an innate trait of respectable women, of universal womanhood. The fact that women—normal, respectable women—might seek out liquor voluntarily does not appear to have entered their consciousness.

From the 1870s through the 1930s, drys accused drinking women of caring more for appearance and status than for morality or reform. And, according to etiquette authorities, editorialists, cookbook writers, and voters, drys were right. Instead of pointing out the decline of reform sentiment in the 1920s, we should perhaps question its applicability to American society beyond reformist circles. Perhaps womanhood was no longer a force in American politics because women, not the minority of reforming woman, now campaigned and voted. This social history of women's drinking expands our understanding of women's political history. Rather than stressing the conservatism or narrow-mindedness of American society generally, we should instead be stressing the impracticality of reformers.

If laws reflect the values of dominant power groups, then repeal marked the emergence of a value system committed to drinking and to the heterosociality associated with it. Drinking (like birth control, an issue of the same period) was increasingly considered a private right beyond the realm of public legislation. Americans who voted for repeal endorsed the possibility, even the probability, of moderate consumption. Progressive Era models of alcohol as inherently addictive and the alcohol industry as inherently corrupt no longer swayed the voting public. The martini rituals of President Franklin Roosevelt attracted national attention, and one could indeed argue that he gave official sanction to the cocktail hour. Repeal also legitimized public drinking, removing much of the underworld atmosphere and mob control of urban speakeasies. Nightclubs thrived during the Depression.[16]

In 1940, seven years after repeal of federal prohibition, three states remained dry. Others continued to grant local-option privileges to municipalities and counties. Sixteen states adopted control systems based on a 1932 report funded by John D. Rockefeller, himself a disgruntled former dry. His Institute of Public Administration described state liquor control boards dispensing alcohol in monopoly systems that would control excess and increase tax revenue. By the end of the 1930s, a handful of national corporations dominated the distilling and brewing industries. These giant corporations spent millions of dollars advertising their wares. But, having been badly burned once, they also sought to control the worst excesses of distributors. Indeed, it may be that alcohol legislation succeeded in the 1930s because the New Deal legitimized oligopolies and government-industry cooperation. Although abuse on the part of officials and manufacturers continued, nothing matched the corruption and lawlessness of pre-Prohibition America.[17]

Prohibition resulted in great part from female efforts to control male drinking. Women's efforts have generally been seen as misguided, and Prohibition as a "a pinched, parochial substitute for reform" (Richard Hofstadter's description in the 1955 *Age of Reform*) or as self-defeating—flappers drinking like men while otherwise acquiescing to them. Both these interpretations fall short. In the context of the liquor industry's extraordinary corruption, the struggling campaign for woman suffrage, and the patriotism and food conservation efforts of World War I, federal prohibition made a great deal of sense. Women sought multiple ways to control male drinking beyond Prohibition as well: moral suasion efforts in the early nineteenth century; campaigns to legitimize divorce from drunkards; saloon-smashing rages of women pushed beyond propriety. And, it must be stressed, many women encouraged their mates to drink at home "and so eliminate the sociability of the saloon that makes one lose thoughts of time and quantity" (as one editorialist phrased it in 1914). Domestic drinking rituals involving both sexes presented a more controlled model of alcoholic sociability. The medium of the wine glass, the decanter, and the cocktail modified alcohol consumption at the same time that it legitimized it. Flappers, contrary to stereotype, did not begin to drink like men. Rather, two different models of drinking melded. If women today drink more than they did one hundred years ago, men drink less.[18]

Because of the manner in which dry legislation was written and the ambivalence surrounding these laws, a woman in the second and third decades of this century could support with no ethical qualms both Prohibition and private consumption. Moreover, by the late 1920s violations of the Eighteenth Amendment and the Volstead Act were severe enough that a dry woman in good conscience could also support repeal. Radical drys never recognized that alcohol control as entailed in federal prohibition was not the only solution to the problem of alcoholism. Prohibition failed because of this dry extremism. A considerable number of Americans endorsing state prohibition in the 1910s had minimal interest in curtailing their own consumption. If prohibitionists had acknowledged this sentiment, allowing the manufacture and sale of light beer and wine for home use, they would have alienated extreme drys who believed that alcohol in any form and in any environment was too dangerous to allow. But they would have retained the support of a large class of Americans who distrusted the liquor industry but saw no harm in an occasional drink. And, arguably, they would have thus circumvented the most egregious legal violations of the decade, incidents that have prejudiced public opinion against Prohibition from the 1920s through the present day. Political and moral extremists ignore at their peril moderate supporters. If there is one lesson to be learned from Prohibition, it is this.

° ° ° EPILOGUE

For all the hoopla surrounding repeal itself, the nation in 1933 greeted legal alcohol with ringing silence. Americans intent on the tragedy of the Depression and exhausted by decades of prohibition controversy had no interest in continuing debate. More effective laws and newly solicitous alcohol producers helped to remove drink from public scrutiny. Equally important to repeal's long-term success were new developments in the treatment of alcohol abuse. In the summer of 1935, alcoholics Bill Wilson and Dr. Robert Smith, in a series of long conversations, talked each other dry. ("Alcoholic," first coined in the mid-nineteenth century, now replaced the dated and pejorative "inebriate" and "drunkard.") Slowly developing their program and inviting others to join, by the end of the decade the two had enlarged their circle to several dozen recovering alcoholics. From these beginnings, Alcoholics Anonymous grew, with eight thousand participants in twenty-two groups by the end of 1941. Fifty years later, AA had eighty-eight thousand groups and a worldwide membership of 1.8 million. AA's support group atmosphere and emphasis on a "greater power" have aided a sizable percentage of participants, particularly middle-class participants. The organization has not eliminated alcoholism as an affliction, but to a remarkable degree it has eliminated alcoholism as a nightmare.[1]

Because of the controversy surrounding alcohol in the 1930s, AA, like the nascent Center for Alcohol Studies at Yale, refused to address Prohibition or drinking within the population generally. Instead, it attended to the small population of problem drinkers. Much of AA's success can be attributed to its canny reading of American attitudes toward drink from the 1930s through today. For members of AA, alcohol abuse is a personal problem—possibly genetic, certainly cultural, but in no way an issue that requires controlling the majority of Americans capable of drinking "moderately." Even Mothers Against Drunk Driving (MADD) takes care to distance itself from its temperance forebears. While successfully using the gendered and emotional imagery of the WCTU, MADD is careful to stress that it does not oppose drinking per se, only irresponsible drinking. For these reasons, America's temperance activists have distrusted and loathed the postwar antialcoholism movement. Traditional temperance groups offered the only formal opposition to Alcoholics Anonymous. As late as the 1970s, the WCTU criticized the National Institute for Alcoholism and Alcohol Abuse for focusing on "moderation and rehabilitation rather than prevention."[2]

So, beyond a curmudgeonly dry press and murmuring agreement on the dangers of drunk driving, Americans faced few inquiries into their social drinking, which increasingly came to mean drinking at home. Beer, which before Prohibition was sold mainly by the glass in saloons, now appeared bottled on supermarket shelves for transport and consumption elsewhere. By the mid-1960s, two-thirds of all alcohol was drunk in homes and private clubs rather than restaurants, public bars, or night clubs. Advertisers stressed "duet drinking," evening cocktails shared by husband and wife. Cocktails and cocktail parties had a prominent place in postwar domestic advice literature. Carolyn Coggins gave them a whole chapter, "More Fun Than Food," in her 1952 *Successful Entertaining at Home.* Prohibition reduced alcohol consumption—not until the late 1960s did per capita drinking match that of the decade preceding federal prohibition, and since the 1980s it has declined again. But etiquette writers emphasized the new dangers of at-home drinking, stressing with disturbing repetition that hosts should not force drinks on unwilling or intoxicated guests. Others praised drinkers' newfound manners: "Gone," wrote James Mayabb in 1962, "are the inebriates who made passes at our wives, burned our walnut tables, and swilled without tasting our second-best liquors."[3] Such praise reappears across the decades, indicating that Americans were ever improving—or ever optimistic.

Given such cultural ambivalence over drink and heterosociality, women's drinking remained a delicate and inflammatory subject. If Americans now viewed male alcoholics as skid-row drunks, they saw women alcoholics as prostitutes. To its credit, AA from its beginnings strove to include women. Marty Mann, one of AA's first female members, began public education campaigns in large part to address problem drinking among women, founding the National Committee for Education on Alcoholism in 1944. From the 1940s through the 1960s, treatment providers within both AA and the psychiatric professions stressed the plight of the female alcohol. Women drank alone, making identification of their problem more difficult, and were harder to help once admitted to treatment.

Discussion of matronly closet drinkers and unsympathetic professionals had at times an eerily Victorian quality. Under the guise of controlling prostitution, states from Connecticut to Washington legislated that women could not drink at the bar but only at tables. Other states banned women from serving alcohol. Until 1958, the Distilled Spirits Council of the United States prohibited images of women in hard-liquor advertisements in order to avoid controversy.[4] Yet throughout this period the proportion of female alcoholics—as measured by the sex ratio of alcoholics admitted to hospitals—remained remarkably stable. In 1947, E. M. Jellinek declared that the ratio of men to women alcoholics was six to one, and the formula soon rigidified into doctrine. Only since the late 1970s has this ratio narrowed. This increase is unquestionably alarming. But it is equally important to point out that women, whose employment patterns and life crises now almost parallel men's, continue to drink much less.[5]

Indeed, analyses and critiques of drinking continue to overlook the vast population of moderate drinkers. Today, approximately 7 percent of the American population drinks abusively. One-third of adults abstain, a figure that has remained remarkably stable in the past thirty years. Roughly two-thirds of Americans use alcohol in moderation. Alcohol scholars have long been loathe to quantify (and thus implicitly endorse) moderate drinking. This attitude has melded with the modern prudery surrounding diet and behavior to keep moderate drinking cloaked in mystery and suspicion. Yet clearly these unsung moderate drinkers hold a critical position in American history, determining the fate of laws and social practices. This oversight particularly affects women, who since at least the 1920s have served as an essential element in the modification and control of male drinking.[6]

The historic connection between drink and masculinity, while still present, has blessedly eased. But another population uses alcohol just as dangerously. The abusive drinking of underage and legal-age Americans in many ways parallels men's abusive drinking in the nineteenth century. Just as males historically have used drinking to define their manhood, these drinkers use alcohol to define their adulthood. While women make up a third of AA membership, the number of younger women and men alcoholics is almost equal.[7] This parity seems to stem not from gender anxiety but from a desperate search by teens and twenty-somethings for some mantle of adult identity, however contrived or destructive it might be. On the positive side, young-adult drinking does not appear to determine lifetime drinking patterns. Women and men over the past several generations have drunk more in their twenties and early thirties than in their forties and fifties. The heavy drinking of young adults today need not be a sign of incipient national alcoholism. On the other hand, the volume consumed in and of itself is worrisome, not to mention the destructive behavior (rape, violence, accidents, suicides) that often accompanies abusive drinking. Recent crusades against drunk driving have succeeded admirably in reducing highway deaths. The crusades imply, however, that abusive drinking is fine so long as the drinker does not operate heavy equipment. Whether campaigns promoting general moderation or abstinence would succeed with high school and collegiate populations remains open to question. Lingering misinterpretation of federal prohibition has done much to undermine the possibility of such a movement.

° ° ° NOTES

INTRODUCTION

1. "Says Women Wets Only Wish to Drink," *New York Times,* 23 May 1932, 8; "We Wonder!" *Union Signal* 55 (1 June 1929): 8.

2. Mark Lender, "Women Alcoholics: Prevalence Estimates and Their Problems as Reflected in Turn-of-the-Century Institutional Data," *International Journal of the Addictions* 16 (1981); Kaye M. Fillmore, "'When Angels Fall': Women's Drinking as Cultural Preoccupation and as Reality," in *Alcohol Problems in Women: Antecedents, Consequences, and Intervention,* ed. Sharon C. Wilsnack and Linda J. Beckman (New York: Guilford, 1984), 8; Cheryl Krasnick Warsh, "'Oh, Lord, Pour a Cordial in Her Wounded Heart': The Alcoholic Woman in Victorian and Edwardian Canada," in *Drink in Canada: Historical Essays,* ed. Cheryl K. Warsh (Montreal: McGill-Queen's University Press, 1993), 76.

3. Earnest H. Cherrington, *Anti-Saloon League Year Book* (Westerville, Ohio: American Issue Press, 1920), 166, passim; Mark E. Lender and James K. Martin, *Drinking in America: A History,* rev. ed. (New York: Free Press, 1987), 129.

CHAPTER ONE: GENDER, PROHIBITION, SUFFRAGE, AND POWER

1. Franklin quoted in Daughters of the American Revolution, *A Book of Beverages* (Boston: Merrymount, 1904).

2. Richard James Hooker, *Food and Drink in America: A History* (New York: Bobbs-Merrill, 1981), 136, 131, passim; Mark E. Lender and James K. Martin, *Drinking in America: A History,* rev. ed. (New York: Free Press, 1987), chs. 1 and 2; Norman H. Clark, *Deliver Us from Evil: An Interpretation of American Prohibition* (New York: Norton, 1976), 8, passim. *Whisky* generally refers to Scotch, *whiskey* to Irish or New World liquor. See *The Compact Edition of the Oxford English Dictionary,* s.v. "whiskey" and "whisky."

3. Hofstadter is cited, for example, in Ian Tyrrell, "Temperance and Economic Change in the Antebellum North," in *Alcohol, Reform, and Society: The Liquor Issue in Social Context,* ed. Jack S. Blocker Jr. (Westport, Conn.: Greenwood, 1979), 46; Harry Gene Levine, "The Discovery of Addiction: Changing

Conceptions of Habitual Drunkenness in America," *Journal of Studies on Alcohol* 39 (1978): 159; Jack S. Blocker Jr., *American Temperance Movements: Cycles of Reform* (Boston: Twayne, 1989), 69. See Richard W. Leeman, *"Do Everything" Reform: The Oratory of Frances E. Willard* (New York: Greenwood, 1992), 26–27, for Frances Willard's views on immigrants.

4. Tyrrell, "Temperance," 47; Levine, "Discovery," 165; Joan L. Silverman, "I'll Never Touch Another Drop: Images of Alcoholism and Temperance in American Popular Culture, 1874–1919" (Ph.D. diss., New York University, 1979), 1; Harry G. Levine and Craig Reinarman, "From Prohibition to Regulation: Lessons from Alcohol Policy for Drug Policy," *Milbank Quarterly* 69 (1991): 462.

5. Perry Duis, *The Saloon: Public Drinking in Chicago and Boston, 1880–1920* (Urbana: University of Illinois Press, 1983), passim; Nuala McGann Drescher, "The Opposition to Prohibition, 1900–1919: A Social and Institutional Study" (Ph.D. diss., University of Delaware, 1964), 8; Andrew Sinclair, *Era of Excess: A Social History of the Prohibition Movement* (New York: Harper Colophon Books, 1964), 76–79; Clark, *Deliver Us,* 45.

6. Leonard Ellis, "Men among Men: An Exploration of All-Male Relationships in Victorian America" (Ph.D. diss., Columbia University, 1982), 133–38; Madelon Powers, "Decay from Within: The Inevitable Doom of the American Saloon," in *Drinking: Behavior and Belief in Modern History,* ed. Susanna Barrows and Robin Room (Berkeley: University of California Press, 1991).

7. Ellis, "Men among Men," 329–57; Patricia Marks, *Bicycles, Bangs, and Bloomers: The New Woman in the Popular Press* (Lexington: University Press of Kentucky, 1990), 127.

8. Robert E. Popham, "The Social History of the Tavern," in *Research Advances in Alcohol and Drug Problems,* vol. 4, ed. Yedi Israel, Frank B. Glaser, Harold Kalant, Robert E. Popham, Wolfgang Schmitt, and Reginald G. Smart (New York: Plenum, 1978), 286; Duis, *The Saloon,* 211; Mark C. Carnes, *Secret Ritual and Manhood in Victorian America* (New Haven: Yale University Press, 1989), 162, passim; Kathy Peiss, *Cheap Amusements: Working Women and Leisure in New York City, 1880 to 1920* (Philadelphia: Temple University Press, 1985), 19; Herbert Asbury, *Carry Nation* (New York: Knopf, 1929), xii, 31.

9. London quoted in Thomas Schlereth, *Victorian America: Transformations in Everyday Life, 1876–1915* (New York: HarperCollins, 1991), 228; Travis Hoke, "The Corner Saloon," *American Mercury,* Mar. 1931, 311, 315; Roy Rosenzweig, *Eight Hours for What We Will: Workers and Leisure in an Industrial City, 1870–1920* (New York: Cambridge University Press, 1983), 106; Jodi Vandenberg-Daves, "The Manly Pursuit of a Partnership between the Sexes: The Debate over YMCA Programs for Women and Girls, 1914–1933," *Journal of American History* 78 (1992): 1325.

10. Robert S. Lynd and Helen Merrell Lynd, *Middletown: A Study in Modern American Culture* (1929; New York: Harcourt Brace Jovanovich, 1957), 41; Rosenzweig, *Eight Hours,* 38–40, 62; Ellis, "Men among Men," 128. In comparison, drunkenness and driving under the influence made up only 15.3 percent of Massachusetts arrests in 1991 and 1992; see *Uniform Crime Reports of the United States: 1992* (Washington, D.C.: U.S. Government Printing Office, 1992), 276.

11. Jack S. Blocker Jr., *"Give to the Wind Thy Fears": The Women's Temperance Crusade, 1873–1874* (Westport, Conn.: Greenwood, 1985), 64; Peter N. Stearns, *Be A Man! Males in Modern Society,* 2d ed. (New York: Holmes and Meier, 1990), esp. 51–71; Thorstein Veblen, *Theory of the Leisure Class: An Economic Study of Institutions* (1899; New York: Modern Library, 1934), 70; *New York Times* quoted in William R. Leach, "Transformations in a Culture of Consumption: Women and Department Stores, 1890–1925," *Journal of American History* 71 (1984): 333; Henry Seidel Canby, *The Age of Confidence: Life in the Nineties* (New York: Farrar and Rinehart, 1934), esp. 46, 118, 210.

12. E. Anthony Rotundo, *American Manhood: Transformations in Masculinity from the Revolution to the Modern Era* (New York: Basic Books, 1993), 180; Stearns, *Be a Man!,* 152–53, 129; George M. Beard, *American Nervousness: Its Causes and Consequences* (1881; New York: Arno, 1972), 33, 31. On terms, see Mark Keller and Masiri McCormick, *A Dictionary of Words about Alcohol,* 2d ed. (New Brunswick, N.J.: Rutgers Center for Alcohol Studies, 1982), 143; *Standard Encyclopedia of the Alcohol Problem* (Westerville, Ohio: American Issue Press, 1925–1930), s.v. "alcoholism" and "inebriety."

13. Harry G. Levine, "Demon of the Middle Class: Self-Control, Liquor, and the Ideology of Temperance in Nineteenth-Century America" (Ph.D. diss., University of California, Berkeley, 1978), 79; Canby, *Age of Confidence,* 168–69; "Can Moderate Drinkers Be Called Inebriates?" *Quarterly Journal of Inebriety* 20 (1898): 445–46; Robert Griswold, "Divorce and the Legal Definition of Victorian Manhood," in *Meanings for Manhood: Constructions of Masculinity in Victorian America,* ed. Mark C. Carnes and Clyde Griffen (Chicago: University of Chicago Press, 1990), 99–100, 103–4.

14. George Packard, *An Address Delivered before the Female Temperance Society of Saco and Biddeford, June 17, 1838* (Saco, Maine: S. and C. Webster, 1839), 10; Ruth Rosen, *The Lost Sisterhood: Prostitution in America, 1900–1918* (Baltimore: Johns Hopkins University Press, 1982), 39; Larry Engelmann, *Intemperance: The Lost War against Liquor* (New York: Free Press, 1979), 9; Barbara Leslie Epstein, *The Politics of Domesticity: Women, Evangelism, and Temperance in Nineteenth-Century America* (Middletown: Wesleyan University Press, 1981), 90, 104.

15. Ian Tyrrell, "Women and Temperance in Antebellum America, 1830–1860," *Civil War History* 28 (1982): 131; Jed Dannenbaum, "The Origins

of Temperance Activism and Militancy among American Women," *Journal of Social History* 15 (1981): 237.

16. H. H. Weld, "Women and Temperance," *American Temperance Magazine* 2 (1851): 249; Mary Ryan, *Cradle of the Middle Class: The Family in Oneida County, New York, 1780–1865* (New York: Cambridge University Press, 1981), 140; Timothy Shay Arthur, *Ten Nights in a Bar-room, And What I Saw There*, ed. Donald A. Koch (1854; Cambridge: Harvard University Press, 1964). *Ten Nights* had sold a million copies by 1900 and was still in print in 1925 (lxiii).

17. Harry Gene Levine, "Temperance and Women in Nineteenth-Century United States," in *Alcohol and Drug Problems in Women*, vol. 5 of *Research Advances in Alcohol and Drug Problems,* ed. Oriana J. Kalant (New York: Plenum, 1980); Elizabeth Cady Stanton, Susan B. Anthony, and Matilda Joslyn Gage, eds., *History of Woman Suffrage* (New York: Fowler and Wells, 1881), 1:512–13; Blocker, *"Give to the Wind Thy Fears,"* 4, 24, passim; John Kobler, *Ardent Spirits: The Rise and Fall of Prohibition* (New York: G. P. Putnam's Sons, 1973), 130.

18. Tyrrell, "Women and Temperance," 144; Eliza D. Stewart, *Memories of the Crusade; A Thrilling Account of the Great Uprising of the Women of Ohio in 1873 against the Liquor Crime* (1889; New York: Arno, 1972), 351, 397; Blocker, *"Give to the Wind,"* 181 ff., 231.

19. David Leigh Colvin, *Prohibition in the United States: A History of the Prohibition Party and the Prohibition Movement* (New York: George H. Doran, 1926); K. Austin Kerr, *Organized for Prohibition: A New History of the Anti-Saloon League* (New Haven: Yale University Press, 1985); Clarence N. Roberts, "The Illinois Intercollegiate Prohibition Association, 1893–1920," *Journal of the Illinois State Historical Society* 70 (1977): 140, 144. Bitter Republicans quipped that the Prohibition Party prohibited only Republican victories.

20. Blocker, *"Give to the Wind,"* 227 ff.; Kerr, *Organized for Prohibition,* 45; Steven Buechler, *Transformation of the Woman Suffrage Movement: The Case of Illinois, 1850–1920* (New Brunswick: Rutgers University Press, 1986), 5; Levine, "Demon," 221.

21. Ruth Bordin, *Woman and Temperance: The Quest for Power and Liberty, 1873–1900* (New Brunswick: Rutgers University Press, 1990), xxv, 3–4, passim.

22. Hooker, *Food and Drink,* 328; Judith B. Erickson, "Making King Alcohol Tremble: The Juvenile Work of the Woman's Christian Temperance Union, 1874–1900," *Journal of Drug Education* 18 (1988): 341 ff.; Estelle Bedell, "Home Hygiene," *Union Signal* 13 (13 Oct. 1887); Harvey Levenstein, *Revolution at the Table: The Transformation of the American Diet* (New York: Oxford University Press, 1988), 49, 103; Epstein, *Politics of Domesticity,* 127–28; Inez Haynes Irwin, *Angels and Amazons: A Hundred Years of American Women*

(1933; New York: Arno, 1974), 328. Leeman reprints Willard's "White Life for Two" speech in *"Do Everything" Reform.*

23. Norton Mezvinsky, "Scientific Temperance Instruction in the Schools," *History of Education Quarterly* 1 (1961): 48 ff.; Philip J. Pauly, "The Struggle for Ignorance about Alcohol: American Physiologists, Wilbur Olin Atwater, and the Woman's Christian Temperance Union," *Bulletin of the History of Medicine* 64 (1990): 371, passim; Colvin, *Prohibition in the United States,* 291. Mark Sullivan, *America Finding Herself,* vol. 2 of *Our Times: The United States, 1900–1925* (New York: Charles Scribner's Sons, 1927–33), 471–53, describes how tinted WCTU diagrams of the human digestive system contributed to the later outcry over artificial coloring: people already knew (they thought) how their innards looked and objected to their being dyed. Thus passed the 1906 Pure Food Act.

24. F. M. Whitaker, "Ohio WCTU and the Prohibition Amendment Campaign of 1883," *Ohio History* 83 (1974): 93 ff.; Frances E. Willard, *Woman and Temperance: or, The Work and Workers of the Woman's Christian Temperance Union* (1883; New York: Arno, 1972), 32–33; Bordin, *Woman,* xiv, 123 ff.

25. Emily Apt Geer, *First Lady: The Life of Lucy Webb Hayes* (Kent: Kent State University Press, 1984), esp. ch. 15.

26. Edward T. James, ed., *Notable American Women, 1607–1950: A Biographical Dictionary* (Cambridge, Mass.: Belknap, 1971), s.v. "Nation, Carry Amelia Moore"; Mark E. Lender, *Dictionary of American Temperance Biography: From Temperance Reform to Alcohol Research, the 1660s to the 1980s* (Westport, Conn.: Greenwood, 1984), 361–62; Robert Day, "Carry from Kansas Became a Nation All unto Herself," *Smithsonian* 20 (Apr. 1989). See also Henry Smith Williams, *Alcohol: How It Affects the Individual, the Community, and the Race* (New York: Century, 1909), 50, on eugenics.

27. Duis, *The Saloon,* 188, 211 ff.; Ray Hutchinson, "Capitalism, Religion, and Reform: The Social History of Temperance in Harvey, Illinois," in *Drinking: Behavior and Belief in Modern History,* ed. Susanna Barrows and Robin Room (Berkeley: University of California Press, 1991), 184.

28. Regina Morantz, "Making Women Modern: Middle-Class Women and Health Reform in Nineteenth-Century America," *Journal of Social History* 10 (1977): 501; Frances Willard, "Annual Address," *Union Signal* 16 (27 Nov. 1890): 7; *History of the Pennsylvania Woman's Christian Temperance Union* (Quincy, Pa.: Quincy Orphanage Press, 1937), 299.

29. Arthur, *Ten Nights,* 154, 168, 170.

30. James Shaw, *History of the Great Temperance Reforms of the Nineteenth Century* (Cincinnati: Hitchcock and Walden, 1875), 262; Packard, *An Address,* 7; Stewart, *Memories of the Crusade,* 310; letter to editor, *Union Signal* 13 (21 July 1887): 7.

31. Levine, "Temperance and Women," 47–48; Tyrrell, "Women and Temperance," 149–51.

32. Levine, "Temperance and Women," 48; "Women's State Temperance Convention," newspaper clipping, ca. 1850, "Temperance" folder, National American Woman Suffrage Association (NAWSA) papers, Library of Congress, Washington, D.C.

33. Ellen DuBois, "The Radicalism of the Woman Suffrage Movement: Notes toward the Reconstruction of Nineteenth-Century Feminism," *Feminist Studies* 3 (1975): 64–67; Stewart, *Memories of the Crusade,* 404.

34. Janet Zollinger Giele, "Social Change and the Feminine Role: A Comparison of Woman's Suffrage and Woman's Temperance, 1870–1920" (Ph.D. diss., Radcliffe College, 1961), 87; Frances E. Willard, *Home Protection Manual, Containing an Argument for the Temperance Ballot for Woman and How to Obtain It as a Means of Home Protection* (New York: *Independent* Office, 1879), 4.

35. Willard, *Woman and Temperance,* 32; Mrs. C. S. Burnett, "Women in Politics," *Union Signal* 9 (5 July 1883): 3; Levine, "Temperance and Women," 42–43.

36. Levine, "Temperance and Women," passim; Dolores Hayden, *The Grand Domestic Revolution: A History of Feminist Designs for American Homes, Neighborhoods, and Cities* (Cambridge: MIT Press, 1981), 118; "Shaw, Anna Howard" folder, NAWSA papers; Carrie Chapman Catt, one-page typewritten manuscript, ca. 1920, "Temperance" folder, NAWSA papers; Elizabeth P. Gordon, *Women Torchbearers: The Story of the Woman's Christian Temperance Union* (Chicago: National Woman's Christian Temperance Union Publishing House, 1924), 187; Aileen Kraditor, *The Ideas of the Woman Suffrage Movement, 1890–1920* (1965; New York: Norton, 1981), 264–82; Naomi Rosenthal, Roberta Karant, Michele Ethier, and Meryl Fingrutd, "Centrality Analysis for Historians," *Historical Methods* 20 (1987): 61, passim.

37. Ross Evans Paulson, *Women's Suffrage and Prohibition: A Study in Equality and Social Control* (Glenview, Ill.: Scott, Foresman, 1973), 114; Kerr, *Organized for Prohibition,* 66 ff., 158–59; Peter Odegard, *Pressure Politics: The Story of the Anti-Saloon League* (New York: Columbia University Press, 1928), 85.

38. Susan Marshall, "In Defense of Separate Spheres: Class and Status Politics in the Antisuffrage Movement," *Social Forces* 65 (1986): 340; William O'Neill, *Everyone Was Brave: A History of Feminism in America,* rev. ed. (Chicago: Quadrangle Books, 1971), 54; Emma Goldman, *Living My Life* (1931; Salt Lake City: Peregrine Smith, 1982), 238–39.

39. Quoted in Alice Stone Blackwell, "Twelve Reasons Why Women Want to Vote," *Union Signal* 16 (19 June 1890): 3; "A Word to the Wise Should be Sufficient!" Sept. 1914, "Temperance" folder, NAWSA papers; Adolph Keitel, "To the Consumer of Malt," 2-page broadside, ca. 1915, "Prohibition and Suf-

frage" folder, NAWSA papers; Drescher, "Opposition," 52, passim; Jane Jerome Camhi, "Women against Women: American Antisuffragism, 1880–1920" (Ph.D. diss., Tufts University, 1973), 202; Carrie Chapman Catt and Nettie Rogers Shuler, *Woman Suffrage and Politics: The Inner Story of the Suffrage Movement* (1923; Seattle: University of Washington Press, 1970), 258, 304, 195, passim.

40. Catt and Shuler, *Woman Suffrage and Politics,* 133, 111, 118, 124–25, 143; National American Woman Suffrage Association, *Victory—How Women Won It: A Centennial Symposium, 1840–1940* (New York: H. W. Wilson, 1940), 89; *Liquor versus Suffrage* (Boston: Woman's Journal, 1913); *Woman Suffrage and the Liquor Interests: Some Exhibits* (New York: National American Woman Suffrage Publishing Company, 1916); Duis, *The Saloon,* 282.

41. Clark, *Deliver Us,* 116–17; "Brewing Propaganda," *New Republic* 4 (21 Aug. 1915): 62–64; Senate Committee on the Judiciary, *Brewing and Liquor Interests and German and Bolshevik Propaganda* (Washington, D.C.: Government Printing Office, 1919); Catt and Shuler, *Woman Suffrage and Politics,* 135, 159, 203, 413, 273, passim; 7.

42. "Hugh F. Fox, of this City, Refutes a Statement Credited to Miss Inez Milholland about Suffrage," *Plainfield (N.J.) Courier-News,* 19 May 1913, "Anti-Suffrage Literature" folder, NAWSA papers; Drescher, "Opposition," 19, passim; Kerr, *Organized for Prohibition,* 26, 32, 161; Gilman Ostrander, *The Prohibition Movement in California, 1848–1933* (Berkeley: University of California Press, 1957), 98, passim; Herbert Asbury, *Carry Nation* (New York: Knopf, 1929), 111.

43. Ella Stewart, "Woman Suffrage and the Liquor Traffic," *Annals of the American Academy of Political and Social Science* 56 (1914): 144; John W. Furlow Jr., "Cornelia Bryce Pinchot: Feminism in the Post-Suffrage Era," *Pennsylvania History* 43 (1976): 341 (the quotation is from a 1925 speech to the New York Woman's Committee for Law Enforcement).

44. Abigail Scott Duniway, *Path Breaking: An Autobiographical History of the Equal Suffrage Movement in Pacific Coast States,* 2d ed. (New York: Schocken, 1971), 205, 113, 143, passim; Kraditor, *Ideas,* 172; Anna Howard Shaw, "Equal Suffrage: A Problem of Political Justice," *Annals of the American Academy of Political and Social Science* 56 (1914): 97; Carrie C. Catt, "The Suffrage Platform," *Woman's Journal* 46 (12 June 1915): 184.

45. Bordin, *Woman,* xv; Giele, "Social Change," 91; Mrs. Dorcas James Spencer, *A History of the Woman's Christian Temperance Union of Northern and Central California* (Oakland, Cal.: West Coast Printing, 1911), 66; B. Sturtevant-Post to Frances E. Willard, 25 January 1896, Frances E. Willard (FEW) correspondence, Woman's Christian Temperance Union microfilm edition, Woman's Christian Temperance Union series, Ohio Historical Society-Michigan Historical Collections; Susan B. Anthony to Frances E. Willard,

23 January 1896, FEW correspondence; Sarah B. Cooper to Frances E. Willard, 25 March 1896, FEW correspondence; Anna M. Hammer to Frances E. Willard, 27 March 1896, FEW correspondence; Lillian M. N. Stevens to Frances E. Willard, 31 January 1896, FEW correspondence; Rheta Childe Dorr, *Susan B. Anthony* (New York: Frederick A. Stokes, 1928), 318.

46. Catt and Shuler, *Woman Suffrage and Politics,* 274–77; L. Ames Brown, "Suffrage and Prohibition," *North American Review* 203 (1916): 94.

47. "Shall State Rights Block Women's after This?" *Woman's Journal* 46 (2 Jan. 1915): 11; Ernest Barron Gordon, *When the Brewer Had the Stranglehold* (New York: Alcohol Information Committee, 1930), 92–93; Frank Foxcroft, "Objections to License Suffrage from a No-License Point of View," address, 1898, "Anti-Suffrage Literature" folder, NAWSA papers; Alice Stone Blackwell, *Suffrage and Temperance* (Boston: Woman's Journal, ca. 1912), 4. The South did not oppose woman suffrage per se: Arkansas granted women the right to vote in primaries (equivalent to full suffrage in a two-party state) in 1917, and Missouri, Tennessee, and Kentucky granted presidential suffrage in 1919 and 1920: Catt and Shuler, *Woman Suffrage and Politics,* 299, 329, 340.

48. Susan E. Marshall, "Ladies against Women: Mobilization Dilemmas of Antifeminist Movements," *Social Problems* 32 (1985): 349, 352; O'Neill, *Everyone,* 57–62; J. A. Haien, comp., *Anti-Suffrage Essays by Massachusetts Women,* intro. Earnest Bernbaum (Boston: Forum Publications, 1916), 98 ff., passim.

49. Priscilla Leonard, *A Help or a Hindrance* (New York: New York State Association Opposed to Woman Suffrage, n.d.), 8. See Thomas J. Jablonsky, "Duty, Nature, and Stability: The Female Anti-Suffragists in the United States, 1894–1920" (Ph.D. diss., University of California, Los Angeles, 1978), 7–8, on suffragists' dismissal of their women opponents.

50. Catt and Shuler, *Woman Suffrage and Politics,* 154; Mrs. Clarence Hale, *Against Woman Suffrage: Maine Women Do Not Want the Vote* (n.p.: Maine Association Opposed to Suffrage to Women, 1916), 8.

51. Alice Stone Blackwell, *The Bubble Pricked: A Reply to "The Case against Woman Suffrage"* (Boston: Woman's Journal, 1916), 35; Ida Husted Harper, "A Brief History of Woman Suffrage in the United States," in *Woman Suffrage: History, Arguments, and Results,* ed. Frances Maule Björkman (New York: National American Woman Suffrage Association, 1913), 32–33; Rosen, *Lost Sisterhood,* 52; Hale, *Against Woman Suffrage,* 8; Margaret C. Robinson, "Against Woman Suffrage," *Zion's Herald* (20 Oct. 1915): 1332; *Some Facts about California's Experiment with Woman Suffrage* (New York: National Association Opposed to Woman Suffrage, ca. 1913), 4–6; Mrs. George A. Caswell, *Address in Opposition to Woman Suffrage* (Boston: Massachusetts Association Opposed to the Further Extension of Suffrage to Women, n.d.), 12.

52. Clark, *Deliver Us,* 127; Paul Aaron and David Musto, "Temperance and Prohibition in America: A Historical Overview," in *Alcohol and Public Policy:*

Beyond the Shadow of Prohibition, ed. M. H. Moore and D. R. Gerstein (Washington, D.C.: National Academy Press, 1981), 156.

53. Clark, *Deliver Us,* 105; Helen L. Sumner, *Equal Suffrage: The Results of an Investigation in Colorado Made for the Collegiate Equal Suffrage League of New York State* (New York: Harper and Brothers, 1909), 208. For more information on woman suffrage and prohibition states, see Gordon, *Women Torchbearers,* 158–59; Odegard, *Pressure Politics,* 86.

54. William F. Ogburn and Inez Goltra, "How Women Vote," *Political Science Quarterly* 34 (1919): 416; Stuart A. Rice and Malcolm M. Willey, "American Women's Ineffective Use of the Vote," *Current History* 20 (1924): 641–47; John E. Caswell, "The Prohibition Movement in Oregon, Part 2, 1904–1915," *Oregon Historical Quarterly* 40 (1939): 79.

55. "The Wettest State," *Collier's* 51 (12 Apr. 1913): 6; London quoted in Stewart, "Woman Suffrage," 147; William M. Bray, "Do Women Want the Vote?" *Atlantic Monthly* 117 (1916): 441.

56. Giele, "Social Change," 184; Buechler, *Transformation,* 179–80.

57. John J. Rumbarger, *Profits, Power, and Prohibition: Alcohol Reform and the Industrialization of America, 1800–1930* (Albany: State University of New York Press, 1989), 184; O'Neill, *Everyone,* 123, 167.

58. Ida Husted Harper, "The Cause of Woman: The Real Relation between Suffragists and Prohibitionists," *New York Sun,* 7 July 1901, 3; Kraditor, *Ideas,* 58–59; *Case against Woman Suffrage* (Boston: Massachusetts Anti-Suffrage Committee, 1915); *Woman Suffrage and the Liquor Question: Facts Show Women's Votes Have NOT Aided Prohibition* (New York: Women's Anti-Suffrage Association, 1915), 4.

59. That is, women in fewer than a quarter of the states voted for national legislators, and in fewer than a third for state legislators, who ratified the amendment. Odegard, *Pressure Politics,* 86; Charles Merz, *The Dry Decade* (1931; Seattle: University of Washington Press, 1969), 18.

60. Stewart, *Memories of the Crusade,* 414; Mary A. Livermore, 1886, quoted in Hayden, *Domestic Revolution,* 127.

61. Catt and Shuler, *Woman Suffrage and Politics,* 422; Katherine Harris, "A Study of Feminine and Class Identity in the Woman's Christian Temperance Union, 1920–1979: A Case Study," *Historicus* 2, no. 2 (1981): 57.

62. T. A. Larson, "Woman Suffrage in Wyoming," *Pacific Northwest Quarterly* 56 (1965): 62; Kay Sloan, "Sexual Warfare in the Silent Cinema: Comedies and Melodramas of Woman Suffragism," *American Quarterly* 33 (1981): 419. The journalist Anne O'Hare McCormick reported that following woman suffrage, the only "safely masculine sport" left was "looking for new polar lands." Kristi Andersen, "Women and Citizenship in the 1920s," in *Women, Politics, and Change in Twentieth-Century America,* ed. Louise A. Tilly and Patricia Gurin (New York: Russell Sage Foundation, 1990), 184.

1. J. Edward Turner, *The History of the First Inebriate Asylum in the World* (New York: privately printed, 1888), 490; Cheryl Krasnick Warsh, "'Oh, Lord, Pour a Cordial in Her Wounded Heart': The Alcoholic Woman in Victorian and Edwardian Canada," in *Drink in Canada: Historical Essays,* ed. Cheryl K. Warsh (Montreal: McGill-Queen's University Press, 1993), 81 ff.; Charles L. Dana, "A Study of Alcoholism As It Occurs in the Bellevue Hospital Cells," *New York Medical Journal* 51 (1890): 647; Ruth M. Alexander, "We Are Engaged as a Band of Sisters: Class and Domesticity in the Washingtonian Temperance Movement, 1840–1850," *Journal of American History* 75 (1988): 780. Prostitutes' drinking at times takes on the quality of an urban legend in the writings of the period.

2. Caroline Lee Hentz, "A Victim of Excitement," in *Love after Marriage; and Other Stories of the Heart* (Philadelphia: T. B. Peterson and Brothers, 1870); H. H. Weld, "Women and Temperance," *American Temperance Magazine* 2 (1851): 245; "The Moderate Drinker of To-day," *Union Signal* 19 (3 Mar. 1893): 1; Mrs. Martha Meir Allen, *Alcohol: A Dangerous and Unnecessary Medicine* (Marcellus, N.Y.: Department of Medical Temperance of the National Woman's Christian Temperance Union, 1900), 417–18. My thanks to Michelle McClellan for the Hentz story.

3. "Female Drinking; or, The Social Gehenna," in *Temperance Tracts* (New York: National Temperance Society and Publication House, 1874), 1:1; Mrs. John Farrar, *The Young Lady's Friend* (1836; New York: Arno, 1974), 194; Allen, *Alcohol,* 162 f., 430, passim.

4. Harriet Martineau, *Society in America,* 3 vols. (London: Sander and Otley, 1837), 1:159–60; "A Mother's Work," in *One Thousand Temperance Anecdotes,* collected and edited by John William Kirton (New York: National Temperance Society and Publication House, ca. 1868), 310–12.

5. Jim Baumohl and Robin Room, "Inebriety, Doctors, and the State: Alcoholism Treatment Institutions before 1940," in *Recent Developments in Alcoholism,* vol. 5, ed. Marc Galanter (New York: Plenum, 1987), 167; T. A. MacNicholl, "Alcohol a Cause of Degeneracy," *Quarterly Journal of Inebriety* 24 (1902): 330–35; T. D. Crothers, "Is Alcoholism Increasing among Women?" *North American Review* 155 (1892): 733; Agnes Sparks, "Alcoholism in Women: Its Cause, Consequence, and Cure," *Quarterly Journal of Inebriety* 20 (1898): 34–36.

6. George Packard, *An Address Delivered before the Female Temperance Society of Saco and Biddeford, June 17, 1838* (Saco, Maine: S. and C. Webster, 1839), 10; Martineau, *Society in America,* 3:160; T. D. Crothers, "Sarah Chandler," *Union Signal* 16 (20 Feb. 1890): 2; "Cursed by Her Appetite," *Quarterly Journal of Inebriety* 7 (1885).

7. Jean Kinney, *Loosening the Grip: A Handbook of Alcohol Information* (St. Louis: Times Mirror, 1987), 16; Harry Gene Levine, "The Alcohol Problem in America: From Temperance to Alcoholism," *British Journal of Addiction* 74 (1984): 111–12. Crothers was something of an outsider within the medical community; other physicians at times questioned his views. He ran an inebriates' hospital in Hartford for decades, as well as managing the *Quarterly Journal of Inebriety*. See Leonard U. Blumberg, "The American Association for the Study and Cure of Inebriety," *Alcoholism: Clinical and Experimental Research* 2 (1978): 238, passim.

8. Jim Baumohl, "On Asylums, Homes, and Moral Treatment: The Case of the San Francisco Home for the Care of the Inebriate, 1849–1870," *Contemporary Drug Problems* 13 (1986): 395–96; Baumohl and Room, "Inebriety, Doctors, and the State," 155; *Fifteenth Annual Report of the Franklin Reformatory Home for Inebriates of Philadelphia* (Philadelphia: Treager and Lamb, 1887), 22, 43, 61; Sparks, "Alcoholism in Women," 34–36.

9. Mark E. Lender, *Dictionary of American Temperance Biography: From Temperance Reform to Alcohol Research, the 1660s to the 1980s* (Westport, Conn.: Greenwood, 1984), 271; Charles S. Clark, *The Perfect Keeley Cure: Incidents at Dwight and 'Through the Valley of the Shadow' into the Perfect Light* (Milwaukee: C. S. Clark, 1892), 18.

10. Alexander, "We Are Engaged," 771; Judith B. Erickson, "Making King Alcohol Tremble: The Juvenile Work of the Woman's Christian Temperance Union, 1874–1900," *Journal of Drug Education* 18 (1988): 337; Frances Willard, "Annual Address," *Union Signal* 9 (8 Nov. 1883): 6; "The Martha Washington Home," *Union Signal* 9 (5 July 1883): 2; Woman's Christian Temperance Union, *Dedication of the W.C.T.U. Mercy Home, Manchester, N.H., January 1, 1890* (Exeter, N.H.: Gazette Printing House, 1890); Woman's Christian Temperance Union of Philadelphia, *Women's Work for Women,* broadside (Philadelphia: Library Company of Philadelphia, n.d.); *Second Annual Report of the Women's Christian Temperance Union of Philadelphia* (Philadelphia: George S. Harris and Son, 1877), 6. The Philadelphia Home for Inebriate Women in 1879 was called the Franklin Reformatory Home for Women, though no association is made in its literature or that of the Franklin Reformatory Home for Inebriates between the two institutions. The women's home is not listed in the 1884 history of the city, indicating it no longer existed (John Thomas Scharf and Thompson Westcott, *History of Philadelphia, 1609–1884,* 3 vols. [Philadelphia: L. H. Everts, 1884]).

11. Turner, *History of the First,* 470–91; George M. Beard, *American Nervousness: Its Causes and Consequences* (1881; New York: Arno, 1972), 308.

12. Patricia M. Tice, *Altered States: Alcohol and Other Drugs in America* (Rochester, N.Y.: Margaret Woodbury Strong Museum, 1992), 78; H[oward] Wayne Morgan, *Drugs in America: A Social History, 1800–1980* (Syracuse:

Syracuse University Press, 1981), 38; Clark, *Perfect Keeley Cure,* 18; John Star-
rett Hughes, "The Madness of Separate Spheres: Insanity and Masculinity in

186

*Notes to
Pages 49–53*

Victorian Alabama," in *Meanings for Manhood: Constructions of Masculinity
in Victorian America,* ed. Mark C. Carnes and Clyde Griffen (Chicago: University of Chicago Press, 1990), 59.

13. Allen, *Alcohol,* 299; Crothers, "Is Alcoholism?" 734; Sparks, "Alcoholism
in Women," 36.

14. "Inebriety among Women in This Country," *Journal of the American
Medical Association* (1892), reprinted in *Journal of the American Medical Asso-
ciation* 268 (1992): 1928; physician quoted in Morgan, *Drugs in America,* 40;
John S. Haller Jr. and Robin M. Haller, *The Physician and Sexuality in Victo-
rian America* (Urbana: University of Illinois Press, 1974), 277–79; Tice, *Altered
States,* 75.

15. *Fifteenth Annual Report,* 16; Crothers, "Is Alcoholism?" 733–34; "Her
First Misstep," *Union Signal* 10 (13 Nov. 1884): 15; Lady Henry Somerset, "A
Sketch in the Sand," *Union Signal* 15 (7 Sept. 1899): 3.

16. Mark Lender, "Women Alcoholics: Prevalence Estimates and Their
Problems as Reflected in Turn-of-the-Century Institutional Data," *Interna-
tional Journal of the Addictions* 16 (1981): 443–48; Baumohl, "Asylums,
Homes," 418; Warsh, "'Oh, Lord.'"

17. Stephen Smith, *Influence and Effects of Social Drinking Usages among
Women* (New York: National Temperance Society and Publication House,
1874), 7; "In a Recent Lecture," *Union Signal* 15 (27 Apr. 1899): 16; H. Smith,
"Alcohol in Relation to Women," *Quarterly Journal of Inebriety* 23 (1901): 190;
Warsh, "'Oh, Lord.'"

18. Catharine Beecher, *Miss Beecher's Domestic Receipt Book, Designed as a
Supplement to Her Treatise on Domestic Economy,* 3d ed. (New York: Harper
and Brothers, 1856), 22; Erickson, "Making King Alcohol," 337; Annie Wittenmyer, *Collection of Recipes for the Use of Special Diet Kitchens in Military Hospitals* (St. Louis: R. P. Studley, 1864), 31–33; Edward B. Foote, *Plain Home Talk*
(New York: Murray Hill, 1876), 76 ff.; Francis E. Anstie, *On the Uses of Wines
in Health and Disease* (1870; London: Macmillan, 1877), passim; *New England
Cook Book* (Boston: Chas. E. Brown, 1905), opp. p. 256; Mary Elizabeth Sherwood, *Manners and Social Usages* (New York: Harper and Brothers, 1884),
466–67.

19. Sarah Stage, *Female Complaints: Lydia Pinkham and the Business of
Women's Medicine* (New York: Norton, 1979), 140–67, Bok quote on 32; *Montgomery Ward and Co. Catalogue and Buyers' Guide,* no. 57 (1895; New York:
Dover, 1969), 260; A. P. Grinnell, "Alcohol and Drugs," *Outlook* 74 (9 May
1903): 142; Haller and Haller, 287–88.

20. Stage, *Female Complaints,* 32; "Liquor-Selling Grocers," *Union Signal*

15 (9 Feb. 1899): 8; Perry Duis, *The Saloon: Public Drinking in Chicago and Boston, 1880–1920* (Urbana: University of Illinois Press, 1983), 223–27.

21. Mrs. H. V. Reed, "Drinking Women," *Union Signal* 13 (29 Dec. 1887): 3; liquor advertisements, Cambridge, Mass., *Chronicle* (1 Nov. 1913): 11; William R. Leach, "Transformations in a Culture of Consumption: Women and Department Stores, 1890–1925," *Journal of American History* 71 (1984): 329; Duis, *The Saloon,* 64–67, 11.

22. Herbert Asbury, *Carry Nation* (New York: Knopf, 1929), 102; Eliza D. Stewart, *Memories of the Crusade; A Thrilling Account of the Great Uprising of the Women of Ohio in 1873 against the Liquor Crime* (1889; New York: Arno, 1972), 227–28; Madelon Powers, "Decay from Within: The Inevitable Doom of the American Saloon," in *Drinking: Behavior and Belief in Modern History,* ed. Susanna Barrows and Robin Room (Berkeley: University of California Press, 1991), 115; Duis, *The Saloon,* 96, 254; Leonard Ellis, "Men among Men: An Exploration of All-Male Relationships in Victorian America" (Ph.D. diss., Columbia University, 1982), 186.

23. Laurel Thatcher Ulrich, *Good Wives: Image and Reality in the Lives of Women in Northern New England, 1650–1750* (New York: Vintage, 1991), 23; *The Compact Edition of the Oxford English Dictionary,* s.v. "Brewster"; *National Cookery Book, Compiled from Original Receipts, for the Women's Centennial Committee of the International Exhibition of 1876* (Philadelphia: Women's Centennial Executive Committee, 1876); Marion Harland, *Common Sense in the Household* (New York: Charles Scribner and Son, 1871), 491–502; Eliza Leslie, *The Ladies' Guide to True Politeness and Perfect Manners* (Philadelphia: T. B. Peterson and Brothers, 1864), 312. It is also worth noting that twentieth-century desserts such as apple pie, gingerbread, ice cream, and shortcake do not require the alcohol that trifles, sweet puddings, or Roman punch would.

24. Mary F. Henderson, *Practical Cooking and Dinner Giving* (New York: Harper and Brothers, 1876), esp. 339–46; Fannie Merritt Farmer, *Boston Cooking-School Cook Book* (Boston: Little, Brown, 1896), 522, 46; Beecher, *Domestic Receipt,* 234; Christine Terhune Herrick, ed. in chief, and Marion Harland, *The Consolidated Library of Modern Cooking and Household Recipes* (New York: R. F. Bodmer, 1905); Linda Hull Larned, *The Hostess of Today* (New York: Charles Scribner's Sons, 1899), 12; Ruth Schwartz Cowan, *More Work for Mother: The Ironies of Household Technology from the Open Hearth to the Microwave* (New York: Basic Books, 1983), 121–22.

25. John F. Kasson, "Rituals of Dinner: Table Manners in Victorian America," in *Dining in America, 1850–1900,* ed. Kathryn Grover (Rochester, N.Y.: Margaret Woodbury Strong Museum, 1987), 119; Farrar, *Young Lady's Friend,* 324–25; Hale quoted in Susan R. Williams, *Savory Suppers and Fashionable Feasts: Dining in Victorian America* (New York: Pantheon Books, 1985), 134;

Mrs. H. O. Ward (pseud. of Clara Sophia [Jessup] Bloomfield-Moore), *The Young Lady's Friend* (Philadelphia: Porter and Coates, 1880), 298 (this is very similar to Farrar's 1836 *Young Lady's Friend* and may have been a revised edition); Leslie, *Ladies' Guide,* 129–30; Mary Elizabeth Wilson Sherwood, *Art of Entertaining* (New York: Dodd, Mead, 1892), 91.

26. Sherwood, *Manners and Social Usages,* esp. 301–4; Henderson, *Practical Cooking,* 38–39; Janet Zollinger Giele, "Social Change and the Feminine Role: A Comparison of Woman's Suffrage and Woman's Temperance, 1870–1920" (Ph.D. diss., Radcliffe College, 1961), 205; Edward T. James, ed., *Notable American Women, 1607–1950: A Biographical Dictionary* (Cambridge, Mass.: Belknap, 1971), s.v. "Sewall, May Elia Wright."

27. Sherwood, *Manners and Social Usages,* 315; *The Successful Housekeeper* (Detroit: M. W. Ellsworth, 1883), 470; Larned, *Hostess of Today,* viii, "Hints to the Novice."

28. Elizabeth F. Ellet, *New Cyclopaedia of Domestic Economy* (1873), paraphrased in Williams, *Savory Suppers,* 80, 86.

29. *Montgomery Ward Catalogue,* 542, 564; *The 1902 Edition of the Sears Roebuck Catalogue,* intro. Cleveland Amory (New York: Bounty Books, 1969), 798–800, 114, 539; *Geo. D. Williams Co. Wholesale Furniture,* catalog (Chicago: Geo. D. Williams Co., 1901), 85, 94–99 (this does not list liquor cabinets by name); Williams, *Savory Suppers,* 64. On locked cabinets, see Hentz, "Victim of Excitement," 52 ff.

30. Stewart, *Memories of the Crusade,* 337–38, 426 ff. (emphasis added); James Shaw, *History of the Great Temperance Reforms of the Nineteenth Century* (Cincinnati: Hitchcock and Walden, 1875), 242; Frances E. Willard, "Editorial Correspondence," *Union Signal* 22 (28 May 1896): 4.

31. Leslie, *Ladies' Guide,* 129–30; Beecher, *Domestic Receipt,* 239–40.

32. Alexander Henry, *Woman and Intemperance, an Address . . .* (Philadelphia: Presbyterian Woman's Temperance Association, 1892), 9–11; Stewart, *Memories of the Crusade,* 463–66; Mrs. D. Bentley, "The Responsibility of Mothers in Regard to Temperance Teaching in Our Schools," *Union Signal* 13 (28 Apr. 1887): 7; Joan L. Silverman, "I'll Never Touch Another Drop: Images of Alcoholism and Temperance in American Popular Culture, 1874–1919" (Ph.D. diss., New York University, 1979), 46–49, 74.

33. Sherwood, *Manners and Social Usages,* 272, 274.

34. Sherwood quotation in Levenstein, *Revolution,* 16; Richard James Hooker, *Food and Drink in America: A History* (New York: Bobbs-Merrill, 1981), 81, 128–31; Dorothy Rainwater, "Victorian Dining Silver," in *Dining in America, 1850–1900,* ed. Kathryn Grover (Rochester, N.Y.: Margaret Woodbury Strong Museum, 1987), 200–201; Timothy Shay Arthur, *Ten Nights in a Bar-room, And What I Saw There,* ed. Donald A. Koch (1854; Cambridge: Harvard University Press, 1964), li; W. J. Rorabaugh, "Beer, Lemonade, and Propri-

ety in the Gilded Age," in *Dining in America, 1850–1900,* ed. Kathryn Grover (Rochester, N.Y.: Margaret Woodbury Strong Museum, 1987), passim.

35. Williams, *Savory Suppers,* 134; Mrs. Burton Kingsland, *Etiquette for All Occasions* (New York: Platt and Peck, 1901), 144; Marion Harland, *Dinner Year-Book* (New York: Charles Scribner's Sons, 1891); Farmer, *Boston Cooking-School* (1896); Mark E. Lender and James K. Martin, *Drinking in America: A History,* rev. ed. (New York: Free Press, 1987), 205; Merton M. Hyman, Marilyn A. Zimmermann, Carol Gurioli, and Alice Helrich, *Drink, Drinking, and Alcohol-Related Mortality and Hospitalization: A Statistical Compendium* (New Brunswick, N.J.: Rutgers Center for Alcohol Studies, 1980), iv.

36. Harry Gene Levine, "The Discovery of Addiction: Changing Conceptions of Habitual Drunkenness in America," *Journal of Studies on Alcohol* 39 (1978): 159; Louise Fiske Bryson, *Every-Day Etiquette: A Manual of Good Manners* (New York: W. D. Kerr, 1890), 83; Larned, *Hostess of Today,* 11–12; Christine Terhune Herrick, ed. in chief, and Marion Harland, *The Modern Hostess,* vol. 1 of *The Consolidated Library of Modern Cooking and Household Recipes* (New York: R. F. Bodmer, 1905), 28.

37. Martineau, *Society in America,* 3:200 ff.; Emily Apt Geer, *First Lady: The Life of Lucy Webb Hayes* (Kent: Kent State University Press, 1984), 153; Nathan D. Urner, *Never: A Hand-Book for the Uninitiated and Inexperienced Aspirants to Refined Society's Giddy Heights and Glittering Attainments* (New York: G. W. Carleton, 1883), 36–48 (emphasis in original); "The Fashionable Drinking of Other Days," *Union Signal* 58 (13 Feb. 1932): 5.

38. Hentz, "Victim of Excitement," 48; Mary E. C. Wyeth, "Florine's Happy New Year," *Union Signal* 13 (6 Jan. 1887): 4; Mrs. E. J. Archibald, "Mrs. Myrtle's Parlor-Meeting, and What Came of It," *Union Signal* 16 (4 Dec. 1890): 2; Bentley, "Responsibility," 7; "The First Glass Is a Glass Too Much," *Union Signal* 22 (1 Oct. 1896): 8.

39. Temperance newspaper quoted in Jed Dannenbaum, "The Origins of Temperance Activism and Militancy among American Women," *Journal of Social History* 15 (1981): 244–45; Helen Saunders Smith Wright, *Old-Time Recipes for Home Made Wines, Cordials, and Liqueurs from Fruits, Flowers, Vegetables, and Shrubs* (Boston: Dana Estes, 1909), 12; Sherwood, *Art of Entertaining,* 91.

40. Kenneth L. Ames, *Death in the Dining Room and Other Tales of Victorian Culture* (Philadelphia: Temple University Press, 1992); Williams, *Savory Suppers,* 31, 46; Edgar de N. Mayhew and Minor Myers, *A Documentary History of American Interiors* (New York: Scribner's, 1980), 325.

41. Henderson, *Practical Cooking,* 346; Sherwood, *Manners and Social Usages,* 315; Larned, *Hostess of Today,* 11–12; Herrick and Harland, *Modern Hostess,* 28.

42. "We Have Preached," *Union Signal* 25 (5 Jan. 1899): 9; temperance

newspaper quoted in *The Report of the Women's National Commission for Law Enforcement and Law Observance* (Cambridge, Mass.: Woman's National Committee for Law Enforcement, 1931), 23; Mark E. Lender, "A Special Stigma: The Origins of Attitudes toward Women Alcoholics," in *Alcohol Interventions: Historical and Sociocultural Approaches,* ed. David L. Strug, S. Priyadarsini, and Merton M. Hyman (New York: Hawthorn, 1981), 49; Faye Huntington, "Mrs. Mannering's 'Why,'" *Union Signal* 19 (6 July 1893): 2.

43. Joseph R. Gusfield, "Social Structure and Moral Reform: A Study of the WCTU," in *Drinking and Intoxication: Selected Readings in Social Attitude and Controls,* ed. Raymond G. McCarthy and Edgar M. Douglass (New Haven: College and University Press, 1959), 403–4, passim; Harry G. Levine, "Demon of the Middle Class: Self-Control, Liquor, and the Ideology of Temperance in Nineteenth-Century America" (Ph.D. diss., University of California, Berkeley, 1978), passim.

44. Jack S. Blocker Jr., *American Temperance Movements: Cycles of Reform* (Boston: Twayne, 1989), 66; Beard, *American Nervousness,* 305.

45. M. E. J. Kelley, "Women and the Drink Problem," *Catholic World* 69 (1899): 678–87, passim.

46. Kelley, "Women and the Drink," 685; Grace Robinson, "Women Wets," *Liberty* 6 (1 Nov. 1930): 30.

47. W. J. Rorabaugh, *The Alcoholic Republic: An American Tradition* (New York: Oxford University Press, 1979), 101; Alice Roosevelt Longworth, *Crowded Hours: Reminiscences of Alice Roosevelt Longworth* (New York: Charles Scribner's Sons, 1934), 61; Anna Steese Richardson, "Grandmother Goes Wet," *Forum* 85 (June 1931): 365.

48. William Seale, *The Tasteful Interlude: American Interiors through the Camera's Eye, 1860–1917,* 2d ed. (Nashville, Tenn.: American Association for State and Local History, 1982), 33, 69, 127, 143, 225; Duis, *The Saloon,* 11; Henry Seidel Canby, *The Age of Confidence: Life in the Nineties* (New York: Farrar and Rinehart, 1934), 18; Sherwood, *Manners and Social Usages,* 272.

49. Packard, *An Address,* 5; Henry Barrett Chamberlin, "The Public Bar versus Private Sideboard," *Chamberlin's* 13 (Nov. 1915): 40; Hentz, "Victim of Excitement," 45; Edith Wharton, *House of Mirth* (1905; New York: Charles Scribner's Sons, 1951), 24.

50. Quoted in Mary Earhart, *Frances Willard: From Prayers to Politics* (Chicago: University of Chicago Press, 1944), 360. See also Ruth Bordin, *Woman and Temperance: The Quest for Power and Liberty, 1873–1900* (New Brunswick: Rutgers University Press, 1990), 141–49, on the union's resentment of Somerset and Willard's time in England.

51. A. William Schmidt, *The Flowing Bowl: When and What to Drink* (New York: Charles L. Webster, 1892), xiv; G. S. Crawford, "Club Life versus Home Life," *Arena* 16 (Aug. 1896): 430–31; "Making Home Comfortable for Him," car-

toon reprinted in Gerald Carson, *The Social History of Bourbon: An Unhurried Account of Our Star-Spangled American Drink* (1963; Lexington: University Press of Kentucky, 1984), [plate 15].

CHAPTER THREE: STARTLING CHANGES IN THE PUBLIC REALM

1. Richard Barry, *What Women Have Actually Done Where They Vote,* reprint from *Ladies' Home Journal* (New York: New York State Association Opposed to Woman Suffrage, ca. 1910), 9; *Woman Suffrage in Practice* (Boston: Massachusetts Association Opposed to the Further Extension of Suffrage to Women, ca. 1914).

2. Charles Dudley Warner, "Editor's Drawer," *Harper's Magazine* 80 (May 1890): 972–73.

3. James B. McGovern, "The American Woman's Pre–World War I Freedom in Manners and Morals," *Journal of American History* 55 (1968): 315–33; Patricia Marks, *Bicycles, Bangs, and Bloomers: The New Woman in the Popular Press* (Lexington: University Press of Kentucky, 1990), 10–11, 123–25; Caroline Ticknor, "The Steel-Engraving Lady and the Gibson Girl," *Atlantic Monthly* 88 (1901): 109; Margaret Deland, "The Change in the Feminine Ideal," *Atlantic Monthly* 105 (1910): 289; *Wesleyan Methodist* reprinted in "Carnality in Song, Dance, and Dress," *Literary Digest* 47 (19 July 1913): 101.

4. Rheta Childe Dorr, *A Woman of Fifty* (New York: Funk and Wagnalls, 1924), 19; Ruth Rosen, *The Lost Sisterhood: Prostitution in America, 1900–1918* (Baltimore: Johns Hopkins University Press, 1982), 43; Margaret Marsh, "Suburban Men and Masculine Domesticity, 1870–1915," in *Meanings for Manhood: Constructions of Masculinity in Victorian America,* ed. Mark C. Carnes and Clyde Griffen (Chicago: University of Chicago Press, 1990), 116.

5. Mark Sullivan, *The Turn of the Century, 1900–1904,* vol. 1 of *Our Times: The United States, 1900–1925* (New York: Charles Scribner's Sons, 1927–33), 393–95; William R. Leach, "Transformations in a Culture of Consumption: Women and Department Stores, 1890–1925," *Journal of American History* 71 (1984): 331.

6. Craig MacAndrew and Robert B. Edgerton, *Drunken Comportment: A Social Explanation* (Chicago: Aldine, 1969), 168, 94; Joseph R. Gusfield, "Passage to Play: Rituals of Drinking Time in American Society," in *Constructive Drinking: Perspectives on Drink from Anthropology,* ed. Mary Douglas (Cambridge: Cambridge University Press, 1987), passim; Elinore Pruitt Stewart, *Letters of a Woman Homesteader* (1914; Boston: Houghton Mifflin, 1988), 205, 234.

7. Leonard Ellis, "Men among Men: An Exploration of All-Male Relationships in Victorian America" (Ph.D. diss., Columbia University, 1982), 135; "The Fashionable Drinking of Other Days," *Union Signal* 58 (13 Feb. 1932): 5; Richard James Hooker, *Food and Drink in America: A History* (New York:

Bobbs-Merrill, 1981), 132; John Kobler, *Ardent Spirits: The Rise and Fall of Prohibition* (New York: G. P. Putnam's Sons, 1973), 120; "Female Drinking; or, The Social Gehenna," in *Temperance Tracts* (New York: National Temperance Society and Publication House, 1874), 1:2; Lewis Erenberg, *Steppin' Out: New York Nightlife and the Transformation of American Culture, 1890–1930* (Westport, Conn.: Greenwood, 1981), 11, 52.

8. Erenberg, *Steppin' Out,* 36, 11, 18, 40–52; Theodore Dreiser, *Sister Carrie* (1900; New York: Norton, 1991), 235.

9. Erenberg, *Steppin' Out,* xii, 123, 135–37; Frederick Lewis Allen, *Only Yesterday: An Informal History of the 1920s* (1931; New York: Harper and Row, 1964), 9–10.

10. Erenberg, *Steppin' Out,* 79, 147; Mrs. Burton Kingsland, *Etiquette for All Occasions* (New York: Platt and Peck, 1901), 101–3; Ethel Mumford, "Where Is Your Daughter This Afternoon?" *Harper's Weekly* 58 (17 Jan. 1914): 28.

11. Perry Duis, *The Saloon: Public Drinking in Chicago and Boston, 1880–1920* (Urbana: University of Illinois Press, 1983), 2; Arthur H. Gleason, "Kitchen Bars, the Secret of Confusion in Maine," *Collier's* 48 (7 Oct. 1911): 20; James Shaw, *History of the Great Temperance Reforms of the Nineteenth Century* (Cincinnati: Hitchcock and Walden, 1875), 228, 232; Eliza D. Stewart, *Memories of the Crusade; A Thrilling Account of the Great Uprising of the Women of Ohio in 1873 against the Liquor Crime* (1889; New York: Arno, 1972), 453–54, 218; Jack S. Blocker Jr., *"Give to the Wind Thy Fears:" The Women's Temperance Crusade, 1873–1874* (Westport, Conn.: Greenwood, 1985), 197.

12. "It Has Been Stated," *Union Signal* 19 (18 May 1893): 16; Dorothy Sue Cobble, "'Practical Women': Waitress Unionists and the Controversies over Gender Roles in the Food Service Industry, 1900–1980," *Labor History* 29 (1988): 16.

13. Madelon Powers, "Women and Public Drinking, 1890–1920," *History Today* 45 (Feb. 1995): 47–48; "Protecting Women Workers," *Outlook* 119 (17 July 1918): 443–44; Harvey Levenstein, *Revolution at the Table: The Transformation of the American Diet* (New York: Oxford University Press, 1988), 186–87.

14. "What We Know about Rum," *Everybody's* 31 (July–Aug. 1914): 132; Koren quoted in Gilman Ostrander, *The Prohibition Movement in California, 1848–1933* (Berkeley: University of California Press, 1957), 79; Clara E. Laughlin, *The Complete Hostess* (New York: D. Appleton, 1906), 42–43.

15. Kathy Peiss, *Cheap Amusements: Working Women and Leisure in New York City, 1880 to 1920* (Philadelphia: Temple University Press, 1985), 95–97; Rheta Louise Childe Dorr, *What Eight Million Women Want* (1910; New York: Kraus Reprint, 1971), 209–15.

16. Roy Rosenzweig, *Eight Hours for What We Will: Workers and Leisure in*

an Industrial City, 1870–1920 (New York: Cambridge University Press, 1983), 63; Peiss, *Cheap Amusements*, 54.

17. Peiss, *Cheap Amusements*, 99, 127; Jane Addams, *A New Conscience and an Ancient Evil* (New York: Macmillan, 1912); Frank M. Goodchild, "The Social Evil in Philadelphia," *Arena* (15 Mar. 1896): 580.

18. Carroll Smith-Rosenberg, "The New Woman as Androgyne: Social Disorder and Gender Crisis, 1870–1936," in *Disorderly Conduct: Visions of Gender in Victorian America* (New York: Oxford University Press, 1986), 256; "Sex O'Clock in America," *Current Opinion* 55 (Aug. 1913): 113; Mark Sullivan, *The War Begins, 1909–1914*, vol. 4 of *Our Times*, 165–63; Dorothy Brown, *Setting a Course: American Women in the 1920s* (Boston: Twayne, 1987), 112–17; William O'Neill, *Everyone Was Brave: A History of Feminism in America*, rev. ed. (Chicago: Quadrangle Books, 1971), 298.

19. Poster quoted in MacAndrew and Edgerton, *Drunken Comportment*, 8.

20. "Protection of the Home," *Independent* 52 (6 Dec. 1900): 648; Walter Clarke, "Prostitution and Alcohol," *Social Hygiene* 3 (1917): 85; Allan M. Brandt, *No Magic Bullet: A Social History of Venereal Disease in the United States since 1880* (New York: Oxford, 1985), 7, 14, 34; Eugene Brieux, *Damaged Goods*, trans. John Pollock (New York: Brentano's, 1912), 69; "The White Slave Traffic before the Supreme Court," *Current Opinion* 54 (Apr. 1913): 273. More rational observers labeled most reports on white slavery *(From the Dance Hall to Hell, Panders and Their White Slaves*, and the film *House of Bondage)* titillating if not pornographic: Agnes Repplier, "The Repeal of Reticence," *Atlantic Monthly* 113 (1914): 297–304.

21. Larry Engelmann, *Intemperance: The Lost War against Liquor* (New York: Free Press, 1979), 15; Ernest A. Grant, "The Liquor Traffic before the Eighteenth Amendment," *Annals of the American Academy of Political and Social Science* 163 (1932): 5.

22. Charles Merz, *Dry Decade* (1931; Seattle: University of Washington Press, 1969), 4–5, 20 ff.; Paul Aaron and David Musto, "Temperance and Prohibition in America: A Historical Overview," in *Alcohol and Public Policy: Beyond the Shadow of Prohibition*, ed. M. H. Moore and D. R. Gerstein (Washington, D.C.: National Academy Press, 1981), 156–57; Ernest A. Dewey, "Cocktails in Kansas," *Commonweal* 11 (5 Feb. 1930): 384; Norman Clark, *The Dry Years: Prohibition and Social Change in Washington*, rev. ed. (Seattle: University of Washington Press, 1988), 130, 138.

23. *New England Cook Book* (Boston: Chas. E. Brown, 1905), 283 (emphasis added).

24. Florence Marion [Howe] Hall, *Social Customs* (Boston: Estes and Lauriat, 1887), 76–82, 91–92; Florence Marion [Howe] Hall, *Social Customs* (Boston: L. C. Page, 1911), 100–108, 173, 413. It is interesting to note that Julia Ward Howe drank: see Edward T. James, ed., *Notable American Women,*

1607–1950: A Biographical Dictionary (Cambridge, Mass.: Belknap, 1971), s.v. "Howe, Julia Ward."

25. Ellin Cravin Learned, *Etiquette of New York To-day* (New York: Frederick A. Stokes, 1906), 83–89, passim; Annie R. Gregory, *Woman's Favorite Cook Book* (n.p.: Annie R. Gregory, 1907), 16–23, passim. See Francis W. Crowninshield, *Manners for the Metropolis: An Entrance Key into the Fantastic Life of the 400* (New York: D. Appleton, 1909), 36, on the correct method of removing an intoxicated male guest from a dinner.

26. Steven Goldberg, "Putting Science into the Constitution: The Prohibition Experience," in *Law, Alcohol, and Order: Perspectives on National Prohibition,* ed. David Kyvig (Westport, Conn.: Greenwood, 1985), 24–25.

27. Man quoted in Sullivan, *The War Begins,* 130–31; Peiss, *Cheap Amusements,* 150 ff.; Rosenzweig, *Eight Hours,* 191, 218 ff.; *Encyclopedia* quoted in Joan L. Silverman, "I'll Never Touch Another Drop: Images of Alcoholism and Temperance in American Popular Culture, 1874–1919" (Ph.D. diss., New York University, 1979), 317.

28. Peiss, *Cheap Amusements,* 125–29, 137; Rosenzweig, *Eight Hours,* 218; Thomas Schlereth, *Victorian America: Transformations in Everyday Life, 1876–1915* (New York: HarperCollins, 1991), 236.

29. Rosenzweig, *Eight Hours,* 56; Madelon Powers, "Decay from Within: The Inevitable Doom of the American Saloon," in *Drinking: Behavior and Belief in Modern History,* ed. Susanna Barrows and Robin Room (Berkeley: University of California Press, 1991), 117; Margaret Marsh, *Suburban Lives* (New Brunswick: Rutgers University Press, 1990), 83–84, 163.

30. Rosenzweig, *Eight Hours,* 188; Powers, "Decay from Within," 115, passim.

31. Aaron and Musto, "Temperance and Prohibition," 157; Rosenzweig, *Eight Hours,* 51.

32. Jane Tompkins, "West of Everything," *South Atlantic Quarterly* 86 (1987); Marsh, *Suburban Lives;* Gail Bederman, "'Teaching Our Sons to Do What We Have Been Teaching the Savages to Avoid': Manhood, Race, and G. Stanley Hall" (paper presented at the American Historical Association Annual Meeting, San Francisco, Jan. 1994); Susan Curtis, "The Son of Man and God the Father: The Social Gospel and Victorian Masculinity," in *Meanings for Manhood: Constructions of Masculinity in Victorian America,* ed. Mark C. Carnes and Clyde Griffen (Chicago: University of Chicago Press, 1990); Paula Baker, "The Domestication of Politics: Women and American Political Society, 1780–1920," *American Historical Review* 89 (1984): 628.

33. John C. Burnham, *Bad Habits: Drinking, Smoking, Taking Drugs, Gambling, Sexual Misbehavior, and Swearing in American History* (New York: New York University Press, 1993), 59; Mary Murphy, "Bootlegging Mothers and Drinking Daughters: Gender and Prohibition in Butte, Montana," *American*

Quarterly 46 (June 1994): 178; Grace C. Root, *Women and Repeal: The Story of the Women's Organization for National Prohibition Reform* (New York: Harper, 1934), 70; editor quoted in Clark, *Dry Years,* 145. For discussion of the scrutiny of men, see Clyde Griffen, "Reconstructing Masculinity from the Evangelical Revival to the Waning of Progressivism: A Speculative Synthesis," in *Meanings for Manhood: Constructions of Masculinity in Victorian America,* ed. Mark C. Carnes and Clyde Griffen (Chicago: University of Chicago Press, 1990).

34. H. H. Weld, "Women and Temperance," *American Temperance Magazine* 2 (1851): 253; Lucy G. Allen, *Table Service* (Boston: Little, Brown, 1915), 88–89.

35. A. William Schmidt, *The Flowing Bowl: When and What to Drink* (New York: Charles L. Webster, 1892), xiv; *Bonfort's Circular* quoted in *The Cyclopedia of Temperance, Prohibition, and Public Morals,* ed. Deets Pickett (New York: Methodist Book Concern, 1917), 396–97; Hutchins Hapgood, "Prohibition," *Forum* 55 (1916): 263–64; Irving Fisher, *Prohibition at Its Worst,* rev. ed. (New York: Alcohol Information Committee, 1927), 204, quoting Hugh Fox of the USBA.

36. Arthur Shadwell, *Drink, Temperance, and Legislation* (New York: Longmans, Green, 1915), 76.

CHAPTER FOUR: PROHIBITION, COCKTAILS, LAW OBSERVANCE, AND THE AMERICAN HOME

1. William Leuchtenburg, *The Perils of Prosperity, 1914–1932* (Chicago: University of Chicago Press, 1958), 236; Gilman Ostrander, *The Prohibition Movement in California, 1848–1933* (Berkeley: University of California Press, 1957), 195.

2. David Kyvig, *Repealing National Prohibition* (Chicago: University of Chicago Press, 1979), 22; John Kobler, *Ardent Spirits: The Rise and Fall of Prohibition* (New York: G. P. Putnam's Sons, 1973), 210.

3. Harry G. Levine and Craig Reinarman, "From Prohibition to Regulation: Lessons from Alcohol Policy for Drug Policy," *Milbank Quarterly* 69 (1991): 463; Kobler, *Ardent Spirits,* 215, 182; Paul Aaron and David Musto, "Temperance and Prohibition in America: A Historical Overview," in *Alcohol and Public Policy: Beyond the Shadow of Prohibition,* ed. M. H. Moore and D. R. Gerstein (Washington, D.C.: National Academy Press, 1981), 159. Legislators had a constitutional right to prohibit possession but chose not to: Mark Sullivan, *Over Here, 1914–1918,* vol. 5 of *Our Times: The United States, 1900–1925* (New York: Charles Scribner's Sons, 1927–33), 638–39.

4. Aaron and Musto, "Temperance and Prohibition," 159–60; Kobler, *Ardent Spirits,* 240; Anne Amateur [pseud.], *Home-Brewed Wines and Unfermented Beverages for All Seasons of the Year* (New York: Charles Scribner's Sons,

1921); Emma Tudor, *October Dawn: A Short and Practical Treatise on the Manufacture of Home Made Wines for the Native Grapes of New England* (Cambridge, Mass.: Riverside, 1926).

5. Levine and Reinarman, "From Prohibition to Regulation," 472; Kobler, *Ardent Spirits,* 238; Larry Engelmann, *Intemperance: The Lost War against Liquor* (New York: Free Press, 1979), 138.

6. Alice Roosevelt Longworth, *Crowded Hours: Reminiscences of Alice Roosevelt Longworth* (New York: Charles Scribner's Sons, 1934), 315; Lucas E. Moore Stave Co., advertisement, *Scribner's* 90 (Nov. 1931): 11; Engelmann, *Intemperance,* 138–34, passim.

7. Preston W. Slosson, *The Great Crusade and After, 1914–1928* (New York: Macmillan, 1930), 114–15; Cointreau advertisement, *New Yorker* 8 (15 Oct. 1932): 62 (other issues carried similar advertisements); Aaron and Musto, "Temperance and Prohibition," 160–62; Slosson, *Great Crusade,* 116.

8. H. L. Mencken, *The American Language,* suppl. 1 (New York: Knopf, 1945), 265; Ernest W. Mandeville, "More Sin and Gin," *Outlook* 139 (25 Feb. 1925): 300; Lewis Erenberg, *Steppin' Out: New York Nightlife and the Transformation of American Culture, 1890–1930* (Westport, Conn.: Greenwood, 1981), 238–55.

9. "Scores Foreigners and the Rich Wets," *New York Times,* 1 June 1924, 3.

10. Andrew Sinclair, *Era of Excess: A Social History of the Prohibition Movement* (New York: Harper Colophon Books, 1964), 86; *Report of the Women's National Commission for Law Enforcement and Law Observance* (Cambridge, Mass.: Woman's National Committee for Law Enforcement, 1931), 39.

11. Sinclair, *Era of Excess,* 332; "Lady Bootlegger," *Scribner's* 92 (Oct. 1932): 229–31; Dayton E. Heckman, "Prohibition Passes: The Story of the Association Against the Prohibition Amendment" (Ph.D. diss., Ohio State University, 1939), 90–97, 101; Charles Merz, *The Dry Decade* (1931; Seattle: University of Washington Press, 1969), 218; Joan L. Silverman, "I'll Never Touch Another Drop: Images of Alcoholism and Temperance in American Popular Culture, 1874–1919" (Ph.D. diss., New York University, 1979), 294; Robin Room, "The Movies and the Wetting of America: The Media as Amplifiers of Cultural Change," *British Journal of Addiction* 83 (1988): 12, passim.

12. Clark Warburton, *The Economic Results of Prohibition* (1932; New York: AMS Press, 1968); Aaron and Musto, "Temperance and Prohibition," 164; Jeffrey Zwiebel and Jeffrey A. Miron, "Alcohol Consumption during Prohibition," *American Economic Review* 81 (1991): 242; Ernest W. Mandeville, "Prohibition Questions Answered," *Outlook* 140 (22 July 1925): 498. Edward T. Lee, "A Page from Anti-Prohibition History," *Union Signal* 58 (11 June 1932): 5, describes how speakeasies differ from the "four saloons yawning on the four corners of all intersecting streets" in pre-Prohibition America.

13. Martha Bensley Bruère, *Does Prohibition Work? . . .* (New York: Harper

and Brothers, 1927), 303, passim; Frederick Lewis Allen, *Only Yesterday: An Informal History of the 1920s* (1931; New York: Harper and Row, 1964), 91–92; Kobler, *Ardent Spirits,* 313–14; Warburton, *Economic Results,* 260, passim.

14. Ernest W. Mandeville, "Booze, Here and There," *Outlook* 139 (11 Mar. 1925): 417; Allen, *Only Yesterday,* 110.

15. A. Lawrence Lowell, "Reconstruction and Prohibition," *Atlantic Monthly* 143 (Feb. 1929): 148; Longworth, *Crowded Hours,* 313–14; Lucy G. Allen, *Table Service* (Boston: Little, Brown, 1915), 91; Mary D. Chambers, *Breakfasts, Luncheons, and Dinners* (Boston: Boston Cooking-School Magazine Company, 1920), 96, 113 ff.; Lillian Eichler, *Book of Etiquette* (Oyster Bay, N.Y.: Nelson Doubleday, 1922), 2:39; Lilian M. Gunn, *Table Service and Decoration* (Philadelphia: J. B. Lippincott, 1928), 32; *How to Entertain at Home* (Boston: Priscilla Publishing, 1928).

16. Sarah Swain Adams, *How to Set the Table for Every Occasion* (New York: Derryvale Linen, 1921), 15; Ellin Craven Learned, *Everybody's Complete Etiquette* (New York: Frederick A. Stokes, 1923), 90; Alice Bradley, *Cooking For Profit: Catering and Food Service Management* (Chicago: American School of Home Economics, 1925), 211.

17. Helen Watkeys Moore, *On Uncle Sam's Water Wagon: Five Hundred Recipes for Delicious Drinks, Which Can Be Made at Home* (New York: G. P. Putnam's Sons, 1919); One Who Knows [pseud.], *Drinks: Formulas for Making Ozonated Non-Alcoholic Drinks to Resemble Alcoholic Cocktails and Mixed Drinks* (New York: Namreh Publishers, 1921); Mrs. Bertha E. L. Stockbridge, *What to Drink: Recipes and Directions for Making and Serving Non-alcoholic Drinks* (New York: D. Appleton, 1920), vii; Ann Batchelder, *Cookery for Today* (Chicago: Butterick, 1932), 125–28; Marjory Swift and Christine T. Herrick, *Feed the Brute* (New York: Stoke, 1926); Harvey Levenstein, *Revolution at the Table: The Transformation of the American Diet* (New York: Oxford University Press, 1988), 168; Fannie Farmer, *Boston Cooking-School Cook Book* (Boston: Little, Brown, 1927), 28–42, 501–7.

18. Learned, *Everybody's Etiquette,* 139; Victor H. Diescher, *The Book of Good Manners: A Guide to Polite Usage for All Social Functions* (New York: Social Culture Publications, 1923), 49; Frederick H. Martens, *The Book of Good Manners: A Guide to Polite Usage for All Social Functions* (New York: Social Culture Publications, 1923), 420–27 (author's note: Martens and Diescher are different books); Lucy G. Allen, *Table Service* (Boston: Little, Brown, 1928), 69, 81–83.

19. John T. Flynn, "Home, Sweet Home-Brew," *Collier's* 84 (1 Sept. 1928): 49; Lit Brothers advertisement, *Philadelphia Inquirer,* 6 Dec. 1923, 5; Mary D. Chambers, *Table Etiquette: Menus and Much Besides* (Boston: Boston Cooking-School Magazine, 1929), 249.

20. George Ade, *The Old-Time Saloon: Not Wet—Not Dry, Just History*

(New York: Ray Long and Richard R. Smith, 1931), 161; Inez Haynes Irwin, "Speaking against Prohibition," *Woman's Journal* 13 (Sept. 1928): 11; Ida M. Tarbell, "Ladies at the Bar," *Liberty* 6 (26 July 1930): 6, 10; Phyllis Mary Blanchard and Carlyn Manasses, *New Girls for Old* (New York: Macaulay, 1930), 4.

21. *The Report of the National Convention, Washington, April 10–11, 1924* (Manchester, Mass.: Woman's National Committee for Law Enforcement, 1924), 26; Ostrander, *Prohibition,* 163.

22. "Prohibition and Propaganda," *Woman's Journal* 15 (July 1930): 18–19; Louise M. Young, *In the Public Interest: The League of Women Voters, 1920–1970* (New York: Greenwood, 1989), 77; Felice D. Gordon, *After Winning: The Legacy of the New Jersey Suffragists* (New Brunswick: Rutgers University Press, 1986), 88; *Report of the WNCLE,* 47; Heckman, "Prohibition Passes," 94.

23. Marguerite M. Wells, "Some Effects of Woman Suffrage," *Annals of the American Academy of Political and Social Science* 143 (1929): 212; Peabody quotation in pamphlet fragment, Lucy Peabody papers, Herbert Hoover Presidential Library, West Branch, Iowa; "The Great Prohibition Poll's Final Week," *Literary Digest* 112 (30 Apr. 1932): 6–7; "Women in the Poll—A Triumphant Test," *Literary Digest* 112 (9 Apr. 1932): 7–9. See criticism of the *Literary Digest* pools in Claude E. Robinson, *Straw Votes: A Study of Political Prediction* (1932; New York: AMS Press, 1979), 151 ff.

24. Mabel Walker Willebrandt, "Will You Help Keep the Law?" *Good Housekeeping* 78 (Apr. 1924): 72–77, 235–40; *Report of National Convention,* 22 (emphasis in original); William John Jackson, "Prohibition as an Issue in New York State Politics, 1836–1933" (Ph.D. diss., Columbia University, 1974), 186; *Washington Convention, April 11–13, 1926* (Cambridge, Mass.: Woman's National Committee for Law Enforcement, 1926), 33, passim; *Report of the WNCLE,* 129, passim; Lucy Peabody, press release dated 30 Apr. 1930, Peabody papers; "Social Leaders Here Reject Cocktail Ban," *New York Times,* 10 June 1930, 27; "Mrs. Willebrandt Calls on Republican Women to Ban Liquor Socially," *Union Signal* 55 (1 June 1929): 6.

25. Ida M. Tarbell, "After the Drink Revolution," in *Save America,* ed. Elizabeth H. Tilton (Boston: Woman's National Committee for Law Enforcement, 1924), 30; Mencken, *American Language,* 264; Edward Longstreth, "How to Be the Life of the Party," *Smart Set* 84 (Mar. 1929): 112; *Report of the WNCLE,* 81; Carrie Chapman Catt, "If Not Prohibition, What?" *Woman's Journal* 15 (July 1930): 303.

26. Henry Seidel Canby, *The Age of Confidence: Life in the Nineties* (New York: Farrar and Rinehart, 1934), 95–96; Peter N. Stearns and Mark Knapp, "Men and Romantic Love: Pinpointing a Twentieth-Century Change," *Journal of Social History* 26 (1993): 775.

27. Susan R. Williams, *Savory Suppers and Fashionable Feasts: Dining in*

Victorian America (New York: Pantheon Books, 1985), 153–56; Richard James Hooker, *Food and Drink in America: A History* (New York: Bobbs-Merrill, 1981), 298; Ruth Schwartz Cowan, *More Work for Mother: The Ironies of Household Technology from the Open Hearth to the Microwave* (New York: Basic Books, 1983), 174–80.

28. Clara E. Laughlin, *The Complete Hostess* (New York: D. Appleton, 1906), 25–26; Chambers, *Breakfasts,* 66; *How to Entertain at Home,* 19; Chambers, *Table Etiquette,* 122.

29. Christine Herrick, *The Chafing-Dish Supper* (New York: C. Scribner's, 1896); Anne Seymour, *A-B-C of Good Form* (New York: Harper and Brothers, 1915).

30. Mrs. Burton Kingsland, *Etiquette for All Occasions* (New York: Platt and Peck, 1901), 103; Florence Marion [Howe] Hall, *Social Customs* (Boston: L. C. Page, 1911), 156; Seymour, *A-B-C of Good Form,* 34; Christine Terhune Herrick, ed. in chief, and Marion Harland, *The Modern Hostess,* vol. 1 of *The Consolidated Library of Modern Cooking and Household Recipes* (New York: R. F. Bodmer, 1905), 183–84; Florence Williams, *Dainties for Home Parties: A Cook-Book for Dance-Suppers, Bridge Parties, Receptions, Luncheons, and Other Entertainments* (New York: Harper and Brothers, 1915), 7–10.

31. Heckman, "Prohibition Passes," 240; Dorothy Dunbar Bromley, "Prohibition? Yes! No!" *McCall's,* July 1930, 34; *The Compact Edition of the Oxford English Dictionary,* s.v. "cocktail"; Allen, *Table Service* (1915), 69, 85. See acknowledgement of the triple definition in *Standard Encyclopedia of the Alcohol Problem* (Westerville, Ohio: American Issue Press, 1925–1930), s.v. "cocktail."

32. Chambers, *Table Etiquette,* 248, 17.

33. Allen Krueger Muhs, *Sunset Host and Hostess Book* (Menlo Park, Calif.: Lane, 1940), 19, 24; Allen, *Only Yesterday,* 9–10, 91, 99; Leon Kroll, *Leon Kroll: A Spoken Memoir,* ed. Nancy Hall and Fredson Bowers (University of Virginia Press, 1983), 62; John Hammond Moore, "The Cocktail: Our Contribution to Humanity's Salvation," *Virginia Quarterly Review* 56 (1980): 336–41.

34. Mrs. Alma Fullford Whitaker, *Bacchus Behave! The Lost Art of Polite Drinking* (New York: Frederick A. Stokes, 1933), 15–16; Irwin, "Speaking Against," 10.

35. Mencken, *American Language,* 260; H. L. Mencken, "From the Vocabulary of the Drinking Chamber," in *Inspired by Drink: An Anthology,* ed. Joan Digby and John Digby (New York: W. Morrow, 1988), 182.

36. Gerald Carson, *The Social History of Bourbon: An Unhurried Account of Our Star-Spangled American Drink* (1963; Lexington: University Press of Kentucky, 1984), 197; Dickens quoted in William Grimes, *Straight Up or On the Rocks: A Cultural History of American Drink* (New York: Simon and Schuster, 1993), 57; Mrs. Alexander Orr Bradley, *Beverages and Sandwiches for Your Husband's Friends (By One Who Knows)* (New York: Brentano's, 1893), passim

(she does not call these cocktails); Leonard Ellis, "Men among Men: An Exploration of All-Male Relationships in Victorian America" (Ph.D. diss., Columbia University, 1982), 329. See Mark Keller and Masiri McCormick, *A Dictionary of Words about Alcohol,* 2d ed. (New Brunswick, N.J.: Rutgers Center for Alcohol Studies, 1982), for drink definitions.

37. A. William Schmidt, *The Flowing Bowl: When and What to Drink* (New York: Charles L. Webster, 1892); Lowell Edmunds, *The Silver Bullet: The Martini in American Civilization* (Westport, Conn.: Greenwood, 1981), 37, 27; Ellis, "Men among Men," 352.

38. Canby, *Age of Confidence,* 95–96; Kate Chopin, *The Awakening* (1899; New York: Bantam, 1981), 116; Linda Hull Larned, *The Hostess of Today* (New York: Charles Scribner's Sons, 1899), 10; Herrick and Harland, *Modern Hostess,* 27; Hall, *Social Customs* (1911), 107; Francis W. Crowninshield, *Manners for the Metropolis: An Entrance Key into the Fantastic Life of the 400* (New York: D. Appleton, 1909), 3.

39. Mary Elizabeth Sherwood, *Manners and Social Usages* (New York: Harper and Brothers, 1884), 313; "Female Drinking; or, The Social Gehenna," in *Temperance Tracts* (New York: National Temperance Society and Publication House, 1874), 1:2.

40. Edmunds, *Silver Bullet,* 30; Belle Linder Israels, "Diverting a Pastime," *Leslie's Weekly* 113 (27 July 1911): 100; Ethel Mumford, "Where Is Your Daughter This Afternoon?" *Harper's Weekly* 58 (17 Jan. 1914): 28; Boston clubwoman quoted in James B. McGovern, "The American Woman's Pre–World War I Freedom in Manners and Morals," *Journal of American History* 55 (1968): 328; London *Truth* quoted in Patricia Marks, *Bicycles, Bangs, and Bloomers: The New Woman in the Popular Press* (Lexington: University Press of Kentucky, 1990), 142.

41. Daughters of the American Revolution, *A Book of Beverages* (Boston: Merrymount, 1904); Christine Terhune Herrick, ed. in chief, and Marion Harland, *Beverages, etc.,* vol. 5 of *The Consolidated Library of Modern Cooking and Household Recipes* (New York: R. F. Bodmer, 1905), 52–125; Sinclair, *Era of Excess,* 113.

42. Jerry Thomas, *The Bon-Vivant's Companion; or, How to Mix Drinks,* ed. and with an introduction by Herbert Asbury (New York: Knopf, 1928); *Giggle Water, Including Eleven Famous Cocktails of the Most Exclusive Club in New York, As Served before the War When Mixing Drinks Was an Art* (New York: C. S. Warnock, 1928); Charlie Roe and Jim Schwenck, *The Home Bartender's Guide and Song Book* (New York: Experimenter Publishing, 1930); Frederick Philip Steiff, *Eat, Drink, and Be Merry in Maryland* (New York: G. P. Putnam's Sons, 1932), xix–xx; Virginia Elliott and Phil D. Stong, *Shake 'Em Up! A Practical Handbook of Polite Drinking* (New York: Brewer and Warren, 1930), 6; Log Cabin Maple Syrup advertisement, *New Yorker* 8 (22 Oct. 1932): 43.

43. Ridgely Hunt and George S. Chappell, comps., *The Saloon in the Home; or, A Garland of Rumblossoms* (New York: Coward-McCann, 1930); Dexter Mason, *The Art of Drinking; or, What to Make with What You Have, Together with Divers Succulent Canapés Suitable to Each Occasion* (New York: Farrar and Rinehart, 1930); William C. Feery, *Wet Drinks for Dry People: A Book of Drinks Based on the Ordinary Home Supplies* (Chicago: Bazner, 1932); Julian Leonard Street, *Civilized Drinking* (n.p.: Redbook Magazine, 1933); Whitaker, *Bacchus Behave!;* Williams, *Dainties for Home Parties,* 7–10; Elliott and Stong, *Shake 'Em Up!,* 13–14.

44. Mary Murphy, "Bootlegging Mothers and Drinking Daughters: Gender and Prohibition in Butte, Montana," *American Quarterly* 46 (June 1994): 187–88; Margaret Culkin Banning, "Anti-Prohibitionette," *Vogue* 76 (1 Sept. 1930): 82; Grace C. Root, *Women and Repeal: The Story of the Women's Organization for National Prohibition Reform* (New York: Harper, 1934), 13, 137; various items in box 33 and letter dated 1 Dec. 1933, Women's Organization for National Prohibition Reform (WONPR) Papers, Hagley Museum and Library, Wilmington, Delaware; Kenneth Rose, *American Women and the Repeal of Prohibition* (New York: New York University Press, 1996), 218.

45. H. Perry Robinson, "The Drink Problem in the United States," *Nineteenth Century and After: A Monthly Review* 94 (Sept. 1923): 444.

46. "Women at Capital a Puzzle on Liquor," *New York Times,* 1 Aug. 1929, 12; Margaret Culkin Banning, "Anti-Prohibitionette," *Vogue* 76 (1 Sept. 1930): 55; Travis Hoke, "The Corner Saloon," *American Mercury,* Mar. 1931, 314.

47. Blanchard and Manasses, *New Girls for Old,* 1, 66–67; Ben B. Lindsey, *The Revolt of Modern Youth* (New York: Boni and Liveright, 1925), 51; Robert Sklar, ed., *The Plastic Age, 1917–1930* (New York: Braziller, 1970), 229; Rufus S. Lusk, "The Drinking Habit," *Annals of the American Association of Political and Social Science* 163 (1932): 50; Engelmann, *Intemperance,* 172–76; Victor G. Vecki, *Alcohol and Prohibition in Their Relation to Civilization and to the Art of Living* (Philadelphia: Lippincott, 1923), 48; Ernest W. Mandeville, "Prohibition, the Law, and the Facts," *Outlook* 139 (1 Apr. 1925): 498.

48. *Report of the Women's National Commission for Law Enforcement and Law Observance* (Cambridge, Mass.: Woman's National Committee for Law Enforcement, 1931), 118, 83.

49. Canby Chambers, "Those Bootleg Blues," *Smart Set* 86 (Mar. 1930): 38–41, 114–17; Allen, *Only Yesterday,* 99; Longworth, *Crowded Hours,* 316; Norman H. Clark, *Deliver Us from Evil: An Interpretation of American Prohibition* (New York: Norton, 1976), 134. Federal income taxes did not "reach . . . the vast majority of citizens" until World War II and the Korean War: John F. Witte, *The Politics and Development of the Income Tax* (Madison: University of Wisconsin Press, 1985), 110.

CHAPTER FIVE: PROHIBITION AND WOMAN'S PUBLIC SPHERE
IN THE 1920S

1. *Standard Encyclopedia of the Alcohol Problem* (Westerville, Ohio: American Issue Press, 1925–30), s.v. "Brehm, Marie C.," and "Prohibition Party."

2. "Feeling the Pulse of Women on Prohibition," *Union Signal* 49 (29 Mar. 1923): 88; Eunice Fuller Barnard, "The Woman Voter Gains Power," *New York Times Magazine,* 12 Aug. 1928, 1; Margaret Culkin Banning, "Anti-Prohibitionette," *Vogue* 76 (1 Sept. 1930): 82; Mabel Walker Willebrandt, "Prohibition and the Future," *Review of Reviews* 80 (Oct. 1929): 55–57.

3. Helen Tyler, *Where Prayer and Purpose Meet* (Evanston, Ill.: Signal, 1949), 192–93; "Float of Woman's Christian Temperance Union of Bucks County, Pennsylvania, in American Legion Parade at Reading," *Union Signal* 55 (6 April 1929): 1; Dorothy E. Johnson, "Organized Women as Lobbyists in the 1920s," *Capital Studies* 1 (1972): 43; Joseph R. Gusfield, "Social Structure and Moral Reform: A Study of the WCTU," in *Drinking and Intoxication: Selected Readings in Social Attitude and Controls,* ed. Raymond G. McCarthy and Edgar M. Douglass (New Haven: College and University Press, 1959), 403, 399; Owen P. White, "The Same Old Fight," *Collier's* 91 (5 Nov. 1932): 19; J. Stanley Lemons, *The Woman Citizen: Social Feminism in the 1920s* (1973; Charlottesville: University of Virginia Press, 1990), 193.

4. Tyler, *Prayer and Purpose,* 175–80; M. Nelson McGeary, *Gifford Pinchot: Forester, Politician* (Princeton: Princeton University Press, 1960), 304; William John Jackson, "Prohibition as an Issue in New York State Politics, 1836–1933" (Ph.D. diss., Columbia University, 1974), 197; K. Austin Kerr, *Organized for Prohibition: A New History of the Anti-Saloon League* (New Haven: Yale University Press, 1985), 263; "Prohibition Punches Prescribed by W.C.T.U.: Christmas Beverages Broadcast at Chicago," *New York Times,* 9 Dec. 1927, 1.

5. "Women and Prohibition," *New York Times,* 29 July 1923, sec. 7, p. 7; Eunice Fuller Barnard, "Madame Arrives in Politics," *North American Review* 226 (1928): 555; White, "Same Old Fight," 19, 41; *Union Signal* 54 (Sept. 1928) and (Oct. 1928).

6. Eunice Fuller Barnard, "Women in the Campaign," *Woman's Journal* 13 (7–9 Dec. 1928): 9; Dorothy Brown, *Setting a Course: American Women in the 1920s* (Boston: Twayne, 1987), 69–71; William F. Ogburn and Inez Goltra, "How Women Vote," *Political Science Quarterly* 34 (1919): 413–33; Stuart A. Rice and Malcolm M. Willey, "American Women's Ineffective Use of the Vote," *Current History* 20 (1924): 320; "Booze Is the Victor," *Collier's* 77 (10 Oct. 1925): 8–9; "Woman Vote Plays Big Part This Year," *New York Times,* 9 July 1928, 2; Marguerite M. Wells, "Some Effects of Woman Suffrage," *Annals of the American Academy of Political and Social Science* 143 (May 1929): 213; Allan

Lichtman, *Prejudice and the Old Politics: The Presidential Election of 1928* (Chapel Hill: University of North Carolina Press, 1979), 86–92, 160–61.

7. Edward T. James, ed., *Notable American Women, 1607–1950: A Biographical Dictionary* (Cambridge, Mass.: Belknap, 1971), s.v. "Peabody, Lucy"; Kerr, *Organized for Prohibition*, 231; "Women Oppose Dry Repeal," *New York Times*, 18 May 1923, 14; *The Report of the National Convention, Washington, April 10–11, 1924* (Manchester, Mass.: Woman's National Committee for Law Enforcement, 1924); pamphlet fragment, "Woman's National Committee for Law Enforcement" folder, 1924–32, Lou Henry Hoover papers, Girl Scouts and Other Groups, Herbert Hoover Presidential Library, West Branch, Iowa; *Washington Convention, April 11–13, 1926* (Cambridge, Mass.: Woman's National Committee for Law Enforcement, 1926); *Standard Encyclopedia of the Alcohol Problem* (Westerville, Ohio: American Issue Press, 1925–30), s.v. "Woman's National Committee for Law Enforcement." For publications, see Woman's National Commission for Law Enforcement and Law Observance, *A Day of Judgment: Who Murdered the Child?* (Marblehead, Mass.: N. A. Lindsey, n.d.); Woman's National Committee for Law Enforcement, *What About the Women?* (Boston: N. A. Lindsey, ca. 1932).

8. *Report of the Women's National Commission for Law Enforcement and Law Observance* (Cambridge, Mass.: Woman's National Committee for Law Enforcement, 1931), 9, 11, 98.

9. Felice D. Gordon, *After Winning: The Legacy of the New Jersey Suffragists* (New Brunswick: Rutgers University Press, 1986), 69–71, 157; "Attack on Crime Begun by Jewelers," *New York Times*, 5 Sept. 1925, 15; "Women Drys to Fight Wets in Many States," *New York Times*, 6 Nov. 1927, sec. 3, p. 6.

10. Nancy Cott, *The Grounding of Modern Feminism* (New Haven: Yale University Press, 1987), 96, 13, 21, 3; *Report of the WNCLE*, 109; Mrs. Alvin T. Hert, "Woman's Work for Herbert Hoover," *Woman's Journal* 13 (Nov. 1928): 21. *The Woman's Journal* was a continuation of a suffrage journal.

11. "Women Drys Fight Smith and Ritchie," *New York Times*, 7 May 1927, 19; "Women Threaten to Name Dry Ticket," *New York Times*, 11 Jan. 1928, 2; "Mrs. Shaver Assails Democratic Chiefs," *New York Times*, 7 July 1928, 14; "Women Drys Seek to Oust Raskob," *New York Times*, 27 Apr. 1930, 2; Lucy Peabody to Walter Newton, Lucy Peabody papers, Herbert Hoover Presidential Library, West Branch, Iowa.

12. Letterhead of Committee Against Repeal of the Eighteenth Amendment, "Temperance" folder, National American Woman Suffrage Association (NAWSA) papers, Library of Congress, Washington, D.C.; Ada Ferguson, "Not All Wet," *Union Signal* 58 (11 June 1932): 7; *Washington Convention*, 1926.

13. Louise M. Young, *In the Public Interest: The League of Women Voters, 1920–1970* (New York: Greenwood, 1989); *Standard Encyclopedia of the Alco-*

hol Problem, s.v. "WNCLE"; "Dry Action Divides the Women Voters," *New York Times,* 29 Apr. 1924, 21; "Women Pledge Aid to Uphold Dry Law: Voters' League Adopts Plan for 'Cooperation and Active Work' to Enforce It," *New York Times,* 30 Apr. 1924, 9.

14. "Women Voters Avoid Dry Act Controversy," *New York Times,* 21 Apr. 1926, 19; "Women Will Fight for Direct Primary," *New York Times,* 8 July 1927, 2; "Women Voters Urge Dry Law for State," *New York Times,* 4 Dec. 1927, 1; "Women Clash over Prohibition," *New York Times,* 26 Apr. 1928, 12; "Women Voters Ban Study of Dry Law," *New York Times,* 27 Apr. 1928, 28; "Program Adopted by Women Voters," *New York Times,* 24 Nov. 1928, 19; Anastatia Sims, "'The Sword of the Spirit': The WCTU and Moral Reform in North Carolina, 1883–1933," *North Carolina Historical Review* 64 (1987): 415.

15. Hert, "Woman's Work," 21; *Who's Who in America* (1928), s.v. "Hert, Mrs. Alvin T."; Nellie Tayloe Ross, "Two Platforms," *Woman's Journal* 13 (Aug. 1928): 115; Wells, "Some Effects," 213, passim; "Prohibition and Propaganda," *Woman's Journal* 15 (July 1930): 18.

16. Johnson, "Organized Women," 43; "Women and Prohibition"; "Standing Committees," "Sub-Committees of the Women's Joint Congressional Commission," and "Legislative Activities of Member Organizations" folders, and minutes of 28 November 1927 meeting, Women's Joint Congressional Committee (WJCC) papers, Library of Congress; Woman's Christian Temperance Union, *Annual Report* (Chicago, 1927), 92; "Women's Federation Reaffirms Dry Stand," *New York Times,* 2 May 1931, 6.

17. Gordon, *After Winning,* 87–88, 96, 121; Gilman Ostrander, *The Prohibition Movement in California, 1848–1933* (Berkeley: University of California Press, 1957), 162–63; Norman Clark, *The Dry Years: Prohibition and Social Change in Washington,* rev. ed. (Seattle: University of Washington Press, 1988), 191–99.

18. Charles Edward Russell, "Is Woman-Suffrage a Failure?" *Century* 85 (Mar. 1924): 728, passim; William Leuchtenburg, *The Perils of Prosperity, 1914–1932* (Chicago: University of Chicago Press, 1958), 115 ff.; Gordon, *After Winning,* 74.

19. Dorothy M. Brown, *Mabel Walker Willebrandt: A Study of Power, Loyalty, and Law* (Knoxville: University of Tennessee Press, 1984), xi, 50–55, 160, 150. Elizabeth P. Gordon, *Women Torchbearers: The Story of the Woman's Christian Temperance Union* (Chicago: National Woman's Christian Temperance Union Publishing House, 1924), 186, claimed her as a WCTU member.

20. Willebrandt, *The Inside of Prohibition* (Indianapolis: Bobbs-Merrill, 1929), 26, 177, passim.

21. "'Dry' Law Scandal Seen by Untermyer; He Blames Coolidge," *New York Times,* 23 Oct. 1924, 1; "Mrs. Willebrandt Gives Out Telegram," *New York Times,* 24 Oct. 1924, 15; Brown, *Mabel Willebrandt,* 150–65; 67, *New York*

Times, 8 Sept. 1928, 1; Emily Newell Blair, "Women in the Political Parties," *Annals of the American Academy of Political and Social Science* 143 (May 1929): 43.

22. Brown, *Mabel Willebrandt*, 180–85; "Says Party Repays Mrs. Willebrandt," *New York Times*, 2 Oct. 1931, 52; "Methodist Board Assails Wine Juice," *New York Times*, 22 Nov. 1930, 2.

23. Lucy Peabody to Walter H. Newton, 6 May 1931, 11 June 1931, Peabody papers; Jefferson Chase, "The Sabines Ravage the Senators," *Vanity Fair*, Aug. 1931, 42; "Plant of Mrs. Willebrandt's Client Is Raided, But McCampbell Denies New Fruit-Juice Policy," *New York Times*, 14 Apr. 1931, 1.

24. Kerr, *Organized for Prohibition*, 209–10, 276, 230; Ostrander, *Prohibition*, 152; *New York Times*, 3 Nov. 1926, 1; Kathleen M. Blee, *Women of the Klan: Racism and Gender in the 1920s* (Berkeley: University of California Press, 1991), 29, 103–21.

25. Joan L. Silverman, "I'll Never Touch Another Drop: Images of Alcoholism and Temperance in American Popular Culture, 1874–1919" (Ph.D. diss., New York University, 1979), 120, 223, 273–74; Duff Gilfond, "Gentlewomen of the House," *American Mercury* (Oct. 1929): 153.

26. Carrie Chapman Catt, "Liquor and Law," *Woman's Journal* 13 (Oct. 1928): 47; Zona Gale, "Speaking for Prohibition," *Woman's Journal* 13 (Aug. 1928): 6; Willebrandt, *Inside;* Alice Stone Blackwell, letter to the editor, 9 June 1932, "Temperance" folder, NAWSA papers. Lillian Wald, of the Henry Street Settlement in New York, and Jane Addams, of Chicago's Hull House, also spoke publicly in support of Prohibition in the early 1930s: Lillian Wald, "Give America's Great Social Adventure a Chance," *Union Signal* 58 (7 May 1932): 4; Dorothy Dunbar Bromley, "Prohibition? Yes! No!" *McCall's*, July 1930.

27. "Mrs. Roosevelt Calls for Dry Enforcement," *New York Times*, 5 Mar. 1929, 5; Norman H. Clark, *Deliver Us from Evil: An Interpretation of American Prohibition* (New York: Norton, 1976), 203; Jackson, "Prohibition Issue," 171, 206; "Says Women Want Smith," *New York Times*, 2 Nov. 1926, 2; "Women Democrats Split on Dry Issue," *New York Times*, 30 Jan. 1928, 4; "Mrs. Shaver Assails"; "Asks Smith to Deny Race Equality View," *New York Times*, 10 July 1928, 2. Eleanor Roosevelt's bitter reactions to Franklin's drinking, and her own and others' statements on her dryness, indicate that she took Prohibition and temperance quite seriously.

28. *New York Times* quoted in Blanche Wiesen Cook, *Eleanor Roosevelt* (New York: Penguin, 1992), 1:375–76; "Beer to Be Served at White House," *New York Times*, 4 Apr. 1933, 5.

29. Gordon, *After Winning*, 86–96.

30. "Lobbyism and the Ladies," *North American Review* 149 (13 June 1928): 247.

31. *Who's Who in America* (1930–31), s.v. "Tilton, Elizabeth"; Elizabeth

Tilton, *Which?* (Boston: Woman's National Committee for Law Enforcement, n.d.). The New York Public Library dates the pamphlet as "1941?", which I question. Tilton's references to hip flasks, Prohibition, and "the law of the land" (10–11) indicate that the story was written while Prohibition was still in effect. The Tilton entry in *Who's Who* does not list *Which?* as a publication between 1930 and 1941, after which she was omitted.

32. Milton MacKaye, "The Wet Crusade," *New Yorker* 8 (22 Oct. 1932): 22. It should be noted that Tilton in 1930 was asked not to chair a campaign but to run for the Senate herself. She declined.

CHAPTER SIX: THE MORAL AUTHORITY OF THE WOMEN'S ORGANIZATION FOR NATIONAL PROHIBITION REFORM

1. "Women in the Poll: A Triumphant Test," *Literary Digest* 112 (9 Apr. 1932): 7.

2. Inez Haynes Irwin, *Angels and Amazons: A Hundred Years of American Women* (1933; New York: Arno, 1974), 331.

3. Walter Lippmann, "Our Predicament under the Eighteenth Amendment," *Harper's Monthly* 154 (Dec. 1926): 51–56, 162.

4. David Kyvig, *Repealing National Prohibition* (Chicago: University of Chicago Press, 1979), 94–96, 48, 69, passim; K. Austin Kerr, *Organized for Prohibition: A New History of the Anti-Saloon League* (New Haven: Yale University Press, 1985), 258. See "Personal Liberty? Yes; But the Saloon? Never," *Outlook* 131 (17 May 1922): 91, for an early, concise, and dismissive summary of the wet arguments that would resound throughout the decade; and Fabian Franklin, "The Fallacies of Prohibition," *Forum* 82 (Oct. 1929): 218–23, for an equally good summation of the constitutional weaknesses of the law.

5. William John Jackson, "Prohibition as an Issue in New York State Politics, 1836–1933" (Ph.D. diss., Columbia University, 1974), 166; Kyvig, *Repealing,* 54, 127 ff.; John C. Gebhart, "Movement against Prohibition," *Annals of the American Academy of Political and Social Science* 163 (1932): 177.

6. Dayton E. Heckman, "Prohibition Passes: The Story of the Association Against the Prohibition Amendment" (Ph.D. diss., Ohio State University, 1939), 26–28; Crystal Fulton, "The Women's Organization for National Prohibition Reform, 1929–1933" (master's thesis, University of Western Ontario, 1990), 95, 86; "Women Anti-Drys Launch New Drive," *New York Times,* 3 Nov. 1927, 10. The WONPR would have little to do with Gross and the WMU, much to Gross's wrath.

7. "Coolidge Stresses Law Observance," *New York Times,* 11 Apr. 1924, 12; Rheta Childe Dorr, *Drink: Coercion or Control* (New York: Frederick A. Stokes, 1929), 2; "Women at Capital a Puzzle on Liquor," *New York Times,* 1

Aug. 1929, 12; Norman Clark, *The Dry Years: Prohibition and Social Change in Washington,* rev. ed. (Seattle: University of Washington Press, 1988), 210.

8. *American Issue* quoted in Heckman, "Prohibition Passes," 27; "We Wonder!" *Union Signal* 55 (1 June 1929): 8.

9. "Ladies at Roslyn," *Time* (18 July 1932): 9; "Born, Reared, and Voting 'Dry,' Mrs. Charles Sabin Now Leads a Fight against Prohibition," *(Wilmington, Del.) Star* (31 July 1932): 2.

10. *United States Congressional Committee Hearings Index,* part III, 69th Congress–73d Congress, December 1925–1934 (Washington, D.C.: Congressional Information Service, 1984), and the *Congressional Master File* (Bethesda, Md.: Congressional Information Service, 1994) include no reference to Boole's testifying in Congress between 1926 and 1930. Hearings such as House Committee on the Judiciary, *Proposing an Amendment to the Constitution of the United States in Lieu of the Eighteenth Amendment,* 70th Congress (Washington, D.C.; Government Printing Office, 1928), and House Committee on the Judiciary, *To Amend the Prohibition Law and to Regulate the Admissibility of Evidence in Certain Cases: Hearings,* 70th Congress (Washington, D.C.: Government Printing Office, 1928), were minor affairs with only a handful of witnesses.

11. David E. Kyvig, "Women against Prohibition," *American Quarterly* 28 (1976): esp. 467; Barbara Sicherman and Carol Hurd Green, eds., *Notable American Women: The Modern Period* (Cambridge, Mass.: Belknap, 1980), s.v. "Sabin, Pauline Morton." Milton MacKaye, "The Wet Crusade," *New Yorker* 8 (22 Oct. 1932): 21–23; "Women Republicans Elect," *New York Times,* 24 Jan. 1922, 2; Dorothy Ducas, "In Miniature: Mrs. Charles H. Sabin, Lady into Tiger," *McCall's,* Sept. 1930, 4; "Mrs. Sabin Debate Winner," *New York Times,* 4 Nov. 1927, 26.

12. Eunice Fuller Barnard, "The Woman Voter Gains Power," *New York Times Magazine,* 12 Aug. 1928, 20.

13. Martin L. Fausold, *James W. Wadsworth Jr.: The Gentleman from New York* (Syracuse: Syracuse University Press, 1975), 125, 132, 183, 191–99; Jackson, "Prohibition Issue," 3, 205; "Returns from Elections Mark Victories but Sound Warnings," *Union Signal* 52 (13 Nov. 1926): 8.

14. Quoted in Pauline Sabin to James W. Wadsworth, 17 Sept. 1926, James W. Wadsworth Jr. papers, Library of Congress, Washington, D.C.; Howard Cobb to Wadsworth, 28 Oct. 1926, Wadsworth papers; telegram to Wadsworth, 3 Nov. 1926, Wadsworth papers. On Sabin's role, see "Women Leaders Back Wadsworth," *New York Times,* 14 Apr. 1926, 2; "Mrs. Sabin Resigns Republican Post," *New York Times,* 9 Mar. 1929, 3.

15. Robert Fowler, *Carrie Catt: Feminist Politician* (Boston: Northeastern University Press, 1986), 96; Fausold, *Wadsworth,* 191–92; "Mrs. C. H. Sabin

Quits Woman Voters' League; Criticizes Campaign as Unethical," *New York Times,* 6 Nov. 1926, 19; "Fitness before Sex," *Guidon* 1 (Mar. 1927): 1; "Opposes Feminine Blocs," *New York Times,* 11 May 1927, 27. Bear in mind that Alice Wadsworth led the antisuffrage movement in the 1910s.

16. Pauline M. Sabin, "I Change My Mind on Prohibition," *Outlook* 149 (13 June 1928): 254, 272; "National Affairs Committee Report on Club Questionnaire," *Guidon* 1 (May 1927): 1; "Mrs. Sabin Brands Dry Law a Menace," *New York Times,* 8 June 1928, 28.

17. MacKaye, "Wet Crusade," 22; "Recent Presidential Campaign," *Guidon* 2 (Nov. 1928): 3; Kyvig, *Repealing,* 111 ff.; Kyvig, "Objection Sustained: Prohibition Repeal and the New Deal," in *Alcohol, Reform, and Society: The Liquor Issue in Social Context,* ed. Jack S. Blocker Jr. (Westport, Conn.: Greenwood, 1979), 100.

18. "Mrs. Sabin Resigns," 3; "Mrs. Sabin Sounds Call for Wet Fight," *New York Times,* 4 Apr. 1929, 1; "Women Organize to Fight Dry Laws," *New York Times,* 29 May 1929, 3; Kyvig, *Repealing,* 49, 118–29; "Women Wets Move to Counteract W.C.T.U.; Plan National Campaign for Modification," *New York Times,* 15 May 1929, 1. The first WONPR office was located in the New York headquarters of the AAPA, and the WONPR throughout its lifetime used literature and statistics prepared by the men's group.

19. Grace C. Root, *Women and Repeal: The Story of the Women's Organization for National Prohibition Reform* (New York: Harper, 1934), 12–14, 206, 209, 182; Fulton, "WONPR," 126–32, 137, 50; "Women at Capital a Puzzle"; WONPR membership card, Women's Organization for National Prohibition Reform (WONPR) Papers, Hagley Museum and Library, Wilmington, Delaware; "Ladies at Roslyn," 9.

20. "411,410 Enrolled by Anti-Dry Women," *New York Times,* 2 Dec. 1931, 6; Kyvig, "Women Against," 474; Crystal Fulton, "A Force Amasses against Prohibition: A Comparison of WONPR Membership at National and State Levels" (paper presented at the International Congress on the Social History of Alcohol, London, Ontario, May 1993), 9.

21. Clarence True Wilson, "License and Liquor or Law and Loyalty?" *Annals of the American Academy of Political and Social Science* 163 (1932): 169; "Doran Hears Wets Condemn Dry Law," *New York Times,* 27 Jan. 1930, 1; Leslie Gordon, ed., *The New Crusade, Including a Report Concerning Prohibition, etc.* (Cleveland: Crusaders, 1932), 10; "Sees Women Voters Improving Politics," *New York Times,* 15 Sept. 1926, 4.

22. "Women Denounce Prohibition Act," *New York Times,* 5 Mar. 1930, 12; Grace Robinson, "Women Wets," *Liberty* 6 (1 Nov. 1930): 30–32; Root, *Women and Repeal,* 30; Felice D. Gordon, *After Winning: The Legacy of the New Jersey Suffragists* (New Brunswick: Rutgers University Press, 1986), 73.

23. "Women Organize to Fight"; "Urges Votes for Wets," *New York Times,*

29 Sept. 1930, 16. Emily Newell Blair, "Neither Wet Nor Dry: How the Non-Combatants Feel about It," *Century Magazine* 94 (Oct. 1928): 762 ff., criticizes this reasoning.

24. Grace Root, ed., *Thirty-Seven Liquor Control Systems of Today* (New York: Women's Organization for National Prohibition Reform, 1932); "Describes Liquor Legislation in Delaware Before and After Repeal of Klair Law and Eighteenth Amendment," WONPR papers; Root, *Women and Repeal,* 122.

25. Root, *Women and Repeal,* 109, 21, 73, 39–40, 63, 106, passim. "Women Become People," *Outlook and Independent* 157 (29 Apr. 1931): 586.

26. Dorothy Dunbar Bromley, "Prohibition? Yes! No!" *McCall's,* July 1930, 17; Margaret Culkin Banning, "Anti-Prohibitionette," *Vogue* 76 (1 Sept. 1930), 84; "Quick Action Urged to Control Liquor," *New York Times,* 10 Sept. 1933, sec. 2, p. 1; "Ladies at Roslyn"; Banning, "Anti-Prohibitionette"; Bromley, "Prohibition?"; Isabel Leighton, "A Charming Aristocrat," *Smart Set,* Mar. 1930; MacKaye, "Wet Crusade," 20; Jefferson Chase, "The Sabines Ravage the Senators," *Vanity Fair,* Aug. 1931, 42; "Born, Reared, and Voting 'Dry.'"

27. "Our Policy Blamed for Britain's Tariff," *New York Times,* 16 July 1932, 22; Root, *Women and Repeal,* 131. For local WONPR campaigns with the GFWC, see box 3, WONPR papers; handwritten history of the Dutchess County WONPR, Women's Organization for National Prohibition Reform papers, Dutchess County Division, Dutchess County Historical Society, Poughkeepsie, N.Y.

28. "Mrs. Sabin Urges Women Wets to Bolt," *New York Times,* 13 Apr. 1931, 2; "Doran Hears Wets Condemn"; "Asks Who Is Paying for Anti-Dry Fight," *New York Times,* 5 Aug. 1929, 20; "Mrs. Boole Replies to Wets' Appeal for Cooperation," *Union Signal* 59 (8 Apr. 1933): 8.

29. "Mrs. Sabin Meets Dry Rival in Debate," *New York Times,* 22 Apr. 1930, 4; "Mrs. Boole Accuses Women Wets Here," *New York Times,* 25 Feb. 1930, 18.

30. Lucy Peabody to Walter H. Newton, 2 Jan. 1931, and Lucy Peabody to President Herbert Hoover, 22 June 1931, 10 Feb. 1932, Peabody papers, Herbert Hoover Presidential Library, West Branch, Iowa; Woman's National Commission for Law Enforcement and Law Observance, *A Day of Judgment: Who Murdered the Child?* (Marblehead, Mass.: N. A. Lindsey, n.d.); "When the 'Antis' Visit Us," *Union Signal* 56 (13 Sept. 1930): 552.

31. "Mrs. Boole Replies"; "Bishop Cannon Asks Tighter Dry Laws," *New York Times,* 25 Jan. 1930, 32.

32. "Women and Prohibition," *New York Times,* 29 July 1923, sec. 7, p. 7; "Roper Urges Dry Council, with Seven-Year Truce by Wets, to Give Law a Fair Trial," *New York Times,* 21 Mar. 1930, 1.

33. "They Shall Not Pass!" *Union Signal* 52 (17 May 1930): 1; Grace M. Putnam, "The Anchor," *Union Signal* 58 (11 June–9 July 1932): 381–82, 399–400, 415–16, 431–32, 447–48.

34. Ada Reed Ferguson, "Not All Wet!" *Union Signal* 58 (11 June 1932): 7; "Says Women Wets Hamper Dry Law," *New York Times,* 8 Jan. 1933, 8; Mark E. Lender, *Dictionary of American Temperance Biography: From Temperance Reform to Alcohol Research, the 1660s to the 1980s* (Westport, Conn.: Greenwood, 1984), 55, passim; *Notable American Women, 1607–1950: A Biographical Dictionary* (Cambridge, Mass.: Belknap, 1971), s.v. "Catt, Carrie Chapman"; Helen Tyler, *Where Prayer and Purpose Meet* (Evanston, Ill.: Signal, 1949), 194.

35. "W.C.T.U. Head Hits Mrs. Sabin's Group," *New York Times,* 17 Oct. 1929, 2; *American Independent* quoted in Root, *Women and Repeal,* 110, 13; Paul A. Carter, *Another Part of the Twenties* (New York: Columbia University Press, 1977), 89; "Privileged People Dissent," in *Report of the WNCLE,* 84; Fletcher Dobyns, *The Amazing Story of Repeal: An Expose of the Power of Propaganda* (Chicago: Willett, Clark, 1940), 106; "Drys Hail Attack on Mrs. Roosevelt," *New York Times,* 15 Jan. 1933, 22.

36. "Prohibition and Propaganda," *Woman's Journal* 15 (July 1930): 18–19; "Repeal Is Not the Answer," *Woman's Journal* 15 (May 1931): 22; Dorothy M. Brown, *Mabel Walker Willebrandt: A Study of Power, Loyalty, and Law* (Knoxville: University of Tennessee Press, 1984), 147, 55; Mabel Walker Willebrandt, *The Inside of Prohibition* (Indianapolis: Bobbs-Merrill, 1929), 277; "Ladies at Roslyn," 9.

37. Ione Nicoll, "Should Women Vote Wet?" *North American Review* 229 (1930): 565; "Social Leaders Here Reject Cocktail Ban," *New York Times,* 10 June 1930, 27; Clark, *Dry Years,* 223.

38. Fausold, *Wadsworth,* 227; Kyvig, *Repealing,* 168, 151, 99; Kyvig, "Objection," 223. See, for example, the *Louisville (Ken.) Courier-Journal* (6 Nov. 1930), which describes election victories solely in wet-dry terms.

39. Gebhart, "Movement Against," 174; Kyvig, *Repealing,* 134–35, 153, 111–14; Walter Lippmann, "The Great Wickersham Mystery," reprinted in *Dry Arguments and Answers* (New York: Women's Organization for National Prohibition Reform, 1932), WONPR papers; Jack S. Blocker Jr., *American Temperance Movements: Cycles of Reform* (Boston: Twayne, 1989), 127–28.

40. "Mrs. Sabin's Hopes Raised," *New York Times,* 11 Sept. 1930, 2; Root, *Women and Repeal,* 67 ff., 93–94, 103, 127; "Ladies at Roslyn"; box 11, "Publicity, General," WONPR papers. For a different view of the WONPR endorsement, see Frank R. Kent, "The Battle Lines Are Drawn," *Scribner's* 92 (Sept. 1932).

41. "Carries on Repeal Drive," *New York Times,* 19 Sept. 1932, 6; Kyvig, *Repealing,* 161; Fausold, *Wadsworth,* 228.

42. David Kyvig, "Sober Thoughts: Myths and Realities of National Prohibition after Fifty Years," in *Law, Alcohol, and Order: Perspectives on National Prohibition,* ed. David Kyvig (Westport, Conn.: Greenwood, 1985), 15 ff.

43. Kyvig, *Repealing,* 173; Clark, *Dry Years,* 236; Clement E. Vose, "Repeal

as a Political Achievement," in *Law, Alcohol, and Order: Perspectives on National Prohibition,* ed. David Kyvig (Westport, Conn.: Greenwood, 1985), 112. Root, *Women and Repeal,* 140, claims that the WONPR was the first repeal organization to propose this system.

44. Kyvig, *Repealing,* 168–75; Jackson, "Prohibition Issue," 246; Root, *Women and Repeal,* 29; "A Vote for Repeal is Intelligent Patriotism," box 4, "Special Publicity," WONPR papers; Roberta W. Nicholson, "Report of Executive Secretary, W.O.N.P.R, May 19th–June 27th, 1933," Women's Organization for National Prohibition Reform (Marion County, Indiana) Collection, Indiana Historical Society Library, Indianapolis, Ind.

45. Kyvig, "Sober Thoughts," 16; Root, *Women and Repeal,* 141–56; Jackson, "Prohibition Issue," 246.

46. "Program of Victory Dinner," box 4, "Special Publicity," WONPR papers; Kyvig, "Women Against," 480–81; Mrs. J. S. Sheppard, "After Five Years, What Has Repeal Achieved?" *New York Times Magazine,* 4 Dec. 1938, 5, 21; Root, *Women and Repeal,* 122.

47. Fulton, "WONPR," 109, 32; Kyvig, "Objection"; *Notable American Women* (1980), s.v. "Sabin, Pauline Morton"; Foster Rhea Dulles, *The American Red Cross: A History* (New York: Harper and Brothers, 1950), 531–32.

48. Kerr, *Organized for Prohibition,* 270 ff.; "Mrs. Boole Reports 600,000 in W.C.T.U.," *New York Times,* 13 May 1931, 21; "They Are Working. Are You?" *Union Signal* 58 (13 Feb. 1932): 13; "'Forgotten Woman' Is Called to Plan Vote Fight on Wets," *New York Times,* 27 Oct. 1932, 1; "W.C.T.U. Neutral on the Presidency," *New York Times,* 4 Nov. 1932, 12. For the "cocktail president" line, see Gilman Ostrander, *The Prohibition Movement in California, 1848–1933* (Berkeley: University of California Press, 1957), 195.

49. W. E. Garrison, "Fitting the Law to the Lawless," *Christian Century* 50 (1933): 1506; Agnes Dubbs Hays, *Heritage of Dedication: One Hundred Years of the National Woman's Christian Temperance Union, 1874–1974* (Evanston, Ill.: Signal, 1973), 65; Tyler, *Prayer and Purpose,* 189, 196, 204; "Mrs. Boole Replies."

50. Joseph R. Gusfield, *Symbolic Crusade* (Urbana: University of Illinois Press, 1963), 149; Jay L. Rubin, "The Wet War: American Liquor Control, 1941–1945" in *Alcohol, Reform, and Society: The Liquor Issue in Social Context,* ed. Jack S. Blocker Jr. (Westport, Conn.: Greenwood, 1979), 239–50; *Union Signal,* passim.

51. Amy Swerdlow, *Women Strike for Peace: Traditional Motherhood and Radical Politics in the 1960s* (Chicago: University of Chicago Press, 1993); Joan Rivière, "Womanliness as a Masquerade," in *Formations of Fantasy,* ed. Victor Burgin, James Donald, and Cora Kaplan (London: Methuen, 1986).

52. Root, *Women and Repeal,* 124–25.

CHAPTER SEVEN: THE DOMESTICATION OF DRINK

1. On the question of modification, see David Kyvig, *Explicit and Authentic Acts: Amending the United States Constitution, 1776–1995* (Lawrence: University Press of Kansas, 1996), ch. 12.

2. Kaye M. Fillmore, "Issues in the Changing Drinking Patterns among Women in the Last Century," in *Women and Alcohol: Health-Related Issues,* National Institute on Alcohol Abuse and Alcoholism Research Monograph no. 16 (Rockville, Md.: U.S. Dept. of Health and Human Services, 1986), 73; Genevieve Knupfer and Robin Room, "Age, Sex, and Social Class as Factors in Amount of Drinking in a Metropolitan Community," *Social Problems* 12 (1964): 233; John W. Riley Jr. and Charles F. Marden, "The Social Pattern of Alcoholic Drinking," *Quarterly Journal of Studies on Alcohol* 8 (1947): 267 ff.; Paula Fass, *The Damned and the Beautiful: American Youth in the 1920s* (New York: Oxford University Press, 1977), 292.

3. Kenneth A. Yellis, "Prosperity's Child: Some Thoughts on the Flapper," *American Quarterly* 21 (1969): 49; Mrs. N. R. C. Morrow, "The New Woman: Has She Come?" *Union Signal* 22 (24 Sept. 1896): 6; H. M. Aubrey, "Liberty and License," *Forum* 53 (1915): 449; "Increase in Smoking by Women a Cause for Alarm," *Union Signal* 46 (12 Feb. 1920): 3; Katherine Harris, "A Study of Feminine and Class Identity in the Woman's Christian Temperance Union, 1920–1979: A Case Study," *Historicus* 2, no. 2 (1981): 61.

4. L. Pierce Clark, "A Psychological Study of Some Alcoholics," *Psychoanalytical Review* 6 (1919): 271–72; Eleanor Rowland Wembridge, "Petting and the Campus," *Survey* 54 (1 July 1925): 393; Dorothy Dunbar Bromley, "Feminist: New Style," *Harper's Monthly* 155 (Oct. 1927): 557, 552. Ellipses in original.

5. Inez Haynes Irwin, *Angels and Amazons: A Hundred Years of American Women* (1933; New York: Arno, 1974), 331, 327; Frederick Lewis Allen, *Only Yesterday: An Informal History of the 1920s* (1931; New York: Harper and Row, 1964), 92; WCTU member quoted in Joseph R. Gusfield, *Symbolic Crusade* (Urbana: University of Illinois Press, 1963), 131.

6. Mrs. Alma Fullford Whitaker, *Bacchus Behave! The Lost Art of Polite Drinking* (New York: Frederick A. Stokes, 1933), 2–3, 5.

7. Lowell Edmunds, *The Silver Bullet: The Martini in American Civilization* (Westport, Conn.: Greenwood, 1981); Gerald Carson, *The Social History of Bourbon: An Unhurried Account of Our Star-Spangled American Drink* (1963; Lexington: University Press of Kentucky, 1984); Ida M. Tarbell, "Ladies at the Bar," *Liberty* 6 (26 July 1930): 8; A. Torelli, *900 Recettes de Cocktails et Boissons Americaines* ("American Drinks") (Paris: S. Bornemann, 1927).

8. Perry Duis, *The Saloon: Public Drinking in Chicago and Boston, 1880–1920* (Urbana: University of Illinois Press, 1983), 289; Harry G. Levine and Craig Reinarman, "From Prohibition to Regulation: Lessons from Alcohol Pol-

icy for Drug Policy," *Milbank Quarterly* 69 (1991): 478; Harry Gene Levine, "The Alcohol Problem in America: From Temperance to Alcoholism," *British Journal of Addiction* 74 (1984): 113.

9. "Killing Bodies and Souls without Regard to Age or Sex," *The American Issue* 42 (Nov. 1935): 3.

10. Phyllis Mary Blanchard and Carlyn Manasses, *New Girls for Old* (New York: Macaulay, 1930), 4; Anna Doll Killip, "Citizens of Philadelphia Present Proof of Prohibition's Beneficial Effects," *Union Signal* 49 (5 July 1923): 5; [Owen Wister], *The Philadelphia Club, 1834–1934* (Philadelphia: privately printed, 1934), 62; George Ade, *The Old-Time Saloon: Not Wet—Not Dry, Just History* (New York: Ray Long and Richard R. Smith, 1931); Don Marquis, *Her Foot Is on the Brass Rail* (New York: Marchbanks, 1935), 7, 9, passim; Frank Shay and John Held Jr., *My Pious Friends and Drunken Companions* (New York: Macaulay, 1927); *New Yorker* cartoon in John C. Burnham, *Bad Habits: Drinking, Smoking, Taking Drugs, Gambling, Sexual Misbehavior, and Swearing in American History* (New York: New York University Press, 1993), fig. I.17; Allen, *Only Yesterday,* 82.

11. Sylvia Lambert and Stephen Israelstam, "The Social History of Alcohol As Portrayed in the Comics Up to the End of the Prohibition Era," *Journal of Drug Issues* 16 (1986): 585–608; Clark, "Psychological Study"; H. Hart, "Personality Factors in Alcoholism," *Archives of Neurology and Psychiatry* 24 116 (July 1930): 120.

12. Clyde Griffen, "Reconstructing Masculinity from the Evangelical Revival to the Waning of Progressivism: A Speculative Synthesis," in *Meanings for Manhood: Constructions of Masculinity in Victorian America,* ed. Mark C. Carnes and Clyde Griffen (Chicago: University of Chicago Press, 1990), 201; Estelle Freedman, "Separatism as Strategy: Female Institution Building and American Feminism, 1870–1930," *Feminist Studies* 5 (1979): 513–15.

13. Gusfield, *Symbolic Crusade,* 29, passim; Mrs. Hattie A. Burr, ed., *The Woman's Suffrage Cook Book* (Boston: Hattie A. Burr, 1886); Catharine Beecher, *Miss Beecher's Domestic Receipt Book, Designed as a Supplement to Her Treatise on Domestic Economy,* 3d ed. (New York: Harper and Brothers, 1856); Fannie Merritt Farmer, *Boston Cooking-School Cook Book* (Boston: Little, Brown, 1896).

14. Nancy Cott, *The Grounding of Modern Feminism* (New Haven: Yale University Press, 1987), intro. and ch. 1.

15. Dorothy Dunbar Bromley, "Prohibition? Yes! No!" *McCall's,* July 1930, 17, quoting Evangeline Booth, commander of the Salvation Army; Frank Stricker, "Cookbooks and Law Books: The Hidden History of Career Women in Twentieth-Century America," in *A Heritage of Her Own: Toward a New Social History of American Women,* ed. Nancy F. Cott and Elizabeth H. Pleck (New York: Touchstone, 1979), 491–92.

16. Edmunds, *Silver Bullet,* 31; Lewis A. Erenberg, "From New York to Middletown: Repeal and the Legitimization of Nightlife in the Great Depression," *American Quarterly* 38 (1986): 761–78.

17. Harry Gene Levine, "The Birth of American Alcohol Control: Prohibition, the Power Elite, and the Problem of Lawlessness," *Contemporary Drug Problems* 12 (1985): 63–115; Levine and Reinarman, "From Prohibition to Regulation," 446; Paul Aaron and David Musto, "Temperance and Prohibition in America: A Historical Overview," in *Alcohol and Public Policy: Beyond the Shadow of Prohibition,* ed. M. H. Moore and D. R. Gerstein (Washington, D.C.: National Academy Press, 1981), 173 ff.; Mrs. J. S. Sheppard, "After Five Years, What Has Repeal Achieved?" *New York Times Magazine,* 4 Dec. 1938, 5, 21.

18. Richard Hofstadter, *The Age of Reform: From Bryan to FDR* (New York: Knopf, 1955), 287; "What We Know about Rum," *Everybody's* 31 (July–Aug. 1914): 278; Margaret Visser, *The Rituals of Dinner: The Origins, Evolution, Eccentricities, and Meaning of Table Manners* (New York: Grove Widenfeld, 1991), 283–84.

EPILOGUE

1. Leonard U. Blumberg with William L. Pittman, *Beware the First Drink! The Washington Temperance Movement and Alcoholics Anonymous* (Seattle: Glen Abbey Books, 1991), 193–95; Mark Keller, "Alcohol Problems and Policies in Historical Perspective," in *Law, Alcohol, and Order: Perspectives on National Prohibition,* ed. David Kyvig (Westport, Conn.: Greenwood, 1985), 166 ff.; Mark Cohen and Joseph Kern, "The Influence of Morality on Alcoholism Treatment: An Historical Analysis," *Journal of Psychiatric Treatment and Evaluation* 5 (1983): 269–771.

2. Harry Gene Levine, "The Alcohol Problem in America: From Temperance to Alcoholism," *British Journal of Addiction* 74 (1984): 117; Kenneth Rose, *American Women and the Repeal of Prohibition* (New York: New York University Press, 1996); Blumberg, *Beware!,* 215; Joseph R. Gusfield, "Moral Passage: The Symbolic Process in Public Designations of Deviance," in *An Introduction to Deviance: Readings in the Process of Making Deviants,* ed. W. J. Filstead (Chicago: Markham, 1972), 72; John Kobler, *Ardent Spirits: The Rise and Fall of Prohibition* (New York: G. P. Putnam's Sons, 1973), 355.

3. Jack S. Blocker Jr., *American Temperance Movements: Cycles of Reform* (Boston: Twayne, 1989), 143, 137; P. Marsteller and K. Karnchanapee, "The Use of Women in the Advertising of Distilled Spirits, 1956–1979," *Journal of Psychedelic Drugs* 12 (1980): 4; Carolyn Coggins, *Successful Entertaining at Home* (New York: Prentice-Hall, 1952), 22–40; Mark E. Lender and James K. Martin, *Drinking in America: A History,* rev. ed. (New York: Free Press, 1987), 205–6; Marguerite Kohl, *The Hostess' Manual* (New York: David McKay, 1954),

40; James Mayabb, *International Cocktail Specialties, from Madison Avenue to Malaya* (New York: Hearthside, 1962), 11.

4. Kaye M. Fillmore, "'When Angels Fall': Women's Drinking as Cultural Preoccupation and as Reality," in *Alcohol Problems in Women: Antecedents, Consequences, and Intervention,* ed. Sharon C. Wilsnack and Linda J. Beckman (New York: Guilford, 1984), 13–14; Blumberg, Beware!, 201–2; Gerald Carson, *The Social History of Bourbon: An Unhurried Account of Our Star-Spangled American Drink* (1963; Lexington: University Press of Kentucky, 1984), 220; Norman Clark, *The Dry Years: Prohibition and Social Change in Washington,* rev. ed. (Seattle: University of Washington Press, 1988), 268–70; Dorothy Sue Cobble, "'Practical Women': Waitress Unionists and the Controversies over Gender Roles in the Food Service Industry, 1900–1980," *Labor History* 29 (1988): 17; Marsteller and Karnchanapee, "Use of Women," 1.

5. Kaye M. Fillmore, "Issues in the Changing Drinking Patterns among Women in the Last Century," in *Women and Alcohol: Health-Related Issues,* National Institute on Alcohol Abuse and Alcoholism Research Monograph no. 16 (Rockville, Md.: U.S. Dept. of Health and Human Services, 1986), 77.

6. Jean Kinney, *Loosening the Grip: A Handbook of Alcohol Information* (St. Louis: Times Mirror, 1987), 22; Robin Room, "Region and Urbanization as Factors in Drinking Practices and Problems," in *The Pathogenesis of Alcoholism: Psychosocial Factors,* vol. 6 of *The Biology of Alcoholism,* ed. Benjamin Kissin and Henri Begleiter (New York: Plenum, 1983), 573.

7. Kinney, *Loosening the Grip,* 263, 216; *Alcoholics Anonymous 1992 Membership Survey* (New York: Alcoholics Anonymous World Services, 1992).

° ° ° ESSAY ON SOURCES

Organizational and private papers used in *Domesticating Drink* include those of the National American Woman Suffrage Association, Congressman James W. Wadsworth, and the Women's Joint Congressional Committee (Library of Congress, Washington, D.C.); the Women's Organization for National Prohibition Reform (Hagley Museum and Library, Wilmington, Delaware, and local branches in Dutchess County, New York, and Marion County, Indiana); the Woman's Christian Temperance Union National Headquarters (on microfilm; Joint Ohio Historical Society—Michigan Historical Collections); and Lucy Peabody and the Woman's National Committee for Law Enforcement (Herbert Hoover Presidential Library, West Branch, Iowa). The NAWSA papers at the Library of Congress include an extensive collection of antisuffrage literature. The Library of Congress also has collected various minor prohibition publications in *Pamphlets on Prohibition in the United States*. The papers of most prominent individuals of the 1920s, whether or not they were publicly associated with Prohibition or repeal, tend to contain some reference to the wet-dry controversy.

Most public libraries have old cookbooks and etiquette guides; the collection at the Winterthur Museum and Library, Wilmington, Delaware, merits particular mention. Such partisan journals as the *Union Signal* (of the Woman's Christian Temperance Union); *American Issue* (of the Anti-Saloon League); and *Woman's Journal* (of the National American Woman Suffrage Association) should also be considered, as well as the *Quarterly Journal of Inebriety* and, after repeal, the *Quarterly Journal of Studies on Alcohol*. Popular journals such as the *Atlantic Monthly, Century, Literary Digest, New Republic, North American Review, Outlook and Independent,* and *Smart Set* discussed Prohibition regularly. The *Annals of the American Academy of Political and Social Science* published a full issue on suffrage in 1914 and another on Prohibition in 1932. The *New York Times* contains a wealth of information on Prohibition, all indexed. Every newspaper large or small reported prohibition controversies and violations with a level of detail that is soon overwhelming.

Corporate histories of the WCTU include Elizabeth P. Gordon, *Women Torchbearers: The Story of the Woman's Christian Temperance Union* (Chicago: National Woman's Christian Temperance Union Publishing House, 1924); Helen Tyler, *Where Prayer and Purpose Meet* (Evanston, Ill.: Signal, 1949); and Agnes Dubbs Hays, *Heritage of Dedication: One Hundred Years of the National Woman's Christian Temperance Union, 1874–1974* (Evanston, Ill.: Signal, 1973). See discussion of the WCTU and other organizations in the *Standard Encyclopedia of the Alcohol Problem,* 6 vols. (Westerville, Ohio: American Issue Press, 1925–30). Grace C. Root's corporate history, *Women and Repeal: The Story of the Women's Organization for National Prohibition Reform* (New York: Harper, 1934), is the most detailed source on the WONPR. For contemporary discussion of the Woman's Organization for National Prohibition Reform, see Margaret Culkin Banning, "Anti-Prohibitionette," *Vogue* 76 (1 Sept. 1930); Jefferson Chase, "The Sabines Ravage the Senators," *Vanity Fair,* Aug. 1931; Dorothy Ducas, "In Miniature: Mrs. Charles H. Sabin, Lady into Tiger," *McCall's,* Sept. 1930; "Ladies at Roslyn," *Time,* 18 July 1932; Isabel Leighton, "A Charming Aristocrat," *Smart Set,* Mar. 1930; Milton MacKaye, "The Wet Crusade," *New Yorker* 8 (22 Oct. 1932); and Grace Robinson, "Women Wets," *Liberty* 6 (1 Nov. 1930).

Other published sources from the period that I have found particularly valuable include Frederick Lewis Allen, *Only Yesterday: An Informal History of the 1920s* (1931; New York: Harper and Row, 1964); Carrie Chapman Catt and Nettie Rogers Shuler, *Woman Suffrage and Politics: The Inner Story of the Suffrage Movement* (1923; Seattle: University of Washington Press, 1970); Abigail Scott Duniway, *Path Breaking: An Autobiographical History of the Equal Suffrage Movement in Pacific Coast States,* 2d ed. (New York: Schocken, 1971); *History of Woman Suffrage,* vols. 1–6 (various publishers, 1881–1922); Inez Haynes Irwin, *Angels and Amazons: A Hundred Years of American Women* (1933; New York: Arno, 1974); Alice Roosevelt Longworth, *Crowded Hours: Reminiscences of Alice Roosevelt Longworth* (New York: Charles Scribner's Sons, 1934); Charles Merz, *The Dry Decade* (1931; Seattle: University of Washington Press, 1969); Eliza D. Stewart, *Memories of the Crusade; A Thrilling Account of the Great Uprising of the Women of Ohio in 1873 against the Liquor Crime* (1889; New York: Arno, 1972); Mark Sullivan, *Our Times: The United States, 1900–1925,* vols. 1–6, (New York: Charles Scribner's Sons, 1927–33); Alma

Fullford Whitaker, *Bacchus Behave! The Lost Art of Polite Drinking* (New York: Frederick A. Stokes, 1933); and Mabel Walker Willebrandt, *The Inside of Prohibition* (Indianapolis: Bobbs-Merrill, 1929). Scholars looking further for primary sources should refer to the notes within each chapter and to the dissertation (University of Pennsylvania, 1995) on which this book is based.

For general reference, I highly recommend Barbara Sicherman and Carol Hurd Green, eds., *Notable American Women: The Modern Period* (Cambridge: Harvard University Press, Belknap Press, 1980); Mark E. Lender, *Dictionary of American Temperance Biography: From Temperance Reform to Alcohol Research, the 1660s to the 1980s* (Westport, Conn.: Greenwood, 1984); and A. W. Noling's underutilized and exhaustive *Beverage Literature: A Bibliography* (Metuchen, N.J.: Scarecrow, 1971).

General histories of prohibition include Jack S. Blocker Jr., *American Temperance Movements: Cycles of Reform* (Boston: Twayne, 1989); Norman H. Clark, *Deliver Us from Evil: An Interpretation of American Prohibition* (New York: W. W. Norton, 1976); Clark, *The Dry Years: Prohibition and Social Change in Washington*, rev. ed. (Seattle: University of Washington Press, 1988); John Kobler, *Ardent Spirits: The Rise and Fall of Prohibition* (New York: G. P. Putnam's Sons, 1973); and Andrew Sinclair, *Era of Excess: A Social History of the Prohibition Movement* (New York: Harper Colophon Books, 1964). Mark E. Lender and James K. Martin, *Drinking in America: A History*, rev. ed. (New York: Free Press, 1987), is unusual for its discussion of actual drinking patterns and contains statistics on per capita consumption. (See also W. J. Rorabaugh's *Alcoholic Republic: An American Tradition* [New York: Oxford University Press, 1979] on consumption rates.) Another tidy, thorough history of prohibition can be found in Paul Aaron and David Musto, "Temperance and Prohibition in America: A Historical Overview," in *Alcohol and Public Policy: Beyond the Shadow of Prohibition*, ed. M. H. Moore and D. R. Gerstein (Washington, D.C.: National Academy Press, 1981). Harry Gene Levine neatly summarizes temperance and prohibition history in "The Alcohol Problem in America: From Temperance to Alcoholism," *British Journal of Addiction* 74 (1984), and Jed Dannenbaum does the same with the historiography in "The Social History of Alcohol," *Drinking and Drug Practices Surveyor* 19 (1984).

I recommend several excellent collections of articles related to prohibition, drinking, and repeal: Susanna Barrows and Robin Room, eds., *Drinking: Behavior and Belief in Modern History* (Berkeley: University of California Press, 1991); Jack S. Blocker Jr., ed., *Alcohol, Reform, and Society: The Liquor Issue in Social Context* (Westport, Conn.: Greenwood, 1979); and David Kyvig, ed., *Law, Alcohol, and Order: Perspectives on National Prohibition* (Westport, Conn.: Greenwood, 1985).

Although *Domesticating Drink* only briefly surveys the antebellum temperance movement, I made great use of Jed Dannenbaum's "The Origins of Temperance Activism and Militancy among American Women," *Journal of Social History* 15 (1981) and Ian Tyrrell's "Women and Temperance in Antebellum America, 1830–1860," *Civil War History* 28 (1982). Historians have also examined thoroughly the first quarter century of the Woman's Christian Temperance Union: Ruth Bordin, *Woman and Temperance: The Quest for Power and Liberty, 1873–1900* (1981; New Brunswick: Rutgers University Press, 1990); Mary Earhart, *Frances Willard: From Prayers to Politics* (Chicago: University of Chicago Press, 1944); and Barbara Leslie Epstein, *The Politics of Domesticity: Women, Evangelism, and Temperance in Nineteenth-Century America* (Middletown: Wesleyan University Press, 1981). Other work on the WCTU includes Joseph R. Gusfield, "Social Structure and Moral Reform: A Study of the WCTU," in *Drinking and Intoxication: Selected Readings in Social Attitude and Controls,* ed. Raymond G. McCarthy and Edgar M. Douglass (New Haven: College and University Press, 1959); and Katherine Harris, "A Study of Feminine and Class Identity in the Woman's Christian Temperance Union, 1920–1979: A Case Study," *Historicus* 2, no. 2 (1981). For a different facet of the WCTU, see Joan Jacobs Brumberg, "'Ruined' Girls: Changing Community Responses to Illegitimacy in Upstate New York, 1890–1920," *Journal of Social History* 18 (1984).

Book-length histories of the twentieth-century prohibition movement unfortunately tend to focus on the men of the Anti-Saloon League: Jack S. Blocker, *American Temperance Movements,* and *Retreat from Reform: The Prohibition Movement in the United States, 1890–1913* (Westport, Conn.: Greenwood, 1976); Larry Engelmann, *Intemperance: The Lost War against Liquor* (New York: Free Press, 1979); K. Austin Kerr, *Organized for Prohibition: A New History of the Anti-Saloon League* (New Haven: Yale University Press, 1985); Gilman Ostrander, *The Prohibition Movement in California, 1848–1933* (Berkeley: University of California Press, 1957); and John J. Rumbarger, *Profits, Power, and Prohibition: Alcohol Reform and the Industrialization of America, 1800–1930* (Albany: State University of New York Press, 1989).

The definitive history of repeal remains David Kyvig, *Repealing Na-*

tional Prohibition (Chicago: University of Chicago Press, 1979). Kyvig's *Law, Alcohol, and Order* is also excellent, as is Dayton E. Heckman's contemporaneous "Prohibition Passes: The Story of the Association Against the Prohibition Amendment" (Ph.D. diss., Ohio State University, 1939). For very different perspectives on repeal, see John C. Burnham, *Bad Habits: Drinking, Smoking, Taking Drugs, Gambling, Sexual Misbehavior, and Swearing in American History* (New York: New York University Press, 1993); Fletcher Dobyns, *The Amazing Story of Repeal: An Exposé of the Power of Propaganda* (Chicago: Willett, Clark, 1940); or Ernest Gordon, *The Wrecking of the Eighteenth Amendment* (Francestown, N.H.: Alcohol Information Press, 1943).

David Kyvig's *American Quarterly* article, "Women Against Prohibition" (1976, vol. 28), introduced the Women's Organization for National Prohibition Reform to modern scholars. His work has been continued in Kenneth Rose's *American Women and the Repeal of Prohibition* (New York: New York University Press, 1996). I also recommend the quantitative analysis in Crystal Fulton's "The Women's Organization for National Prohibition Reform, 1929–1933" (master's thesis, University of Western Ontario, 1990). Parenthetical discussion of the WONPR can be found in a variety of histories of Prohibition or of American women.

For general histories of the woman suffrage campaign, see Ellen DuBois, "The Radicalism of the Woman Suffrage Movement: Notes toward the Reconstruction of Nineteenth-Century Feminism," *Feminist Studies* 3 (1975); Eleanor Flexner, *Century of Struggle: The Woman's Rights Movement in the United States,* rev. ed. (Cambridge: Harvard University Press, 1979); William O'Neill, *Everyone Was Brave: A History of Feminism in America,* rev. ed. (Chicago: Quadrangle Books, 1971). Regional studies include Steven Buechler, *Transformation of the Woman Suffrage Movement: The Case of Illinois, 1850–1920* (New Brunswick: Rutgers University Press, 1986); Carol Hoffecker, "Delaware's Woman Suffrage Campaign," *Delaware History* 20 (1987); and T. A. Larson, "Woman Suffrage in Wyoming," *Pacific Northwest Quarterly* 56 (1965). Aileen Kraditor's *Ideas of the Woman Suffrage Movement, 1890–1920* (1965; New York: W. W. Norton, 1981) is unusual in its discussion of suffragists' dry sympathies.

The most helpful secondary sources on antisuffragism include Jane Jerome Camhi, "Women against Women: American Antisuffragism, 1880–1920" (Ph.D. diss., Tufts University, 1973); Elna Green, "Those Opposed: The Antisuffragists in North Carolina, 1900–1920," *North Carolina Historical Review* 67 (1990); and Susan E. Marshall, "Ladies against Women: Mobilization Dilemmas of Antifeminist Movements," *Social Problems* 32 (1985).

Scholars who have analyzed the relationship between woman suffrage and prohibition include Janet Zollinger Giele, "Social Change and the Feminine Role: A Comparison of Woman's Suffrage and Woman's Temperance, 1870–1920" (Ph.D. diss., Radcliffe College, 1961); Harry G. Levine, "Demon of the Middle Class: Self-Control, Liquor, and the Ideology of Temperance in Nineteenth-Century America" (Ph.D. diss., University of California, Berkeley, 1978); and Ross Evans Paulson, *Women's Suffrage and Prohibition: A Study in Equality and Social Control* (Glenview, Ill.: Scott, Foresman, 1973). Eileen L. McDonagh and H. Douglas Price quantify the relationship between drys and suffragists in "Woman Suffrage in the Progressive Era," *American Political Science Review* 79 (1985). See also Levine's "Temperance and Women in Nineteenth-Century United States," in *Alcohol and Drug Problems in Women,* vol. 5 of *Research Advances in Alcohol and Drug Problems,* ed. Oriana J. Kalant (New York: Plenum, 1980).

Histories of women in the 1920s after passage of woman suffrage include Dorothy Brown, *Setting a Course: American Women in the 1920s* (Boston: Twayne, 1987); Paul A. Carter, *Another Part of the Twenties* (New York: Columbia University Press, 1977); William Chafe, *The American Woman: Her Changing Social, Economic, and Political Roles, 1920–1970* (New York: Oxford University Press, 1972); Nancy Cott, *The Grounding of Modern Feminism* (New Haven: Yale University Press, 1987); J. Stanley Lemons, *The Woman Citizen: Social Feminism in the 1920s* (1973; Charlottesville: University of Virginia Press, 1990); Rayna Rapp and Ellen Ross, "The 1920s: Feminism, Consumerism, and Political Backlash in the United States," in *Women in Culture and Politics: A Century of Change,* ed. Judith Friedlander (Bloomington: Indiana University Press, 1986); Lois Scharf and Joan Jensen, eds., *Decades of Discontent: The Women's Movement, 1920–1940* (Westport, Conn.: Greenwood, 1983); and Louise A. Tilly and Patricia Gurin, eds., *Women, Politics, and Change in Twentieth-Century America* (New York: Russell Sage Foundation, 1990). Other sources on the period that I have found useful include Paula Baker, *Moral Frameworks of Public Life: Gender, Politics, and the State in Rural New York, 1870–1930* (New York: Oxford University Press, 1991); Blanche Wiesen Cook, *Eleanor Roosevelt,* vol. 1 (New York: Penguin, 1992); Robert Fowler, *Carrie Catt: Feminist Politician* (Boston: Northeastern University Press, 1986); Allan Lichtman, *Prejudice and the Old Politics: The Presidential Election of*

1928 (Chapel Hill: University of North Carolina Press, 1979); and Susan Zeiger, "Finding a Cure for War: Women's Politics and the Peace Movement in the 1920s," *Journal of Social History* 24 (1990).

Detailed regional histories such as Felice D. Gordon's *After Winning: The Legacy of the New Jersey Suffragists* (New Brunswick: Rutgers University Press, 1986) tend to address more thoroughly women's prohibition issues in the 1920s. Indeed, it remains a historiographic challenge to deconstruct the silences—the omissions—in many of these works. Modern historians' discomfort with the issue notwithstanding, Prohibition was among the most polarizing, debated issues of American voters, male and female, throughout the decade of the 1920s. With enough diligence, prohibition scholars can find very useful information, couched as it might be, in articles such as John W. Furlow Jr., "Cornelia Bryce Pinchot: Feminism in the Post-Suffrage Era," *Pennsylvania History* 43 (1976).

The scholarship on masculinity, while not quite up to the volume of women's history, is rapidly gaining. Most useful to *Domesticating Drink* have been Mark C. Carnes, *Secret Ritual and Manhood in Victorian America* (New Haven: Yale University Press, 1989); Mark C. Carnes and Clyde Griffen, eds., *Meanings for Manhood: Constructions of Masculinity in Victorian America* (Chicago: University of Chicago Press, 1990): 116; Christopher Lasch, "The Mismeasure of Man," *New Republic* 208 (19 Apr. 1993); E. Anthony Rotundo, *American Manhood: Transformations in Masculinity from the Revolution to the Modern Era* (New York: Basic Books, 1993); and Peter N. Stearns, *Be A Man! Males in Modern Society,* 2d ed. (New York: Holmes and Meier, 1990).

Much of the writing on drinking behavior historically and today tends to focus on temperance, alcohol abuse, or the relation between the two. Even these sources, however, have a wealth of information for anyone interested in moderate as well as immoderate drinking. Harry Levine in particular has done excellent work on drinker-abstainer tensions. In addition to his dissertation, "Demon of the Middle Class," and the article "Temperance and Women in Nineteenth-Century United States," I recommend "From Prohibition to Regulation: Lessons from Alcohol Policy for Drug Policy," *Milbank Quarterly* 69 (1991), coauthored with Craig Reinarman, and his "Discovery of Addiction: Changing Conceptions of Habitual Drunkenness in America," *Journal of Studies on Alcohol* 39 (1978). See also Peter Park, "The Supply Side of Drinking: Alcohol Production and Consumption in the United States before Prohibition," *Contemporary Drug Problems* 12 (1985); Harold W. Pfautz, "The Image of Alcohol in Popular Fiction: 1900–1904 and 1945–1950," *Quarterly Journal of Studies on Alcohol* 23 (1962); Robin Room, "'A Reverence for Strong Drink': The Lost Generation and the Elevation of Alcohol in American Culture," *Journal of Studies on Alcohol* 45 (1984); and W. J. Rorabaugh, "Beer, Lemonade, and Propriety in the Gilded Age," *Dining in America, 1850–1900,* ed. Kathryn Grover (Rochester, N.Y.: Margaret Woodbury Strong Museum, 1987). John C. Burnham's "New Perspectives on the Prohibition 'Experiment' in the 1920s," *Journal of Social History* 2 (1968), remains significant to the alcohol studies field. See also Jeffrey Zwiebel and Jeffrey A. Miron, "Alcohol Consumption during Prohibition," in *American Economic Review* 81 (1991).

For more theoretical discussion of drinking cross-culturally, see Mary Douglas, ed., *Constructive Drinking: Perspectives on Drink from Anthropology* (Cambridge: Cambridge University Press, 1987); Marja Holmila, *Wives, Husbands, and Alcohol: A Study of Informal Drinking Control within the Family* (Helsinki: Finnish Foundation for Alcohol Studies, 1988); Craig MacAndrew and Robert B. Edgerton, *Drunken Comportment: A Social Explanation* (Chicago: Aldine Publishing, 1969); and Juha Partanen, *Sociability and Intoxication: Alcohol Drinking in Keyna, Africa, and the Modern World* (Helsinki: Finnish Foundation for Alcohol Studies, 1991).

Standard sources on food and drink (or rather drink and food) include Hugh Barty-King and Anton Massel, *Rum: Yesterday and Today* (London: Heinemann, 1983); Gerald Carson, *The Social History of Bourbon: An Unhurried Account of Our Star-Spangled American Drink* (1963; Lexington: University Press of Kentucky, 1984); Lowell Edmunds, *The Silver Bullet: The Martini in American Civilization* (Westport, Conn.: Greenwood, 1981); William Grimes, *Straight Up or On the Rocks: A Cultural History of American Drink* (New York: Simon and Schuster, 1993); Kathryn Grover, ed., *Dining in America, 1850–1900* (Rochester, N.Y.: Margaret Woodbury Strong Museum, 1987); Richard James Hooker, *Food and Drink in America: A History* (New York: Bobbs-Merrill, 1981); Harvey Levenstein, *Revolution at the Table: The Transformation of the American Diet* (New York: Oxford University Press, 1988); John Hammond Moore, "The Cocktail: Our Contribution to Humanity's Salvation," *Virginia Quarterly Review* 56 (1980); and Susan R. Williams, *Savory Suppers and Fashionable Feasts: Dining in Victorian America* (New York: Pantheon Books, 1985).

For histories of the American saloon, see such standard works as Perry Duis, *The Saloon: Public Drinking in Chicago and Boston, 1880–1920* (Urbana: University of Illinois Press, 1983); Leonard Ellis, "Men among Men: An Exploration of All-Male Relationships in Victorian America" (Ph.D. diss., Columbia University, 1982); Jon M. Kingsdale, "The 'Poor Man's Club': Social Functions of the Urban Working-Class Saloon," in *The American Man*, ed. Elizabeth H. and Joseph H. Pleck (Englewood Cliffs, N.J.: Prentice-Hall, 1980); Robert E. Popham, "The Social History of the Tavern," in *Research Advances in Alcohol and Drug Problems*, vol. 4, ed. Yedi Israel, Frank B. Glaser, Harold Kalant, Robert E. Popham, Wolfgang Schmitt, and Reginald G. Smart (New York: Plenum, 1978); and Madelon Powers, "Decay from Within: The Inevitable Doom of the American Saloon," in *Drinking: Behavior and Belief in Modern History*, ed. Susanna Barrows and Robin Room (Berkeley: University of California Press, 1991).

Reference works on material culture are still rare. Thomas Schlereth remains a leading authority; see his *Material Culture: A Research Guide* (Lawrence: University Press of Kansas, 1985) and *Victorian America: Transformations in Everyday Life, 1876–1915* (New York: HarperCollins, 1991). For discussion of prohibition and temperance in fiction of the period, see Joan L. Silverman's "I'll Never Touch Another Drop: Images of Alcoholism and Temperance in American Popular Culture, 1874–1919" (Ph.D. diss., New York University, 1979). Ruth Schwartz Cowan's *More Work for Mother: The Ironies of Household Technology from the Open Hearth to the Microwave* (New York: Basic Books, 1983) excels in its use of material culture and social history. Histories of etiquette, particularly as a subfield within material culture, may be found in Gerald Carson, *The Polite Americans: A Wide-angle View of Our More or Less Good Manners over Three Hundred Years* (New York: Morrow, 1966); and Margaret Visser, *The Rituals of Dinner: The Origins, Evolution, Eccentricities, and Meaning of Table Manners* (New York: Grove Widenfeld, 1991).

The most thorough discussions of women's moderate drinking have been carried out by labor historians examining working-class leisure: Kathy Peiss, *Cheap Amusements: Working Women and Leisure in New York City, 1880 to 1920* (Philadelphia: Temple University Press, 1985); Madelon Powers, "Decay from Within;" Roy Rosenzweig, *Eight Hours for What We Will: Workers and Leisure in an Industrial City, 1870–1920* (New York: Cambridge University Press, 1983). Beyond labor historians, a second group of scholars discusses women's drinking within the context of popular culture. These works include Lewis Erenberg, *Steppin' Out: New York Nightlife and the Transformation of American Culture, 1890–1930* (Westport, Conn.: Greenwood, 1981), and Paula Fass, *The Damned and the Beautiful: American Youth in the 1920s* (New York: Oxford University Press, 1977).

Women's histories that relate on some level to drinking patterns include William Chafe, *The Paradox of Change: American Women in the Twentieth Century* (New York: Oxford University Press, 1991); Estelle Freedman, "Separatism as Strategy: Female Institution Building and American Feminism, 1870–1930," *Feminist Studies* 5 (1979); James B. McGovern, "The American Woman's Pre–World War I Freedom in Manners and Morals," *Journal of American History* 55 (1968); and Carroll Smith-Rosenberg, "The New Woman as Androgyne: Social Disorder and Gender Crisis, 1870–1936," in *Disorderly Conduct: Visions of Gender in Victorian America* (New York: Oxford University Press, 1986). These scholars tend to present alcohol consumption as evidence of the decline of feminism and feminist support.

Kaye M. Fillmore's "'When Angels Fall': Women's Drinking as Cultural Preoccupation and as Reality," in *Alcohol Problems in Women: Antecedents, Consequences, and Intervention,* ed. Sharon C. Wilsnack and Linda J. Beckman (New York: Guilford, 1984), is an excellent introduction to scholarship on women's abusive drinking. See also Roberta G. Ferrence, "Sex Differences in the Prevalence of Problem Drinking," in *Alcohol and Drug Problems in Women,* vol. 5 of *Research Advances in Alcohol and Drug Problems,* ed. Oriana J. Kalant (New York: Plenum, 1980); Edith S. Gomberg, "Alcoholism in Women," in *Social Aspects of Alcoholism,* vol. 4 of *The Biology of Alcoholism,* ed. Benjamin Kissin and Henri Begleiter (New York: Plenum, 1976); Mark E. Lender, "A Special Stigma: The Origins of Attitudes toward Women Alcoholics," in *Alcohol Interventions: Historical and Sociocultural Approaches,* ed. David L. Strug, S. Priyadarsini, and Merton M. Hyman (New York: Hawthorn, 1986); and Cheryl Krasnick Warsh, "'Oh, Lord, Pour a Cordial in Her Wounded Heart': The Alcoholic Woman in Victorian and Edwardian Canada," in *Drink in Canada: Historical Essays,* ed. Cheryl K. Warsh (Montreal: McGill-Queen's University Press, 1993).

The best history of Alcoholics Anonymous is Ernest Kurtz's *Not-God: A History of Alcoholics Anonymous* (Center City, Minn.: Hazelden Educational Services, 1979). For a general introduction to the field, see Jean Kinney, *Loosening the Grip: A Handbook of Alcohol Information* (St. Louis: Times Mirror, 1987). Historical discussion of alcohol and drug abuse may be found in John S. Haller Jr. and Robin M. Haller, *The Physician and Sexu-*

ality in Victorian America (Urbana: University of Illinois Press, 1974); H[oward] Wayne Morgan, *Drugs in America: A Social History, 1800–1980* (Syracuse: Syracuse University Press, 1981); and Patricia M. Tice, *Altered States: Alcohol and Other Drugs in America* (Rochester, N.Y.: Margaret Woodbury Strong Museum, 1992).

° ° ° INDEX

Numbers in italic type denote illustrations.

bootlegging, 91, 93, 137
Boston Cooking-School Cook Book, 55, 61, 97
Bradley, Mrs. Alexander Orr, 106
Breakfasts, Lunches, and Dinners, 103
Brehm, Marie C., 114
brewers, 9–12, 86, 127, 160; antisuffrage activities, 28–30, 37–38, 41, 100; and prohibition movement, 28, 30, 36; since repeal, 169, 171. *See also* distillers; liquor interests; vintners; wets
Brewing and Liquor Interests and German and Bolshevik Propaganda, 29–30
brewster, 54
Briggs, Emily Edson, 61
Bromley, Dorothy Dunbar, 162

cabarets, 73–74, 76, 92; and public drinking, 7, 159; and women's drinking, 87, 108. *See also* women's drinking
Café des Beaux Arts, New York, 74
California, 36, 99, 107, 137; alcohol asylums, 51; wine industry, 30, 126–27; woman suffrage in, 32, 35. *See also* San Francisco
California Red Light Injunction and Abatement Act, 35, 39
Canada, 38, 51
Canby, Henry, 15
Case against Woman Suffrage, 33–34
Castle, Irene, 72
Catholic World, 65
Catt, Carrie C., 29, 35, 120, 121, 140; on drinking, 101, 128, 160; on liquor interests, 30, 40–41; on temperance and prohibition, 28, 31, 122, 123, 149, 151
Chambers, Mary, 98, 103, 104
champagne, 57–58; in Prohibition era, 97–98; at social events, 56, 62; women's drinking, 53, 56, 60, 63, 66, 73, 105. *See also* beverages; glassware; women's drinking
charity girls, 77
Chautauqua, New York, 68
Chicago, 47, 165; and lawbreaking in

Prohibition era, 91, 93; women's voting in, 36, 118; women's work in saloons, 75
Chicago Tribune, 39, *40*
child labor, 37, 114, 123; and prohibition movement, 31, 33
Chopin, Kate, 107
Christianity, 23, 31, 85; and 1928 presidential campaign, 118, 126; and temperance movement, 11, 18, 20, 119; and women's alcohol abuse, 47
Christman, Frank, 139
cider, 10, 11, 52; home production of, 5, 54, 90, 126. *See also* beverages
Civilized Drinking, 109
Clark, Fred G., 142
Cleveland Press, 143
Cleveland, Sarah, 22
cocktail parties, 43, 104–5, 165; in etiquette manuals, 104–7; and Prohibition Amendment, 112, 164; in temperance literature, 108–9. *See also* women's drinking
cocktails, 97, 102–10; as appetizer, 107, 108; drinking in Prohibition era, 95, 99, 102–10, *129,* 151; and home drinking, 52, 98, 170, 172; meaning of, 88, 107, 162, 163, 164; in men's clubs, 13, 82; popularity of, 94, 109; supplies for, 92, 98–99, 104–5, 108, 110, 164; vs. drugs, 49, *50;* as women's drink, 73, 74, 98, 105, 108, 110. *See also* beverages; glassware; material culture
coffee, 56, 60, 61. *See also* beverages; temperance beverages
Coggins, Carolyn, 172
Collection of Recipes for the Use of Special Diet Kitchens in Military Hospitals, 52
colleges, 20, 111, 148, 162, 173. *See also* youth; youth drinking
Collier's, 36, 98
Colorado, 29, 36, 70
Colvin, Mamie (Mrs. D. Leigh), 146, 148–49, 150
Complete Hostess, The, 102

Norton, Mary, 137
nullification, 135

consumption, 6, 30, 84, 103, 160, 170, 195n. 3; and home delivery, 54, 67; and woman movement, 17, 19, 26, 75. *See also* alcohol laws; high-license movement; local option; Prohibition Amendment

prohibition laws, state, 5, 19, 36; Alabama, 80; California, 35; Iowa, 23; Kansas, 23, 80; Maine, 12, 75, 80; New York, 116, 119; North Carolina, 80; North Dakota, 80; Oregon, 80; Pennsylvania, 116; and private drinking, 79–80, 89, 94; and Prohibition Amendment, 93; since repeal, 144, 153–55, 158, 169; South Carolina, 80; Tennessee, 40; Virginia, 80; Washington, 80; West Virginia, 80

prohibition movement, 12, 23; and gender roles, 32, 39, 85, 86, 159; opponents, 28–29; regional differences, 121, 128, 152; 20th-century support, 21, 35, 38, 79, 80, 95. *See also* Prohibition Amendment; temperance movement

Prohibition Party, 19, 36, 114, 139, 178n. 19; and WCTU, 21–22, 116, 117; and woman suffrage, 28. *See also* Anti-Saloon League (ASL); National Woman's Democratic Law Enforcement League (NWDLEL); temperance movement; Woman's Christian Temperance Union (WCTU); Woman's National Committee for Law Enforcement (WNCLE); woman suffrage and prohibition

prostitution, 6, 35; and alcohol, 44, 79, 173; charity girls, 77; and prohibition movement, 25, 115; in public venues, 73, 74, 76, 77, 83; and saloons, 12, 17, 43, 54, 75, 107; and white slavery, 78, 183n. 1. *See also* sexuality, women's

punch, 13, 55; at social events, 56, 103, 106, 109; as women's drink, 107. *See also* beverages

Pure Food and Drug Act, 48, 179

Quarterly Journal of Inebriety, 46, 51

race, 92, 120

racism: and Prohibition Amendment, 32, 130, 135; and woman suffrage, 29. *See also* ethnicity; nativism

Raskob, John J., 121, 135, 152

receptions, 103

Redbook, 109

Red Cross, 155

Repeal Amendment, 135, 142, 153–54, 156. *See also* Constitution, U.S.; modification; Prohibition Amendment; Woman Suffrage Amendment

repeal movement, 123, 134–36, 152–54, 171; attitudes toward, 112, 128, 147, 156, 164, 170; and drink-mixing manuals, 109; and gender, 115, 134–58; meaning of, 120, 145, 169. *See also* Association against the Prohibition Amendment (AAPA); social class; wets; Women's Organization for National Prohibition Reform (WONPR)

Report of the Women's National Commission for Law Enforcement and Law Observance, 119–20, 150–51

Republican National Committee, 118, 138, 140

Republican National Conventions, 138, 153

Republican Party, 120, 155; connections to WONPR, 138, 141; and 1928 presidential campaign, 118, 122–23, 126, 139; and Prohibition Amendment, 22, 117, 120, 124–25, 139, 152; and Prohibition Party, 19, 178n. 19; and women, 125, 131, 167

restaurants, 7, 12, 76, *96,* 103; as heterosocial drinking space, 86, 159; temperance, 21; and women's drinking, 70, 73, 84, 98. *See also* women's drinking

Riley, Edith Dolan, 137

Rivière, Joan, 157

Robinson, Margaret C., 33

Rockefeller, John D., 169

Rockefeller, Mrs. John D., Jr., 137

Roosevelt, Eleanor: and Prohibition Amendment, 129–31, 139, 150, 205n. 27; and Sabin, 138–39

The Library of Congress
has cataloged the hardcover edition of this book as follows:

Murdock, Catherine Gilbert.
    Domesticating drink : women, men, and alcohol in America,
1870–1940 / Catherine Gilbert Murdock.
        p. cm.—(Gender relations in the American experience)
    Includes bibliographical references and index.
    ISBN 0-8018-5940-9 (alk. paper)
        1. Drinking of alcoholic beverages—United States—History.
2. Men—Alcohol use—United States—History. 3. Women—Alcohol
use—United States—History. 4. Women social reformers—United
States—History. 5. Drinking customs—United States.
    I. Title. II. Series.
HV5292.M86 1998
394.1′3′0973—dc21   98-4285

ISBN 0-8018-6870-X (pbk.)